HTML & CSS

Design and Build Websites

JON DUCKETT

WILEY

JOHN WILEY & SONS, INC.

HTML & CSS
DESIGN AND BUILD WEBSITES

Published by
John Wiley & Sons, Inc.
10475 Crosspoint Boulevard
Indianapolis, IN 46256
www.wiley.com

©2014 by John Wiley & Sons, Inc., Indianapolis, Indiana
ISBN: 978-1-118-87164-5
Manufactured in the United States of America
Published simultaneously in Canada
10 9 8 7 6 5 4 3 2

CREDITS

For John Wiley & Sons, Inc.

EXECUTIVE EDITOR
Carol Long

MARKETING MANAGER
Ashley Zurcher

PRODUCTION MANAGER
Tim Tate

PRODUCTION EDITOR
Daniel Scribner

VICE PRESIDENT AND
EXECUTIVE GROUP PUBLISHER
Richard Swadley

VICE PRESIDENT AND
EXECUTIVE PUBLISHER
Barry Pruett

ASSOCIATE PUBLISHER
Jim Minatel

PRODUCTION COORDINATOR,
COVER
Katie Crocker

AUTHOR
Jon Duckett

COVER DESIGNER
Emme Stone

DESIGN AND LAYOUT
Jon Duckett
Emme Stone

TECHNICAL EDITOR
Chris Mills

TECHNICAL REVIEWERS
Andy Stone
Angela Shimell
Donna Watson
Martin Callanan
Rob Jacoby
Tony Berry

PHOTOGRAPHY
John Stewardson
johnstewardson.com

ADDITIONAL PHOTOGRAPHY
Hesperian
Joe Robertson
flickr.com/photos/mindfire
Jules Clancy
thestonesoup.com
Kylie Gusset
gusset.net
Michael Stillwell
beebo.org

Try out and download all of the code for this book online at:
http://www.htmlandcssbook.com/code/

CONTENTS

INTRODUCTION

- ▸ About this book
- ▸ How the web works
- ▸ Learning from other pages

Firstly, thank you for picking up this book. It has been written with two very different types of people in mind:

- Those who want to learn how to design and build websites from scratch

- Anyone who has a website (that may be built using a content management system, blogging software, or an e-commerce platform) and wants more control over the appearance of their pages

The only things you need in order to use this book are a computer with a web browser and a text editor (such as Notepad, which comes with Windows, or TextEdit, which comes with Macs).

Introduction pages come at the beginning of each chapter. They introduce the key topics you will learn about.

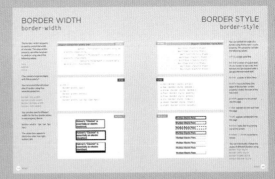

Reference pages introduce key pieces of HTML & CSS code. The HTML code is shown in blue and CSS code is shown in pink.

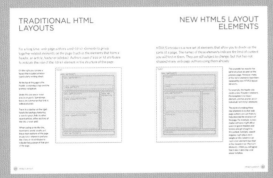

Background pages appear on white; they explain the context of the topics covered that are discussed in each chapter.

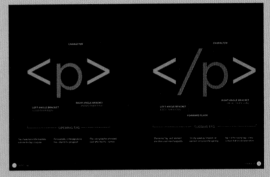

Diagram and infographics pages are shown on a dark background. They provide a simple, visual reference to topics discussed.

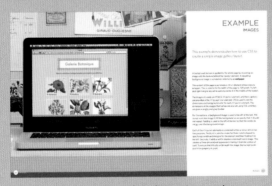

Example pages put together the topics you have learned and demonstrate how they can be applied in each.

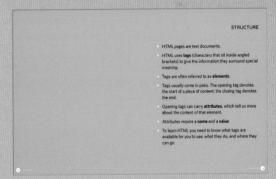

Summary pages come at the end of each chapter. They remind you of the key topics that were covered in each chapter.

IS IT HARD TO LEARN?

Many books that teach HTML and CSS resemble dull manuals. To make it easier for you to learn, we threw away the traditional template used by publishers and redesigned this book from scratch.

I've focussed on the code you need to use 90% of the time and omitted the code that you would rarely see even if writing websites is your full time job. By the end of the book, if you come across the other 10% you will be able to Google it to find out what it means quickly and easily.

At work, when people look at my screen and see it full of code, it's not unusual to get a comment about it looking very complicated or how clever I must be to understand it. The truth is, it's not that hard to learn how to write web pages and read the code used to create them; you certainly don't have to be a "programmer."

Understanding HTML and CSS can help anyone who works with the web; designers can create more attractive and usable sites, website editors can create better content, marketers can communicate with their audience more effectively, and managers can commission better sites and get the best out of their teams.

I have also added practical information on topics I am commonly asked about, such as how to prepare images, audio and video for the web, how to approach the design and build of a new site, how to improve your rankings in search engines (SEO), and how to use Google Analytics to learn about visitors to your site.

THE STRUCTURE OF THIS BOOK

In order to teach you about creating web pages, this book is divided into three sections:

1: HTML

We will spend the first chapter looking at how HTML is used to create web pages. You will see that you start by writing down the words you want to appear on your page. You then add tags or elements to the words so that the browser knows what is a heading, where a paragraph begins and ends, and so on.

The rest of this section introduces the tags you have at your disposal to create web pages, grouped into chapters on: text, lists, links, images, tables, forms, video audio and flash, and miscellaneous elements.

I should warn you that the examples in the first nine chapters are not exciting to look at, yet they are the foundation of every web page. The following chapters on CSS will show you how to make your pages look a lot more interesting.

2: CSS

We start this section with a chapter that explains how CSS uses rules to enable you to control the styling and layout of web pages. We then go on to look at the wide variety of CSS properties you can use in your CSS rules. These properties generally fall into one of two categories:

Presentation: How to control things like the color of text, the fonts you want to use and the size of those fonts, how to add background colors to pages (or parts of a page), and how to add background images.

Layout: How to control where the different elements are positioned on the screen. You will also learn several techniques that professionals use to make their pages more attractive.

3: PRACTICAL

We end up with some helpful information that will assist you in building better websites.

We look at some new tags that will be introduced in HTML5 to help describe the structure of your pages. HTML5 is the latest version of HTML (still under development at the time of writing). Before learning about these elements, you need a good grasp of how CSS is used to control the design of web pages. There is a chapter that talks you through a design process that you might like to follow when creating a new website.

Finally, we end up looking at topics that will help you once you have built your site, such as putting it on the web, search engine optimisation (SEO) and using analytics software to track who comes to your site and what they are looking at.

HOW PEOPLE ACCESS THE WEB

Before we look at the code used to build websites it is important to consider the different ways in which people access the web and clarify some terminology.

BROWSERS

People access websites using software called a **web browser**. Popular examples include Firefox, Internet Explorer, Safari, Chrome, and Opera.

In order to view a web page, users might type a web address into their browser, follow a link from another site, or use a bookmark.

Software manufacturers regularly release new versions of browsers with new features and supporting new additions to languages. It is important, however, to remember that many computer owners will not be running the latest versions of these browsers. Therefore you cannot rely on all visitors to your site being able to use the latest functionality offered in all browsers.

You will learn how to tell which browsers visitors use to access your website in Chapter 19.

WEB SERVERS

When you ask your browser for a web page, the request is sent across the Internet to a special computer known as a **web server** which hosts the website.

Web servers are special computers that are constantly connected to the Internet, and are optimized to send web pages out to people who request them.

Some big companies run their own web servers, but it is more common to use the services of a **web hosting** company who charge a fee to host your site.

DEVICES

People are accessing websites on an increasing range of devices including desktop computers, laptops, tablets, and mobile phones. It is important to remember that various devices have different screen sizes and some have faster connections to the web than others.

SCREEN READERS

Screen readers are programs that read out the contents of a computer screen to a user. They are commonly used by people with visual impairments.

In the same way that many countries have legislations that require public buildings to be accessible to those with disabilities, many laws have also been passed that require websites be accessible to those with disabilities.

Throughout this book you will see several references to screen readers. These notes will help ensure that the sites you create are accessible to people who use such software.

It is interesting to note that technologies similar to those employed by screen readers are also being used in other areas where people are unable read a screen, such as when they are driving or jogging.

HOW WEBSITES ARE CREATED

All websites use HTML and CSS, but content management systems, blogging software, and e-commerce platforms often add a few more technologies into the mix.

WHAT YOU SEE

When you are looking at a website, it is most likely that your browser will be receiving HTML and CSS from the web server that hosts the site. The web browser interprets the HTML and CSS code to create the page that you see.

Most web pages also include extra content such as images, audio, video, or animations and this book will teach you how to prepare them for use on the web and then how to insert them into your web pages.

Some sites also send JavaScript or Flash to your browser, and you will see how to add JavaScript and Flash in your web pages. Both of these technologies are advanced topics that you can go on to learn more about once you have mastered HTML and CSS, if you want to.

HOW IT IS CREATED

Small websites are often written just using HTML and CSS.

Larger websites — in particular those that are updated regularly and use a content management system (CMS), blogging tools, or e-commerce software — often make use of more complex technologies on the web server, but these technologies are actually used to produce HTML and CSS that is then sent to the browser. So, if your site uses these technologies, you will be able to use your new HTML and CSS knowledge to take more control over how your site looks.

Larger, more complex sites like these may use a database to store data, and programming languages such as PHP, ASP.Net, Java, or Ruby on the web server, but you do not need to know these technologies to improve what the user sees. The skills you'll learn in this book should be enough to help you on that road.

HTML5 & CSS3

Since the web was first created there have been several versions of HTML and CSS — each intended to be an improvement on the previous version.

At the time of writing this book, HTML5 & CSS3 were still being developed. Although they had not been finalized, many browsers were already supporting some features of these languages and a lot of people were using the latest code on their websites. I have therefore chosen to teach you these latest versions.

Because HTML5 and CSS3 build on previous versions of these languages, learning these means you will also be able to understand the earlier versions of them. I have added clear notes when the code is new and also when it might not work in older browsers.

HOW THE WEB WORKS

When you visit a website, the web server hosting that site could be anywhere in the world. In order for you to find the location of the web server, your browser will first connect to a Domain Name System (DNS) server.

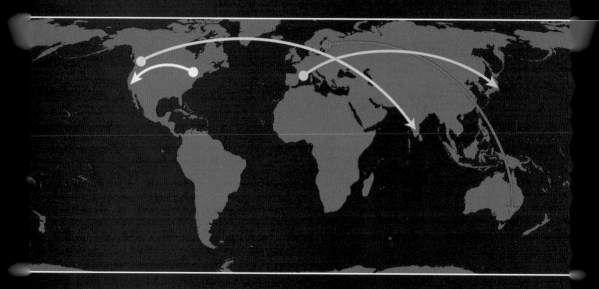

On this page you can see examples that demonstrate how the web server that hosts the website you are visiting can be anywhere in the world. It is the DNS servers that tell your browser how to find the website

A user in Barcelona visits sony.jp in Tokyo

A user in New York visits google.com in San Francisco

A user in Stockholm visits qantas.com.au in Sydney

On the right you can see what happens when a web user in England wants to view the website of the Louvre art gallery in France which is located at www.louvre.fr. Firstly, the browser in Cambridge contacts

1

When you connect to the web, you do so via an Internet Service Provider (ISP). You type a domain name or web address into your browser to visit a site; for example: `google.com`, `bbc.co.uk`, `microsoft.com`.

2

Your computer contacts a network of servers called Domain Name System (DNS) servers. These act like phone books; they tell your computer the IP address associated with the requested domain name. Every device on the web has a unique IP address; it is like the telephone number for that computer. Traditionally these were numbers of up to 12 digits separated by periods/full stops but they are now being updated to sets of up to 32 characters.

3

The unique number that the DNS server returns to your computer allows your browser to contact the web server that hosts the website you requested. A web server is a computer that is constantly connected to the web, and is set up especially to send web pages to users.

4

The web server then sends the page you requested back to your web browser.

Cambridge

LONDON

PARIS

1

STRUCTURE

- ▸ Understanding structure
- ▸ Learning about markup
- ▸ Tags and elements

We come across all kinds of documents every day of our lives. Newspapers, insurance forms, shop catalogues... the list goes on.

Many web pages act like electronic versions of these documents. For example, newspapers show the same stories in print as they do on websites; you can apply for insurance over the web; and stores have online catalogs and e-commerce facilities.

In all kinds of documents, structure is very important in helping readers to understand the messages you are trying to convey and to navigate around the document. So, in order to learn how to write web pages, it is very important to understand how to structure documents. In this chapter you will:

- See how HTML describes the structure of a web page
- Learn how tags or elements are added to your document
- Write your first web page

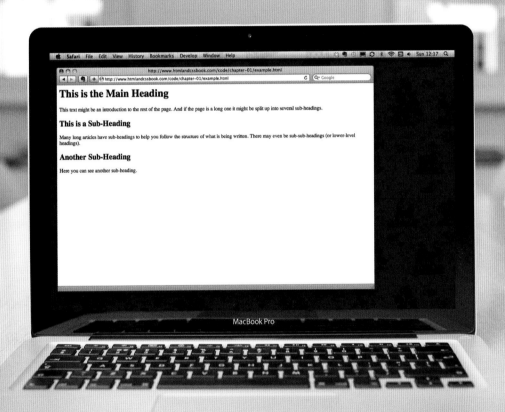

HOW PAGES USE STRUCTURE

Think about the stories you read in a newspaper: for each story, there will be a headline, some text, and possibly some images. If the article is a long piece, there may be subheadings that split the story into separate sections or quotes from those involved. Structure helps readers understand the stories in the newspaper.

The structure is very similar when a news story is viewed online (although it may also feature audio or video). This is illustrated on the right with a copy of a newspaper alongside the corresponding article on its website.

Now think about a very different type of document — an insurance form. Insurance forms often have headings for different sections, and each section contains a list of questions with areas for you to fill in details or checkboxes to tick. Again, the structure is very similar online.

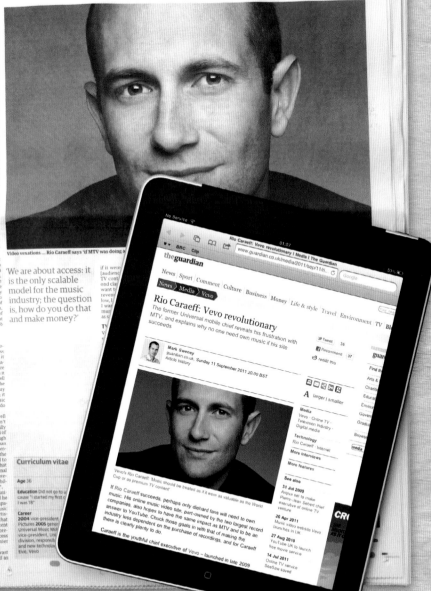

STRUCTURING WORD DOCUMENTS

The use of headings and subheadings in any document often reflects a hierarchy of information. For example, a document might start with a large heading, followed by an introduction or the most important information.

This might be expanded upon under subheadings lower down on the page. When using a word processor to create a document, we separate out the text to give it structure. Each topic might have a new paragraph, and each section can have a heading to describe what it covers.

On the right, you can see a simple document in Microsoft Word. The different styles for the document, such as different levels of heading, are shown in the drop down box. If you regularly use Word, you might have also used the formatting toolbar or palette to do this.

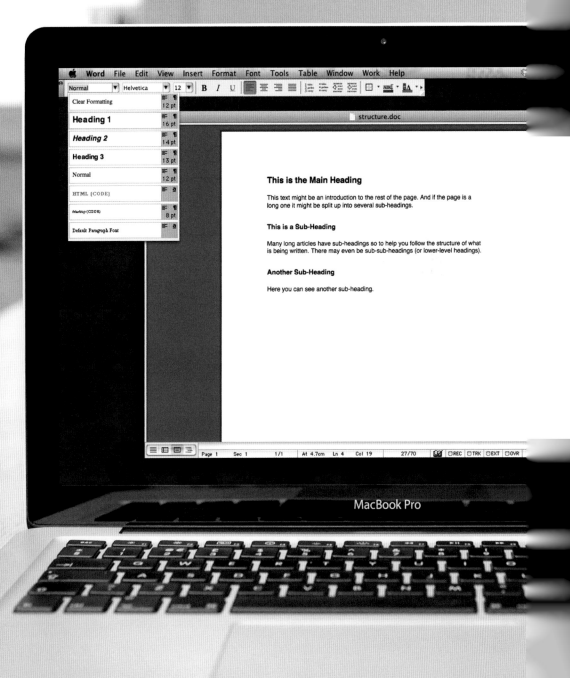

This is the Main Heading

This text might be an introduction to the rest of the page. And if the page is a long one it might be split up into several sub-headings.

This is a Sub-Heading

Many long articles have sub-headings so to help you follow the structure of what is being written. There may even be sub-sub-headings (or lower-level headings).

Another Sub-Heading

Here you can see another sub-heading.

On the previous page you saw
how structure was added to
a Word document to make it
easier to understand. We use
structure in the same way when
writing web pages.

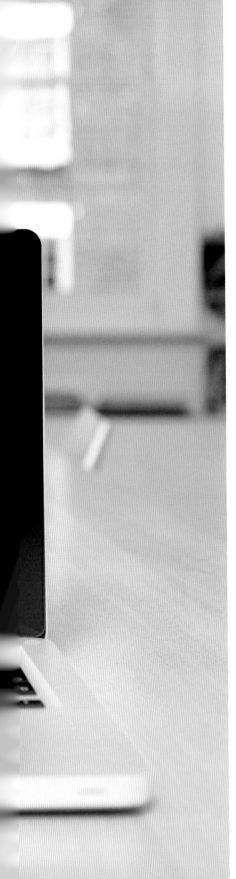

HTML DESCRIBES THE STRUCTURE OF PAGES

In the browser window you can see a web page that features exactly the same content as the Word document you met on the page 18. To describe the structure of a web page, we add code to the words we want to appear on the page.

You can see the HTML code for this page below. Don't worry about what the code means yet. We start to look at it in more detail on the next page. Note that the HTML code is in blue, and the text you see on screen is in black.

```
<html>
  <body>
    <h1>This is the Main Heading</h1>
    <p>This text might be an introduction to the rest of
        the page. And if the page is a long one it might
        be split up into several sub-headings.</p>
    <h2>This is a Sub-Heading</h2>
    <p>Many long articles have sub-headings to help you
        follow the structure of what is being written.
        There may even be sub-sub-headings (or lower-level
        headings).</p>
    <h2>Another Sub-Heading</h2>
    <p>Here you can see another sub-heading.</p>
  </body>
</html>
```

The HTML code (in blue) is made up of characters that live inside angled brackets — these are called HTML **elements**. Elements are usually made up of two **tags**: an opening tag and a closing tag. (The closing tag has an extra forward slash in it.) Each HTML element tells the browser something about the information that sits between its opening and closing tags.

HTML USES ELEMENTS TO DESCRIBE THE STRUCTURE OF PAGES

Let's look closer at the code from the last page.
There are several different elements. Each
element has an opening tag and a closing tag.

CODE

```
<html>
    <body>
        <h1>This is the Main Heading</h1>

        <p>This text might be an introduction to the rest of
            the page. And if the page is a long one it might
            be split up into several sub-headings.</p>

        <h2>This is a Sub-Heading</h2>

        <p>Many long articles have sub-headings to help you
            follow the structure of what is being written.
            There may even be sub-sub-headings (or lower-level
            headings).</p>

        <h2>Another Sub-Heading</h2>

        <p>Here you can see another sub-heading.</p>

    </body>
</html>
```

Tags act like containers. They tell you something about the information that lies between their opening and closing tags.

DESCRIPTION

The opening `<html>` tag indicates that anything between it and a closing `</html>` tag is HTML code.

The `<body>` tag indicates that anything between it and the closing `</body>` tag should be shown inside the main browser window.

Words between `<h1>` and `</h1>` are a main heading.

A paragraph of text appears between these `<p>` and `</p>` tags.

Words between `<h2>` and `</h2>` form a sub-heading.

Here is another paragraph between opening `<p>` and closing `</p>` tags.

Another sub-heading inside `<h2>` and `</h2>` tags.

Another paragraph inside `<p>` and `</p>` tags.

The closing `</body>` tag indicates the end of what should appear in the main browser window.

The closing `</html>` tag indicates that it is the end of the HTML code.

A CLOSER LOOK AT TAGS

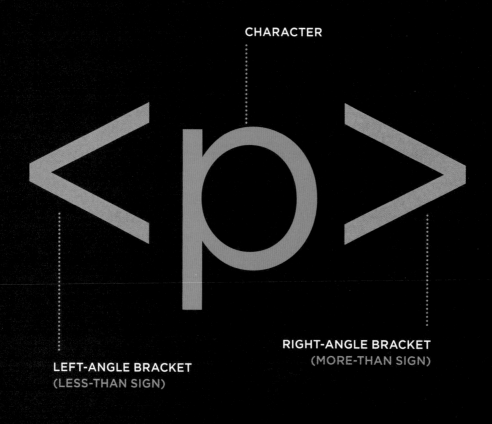

CHARACTER

LEFT-ANGLE BRACKET
(LESS-THAN SIGN)

RIGHT-ANGLE BRACKET
(MORE-THAN SIGN)

OPENING TAG

The characters in the brackets indicate the tag's purpose.

For example, in the tags above the p stands for paragraph.

The closing tag has a forward slash after the the < symbol.

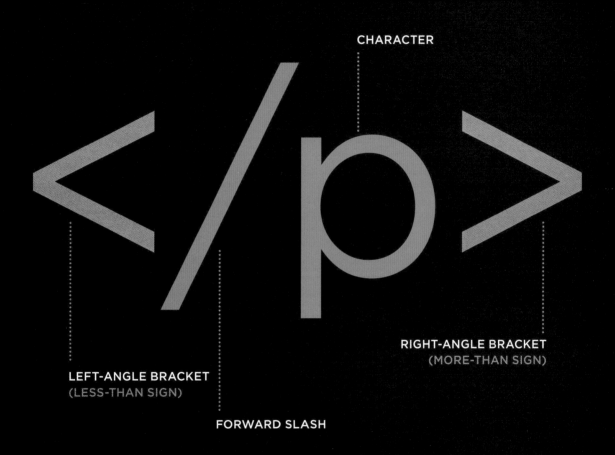

CHARACTER

LEFT-ANGLE BRACKET
(LESS-THAN SIGN)

FORWARD SLASH

RIGHT-ANGLE BRACKET
(MORE-THAN SIGN)

CLOSING TAG

The terms "tag" and "element" are often used interchangeably. Strictly speaking, however, an element comprises the opening tag *and* the closing tag *and* any content that lies between them.

ATTRIBUTES TELL US MORE ABOUT ELEMENTS

Attributes provide additional information about the contents of an element. They appear on the opening tag of the element and are made up of two parts: a name and a value, separated by an equals sign.

ATTRIBUTE NAME

```
<p lang="en-us">Paragraph in English</p>
```

ATTRIBUTE VALUE

The attribute **name** indicates what kind of extra information you are supplying about the element's content. It should be written in lowercase.

The **value** is the information or setting for the attribute. It should be placed in double quotes. Different attributes can have different values.

Here an attribute called lang is used to indicate the language used in this element. The value of this attribute on this page specifies it is in US English.

HTML5 allows you to use
uppercase attribute names and
omit the quotemarks, but this is
not recommended.

ATTRIBUTE
NAME

`<p lang="fr">Paragraphe en Français</p>`

ATTRIBUTE
VALUE

The majority of attributes can only be used on certain elements, although a few attributes (such as `lang`) can appear on any element.

Most attribute values are either pre-defined or follow a stipulated format. We will look at the permitted values as we introduce each new attribute.

The value of the `lang` attribute is an abbreviated way of specifying which language is used inside the element that all browsers understand.

BODY, HEAD & TITLE

\<body\>

You met the \<body\> element in the first example we created. Everything inside this element is shown inside the main browser window.

\<head\>

Before the \<body\> element you will often see a \<head\> element. This contains information *about* the page (rather than information that is shown within the main part of the browser window that is highlighted in blue on the opposite page). You will usually find a \<title\> element inside the \<head\> element.

\<title\>

The contents of the \<title\> element are either shown in the top of the browser, above where you usually type in the URL of the page you want to visit, or on the tab for that page (if your browser uses tabs to allow you to view multiple pages at the same time).

/chapter-01/body-head-title.html `HTML`

```
<html>
  <head>
    <title>This is the Title of the Page</title>
  </head>
  <body>
    <h1>This is the Body of the Page</h1>
    <p>Anything within the body of a web page is
    displayed in the main browser window.</p>
  </body>
</html>
```

`RESULT`

This is the Body of the Page

Anything within the body of a web page is displayed in the main browser window.

Anything written between the
`<title>` tags will appear in the
title bar (or tabs) at the top of
the browser window, highlighted
in orange here.

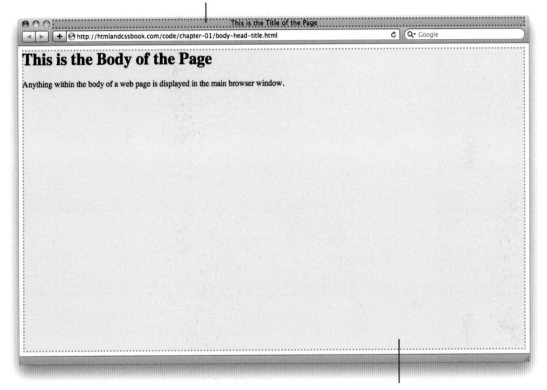

Anything written between
the `<body>` tags will appear
in the main browser window,
highlighted in blue here.

You may know that HTML stands for HyperText Markup Language. The HyperText part refers to the fact that HTML allows you to create links that allow visitors to move from one page to another quickly and easily. A markup language allows you to annotate text, and these annotations provide additional meaning to the contents of a document. If you think of a web page, we add code around the original text we want to display and the browser then uses the code to display the page correctly. So the tags we add are the markup.

CREATING A WEB PAGE ON A PC

To create your first web page on a PC, start up Notepad. You can find this by going to:

Start
   All Programs (or Programs)
      Accessories
         Notepad

You might also like to download a free editor called Notepad++ from notepad-plus-plus.org.

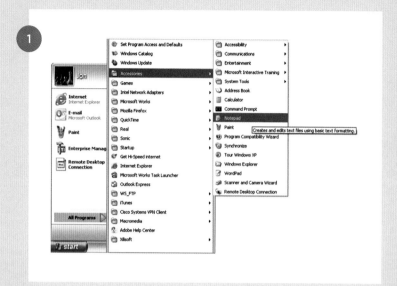

Type the code shown on the right.

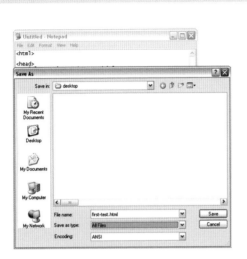

Go to the File menu and select **Save as...** You will need to save the file somewhere you can remember. If you like, you could create a folder for any examples that you try out from this book.

Save this file as `first-test.html`. Make sure that the **Save as type** drop down has **All Files** selected.

Start your web browser. Go to the **File** menu and select **Open**. Browse to the file that you just created, select it and click on the **Open** button. The result should look something like the screen shot to the left.

If it doesn't look like this, find the file you just created on your computer and make sure that it has the file extension `.html` (if it is `.txt` then you need to go back to Notepad and save the file again, but this time put quote marks around the name "`first-test.html`").

CREATING A WEB PAGE ON A MAC

To create your first web page on a Mac, start up TextEdit. This should be in your **Applications** folder.

You might also like to download a free text editor for creating web pages called TextWrangler which is available from barebones.com.

Type the code shown on the right.

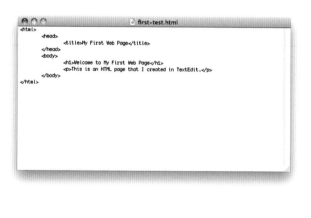

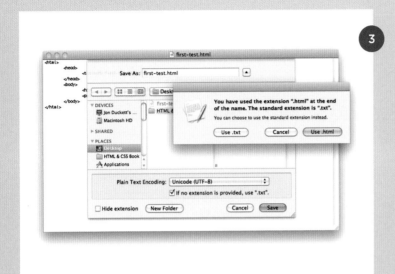

Now go to the **File** menu and select **Save as...** You will need to save the file somewhere you can remember.

If you like, you could create a folder for any examples that you try out from this book. Save this file as `first-test.html`. You will probably see a window like the screen shot to the left.

You want to select the **Use .html** button.

Next, start your web browser, go to the **File** menu, and select **Open**. You should browse to the file that you just created, select it and click on the **Open** button. The result should look like the screen shot to the left.

If it doesn't look like this, you might need to change one of the settings in TextEdit. Go to the TextEdit menu and select **Preferences**. Then on the preferences for **Open and Save**, tick the box that says **Ignore rich text commands in HTML files**. Now try to save the file again.

CODE IN A CONTENT MANAGEMENT SYSTEM

If you are working with a content management system, blogging platform, or e-commerce application, you will probably log into a special administration section of the website to control it. The tools provided in the administration sections of these sites usually allow you to edit parts of the page rather than the entire page, which means you will rarely see the `<html>`, `<head>`, or `<body>` elements.

Looking at the content management system on the opposite page, you have a box

that allows you to enter a title for the page, another box for the main article, a way to enter a publication date, and something to indicate which section of the site this page belongs in.

For an e-commerce store, you might have boxes that allow you to enter a title for the product, a description of the product, its price, and the quantity available.

That is because they use a single 'template' to control all of the pages for a section of the site. (For example, an e-commerce

system might use the same template to show all of their products.) The information you supply is placed into the templates.

The advantage of this approach is that people who do not know how to write web pages can add information to a website and it is also possible to change the presentation of something in the template, and it will automatically update every page that uses that template. If you imagine an e-commerce store with 1,000 items for sale, just

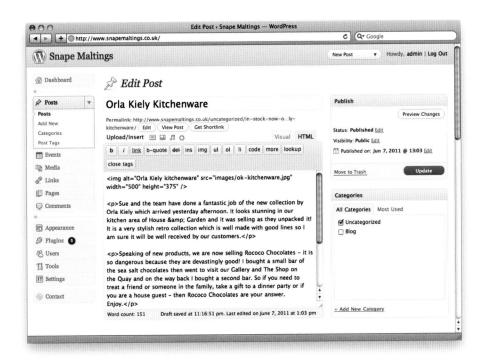

altering one template is a lot easier than changing the page for each individual product. In systems like this, when you have a large block of text that you can edit, such as a news article, blog entry or the description of a product in an e-commerce store, you will often see a text editor displayed.

Text editors usually have controls a little like those on your word processor, giving you different options to style text, add links or insert images. Behind the scenes these editors

are adding HTML code to your text, just like the code you have seen earlier in this chapter. Many of these editors will have an option that allows you to see (and edit) the code that they produce.

Once you know how to read and edit this code, you can take more control over these sections of your website.

In the example above, you can see that the text editor has a tab for Visual / HTML views of what the user enters. Other systems

might have a button (which often shows angle brackets) to indicate how to access the code.

Some content management systems offer tools that also allow you to edit the template files. If you do try to edit template files you need to check the documentation for your CMS as they all differ from each other. You need to be careful when editing template files because if you delete the wrong piece of code or add something in the wrong place the site may stop working entirely.

LOOKING AT HOW OTHER SITES ARE BUILT

When the web was first taking off, one of the most common ways to learn about HTML and discover new tips and techniques was to look at the source code that made up web pages.

These days there are many more books and online tutorials that teach HTML, but you can still look at the code that a web server sends to you. To try this out for yourself, simply go to the sample code for this chapter, at `www.htmlandcssbook.com/view-source/` and click on the link called "View Source."

Once you have opened this page, you can look for the **View** menu in your browser, and select the option that says **Source** or **View source**. (The title changes depending on what browser you are using.)

You should see a new window appear, and it will contain the source code that was used to create this page.

You can see this result in the photograph on the right. The page you see is the window at the top; the code is below.

At first this code might look complicated but don't be discouraged. By the time you have finished the next chapter of this book, you will be able to understand it.

All of the examples for this book are on the website, and you can use this simple technique on any of the example pages to see how they work.

You can also download all of the code for this book from the same website by clicking on the "Download" link.

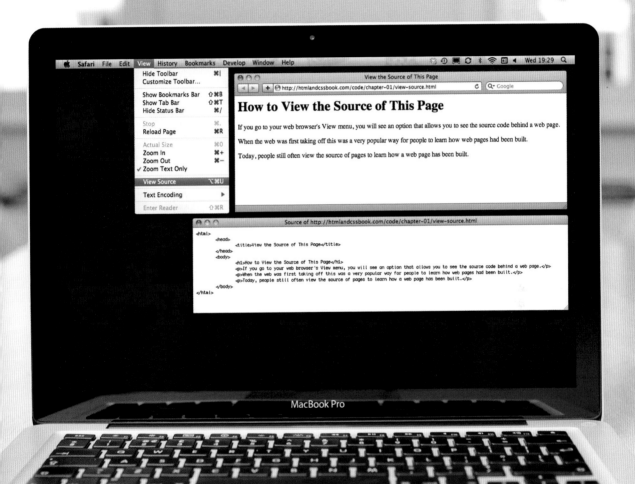

- HTML pages are text documents.

- HTML uses tags, which are characters that sit inside angled brackets. They act like containers and tell you something about the information that lies between them.

- Tags are often referred to as elements.

- Tags usually come in pairs. The opening tag denotes the start of a piece of content; the closing tag denotes the end.

- Opening tags can carry attributes, which tell us more about the content of that element.

- Attributes require a name and a value.

- To learn HTML you need to know what tags are available for you to use, what they do, and where they can go.

2

TEXT

- ▸ Headings and paragraphs
- ▸ Bold, italic, emphasis
- ▸ Structural and semantic markup

When creating a web page, you add tags (known as markup) to the contents of the page. These tags provide extra meaning and allow browsers to show users the appropriate structure for the page.

In this chapter we focus on how to add markup to the text that appears on your pages. You will learn about:

- **Structural markup:** the elements that you can use to describe both headings and paragraphs

- **Semantic markup:** which provides extra information; such as where emphasis is placed in a sentence, that something you have written is a quotation (and who said it), the meaning of acronyms, and so on

The Story in the Book

Chapter 1

Molly had been staring out of her window for about an hour now. On her desk, lying between the copies of *Nature*, *New Scientist*, and all the other scientific journals her work had appeared in, was a well thumbed copy of *On The Road*. It had been Molly's favorite book since college, and the longer she spent in these four walls the more she felt she needed to be free.

She had spent the last ten years in this room, sitting under a poster with an Oscar Wilde quote proclaiming that "Work is the refuge of people who have nothing better to do." Although many considered her pioneering work, unraveling the secrets of the llama DNA, to be an outstanding achievement, Molly *did* think she had something better to do.

HEADINGS

`<h1>`

`<h2>`

`<h3>`

`<h4>`

`<h5>`

`<h6>`

HTML has six "levels" of headings:

`<h1>` is used for main headings

`<h2>` is used for subheadings

If there are further sections under the subheadings then the `<h3>` element is used, and so on...

Browsers display the contents of headings at different sizes. The contents of an `<h1>` element is the largest, and the contents of an `<h6>` element is the smallest. The exact size at which each browser shows the headings can vary slightly. Users can also adjust the size of text in their browser. You will see how to control the size of text, its color, and the fonts used when we come to look at CSS.

chapter-02/headings.html   HTML

```
<h1>This is a Main Heading</h1>
<h2>This is a Level 2 Heading</h2>
<h3>This is a Level 3 Heading</h3>
<h4>This is a Level 4 Heading</h4>
<h5>This is a Level 5 Heading</h5>
<h6>This is a Level 6 Heading</h6>
```

RESULT

This is a Main Heading

This is a Level 2 Heading

This is a Level 3 Heading

This is a Level 4 Heading

This is a Level 5 Heading

This is a Level 6 Heading

PARAGRAPHS

<p>A paragraph consists of one or more sentences that form a self-contained unit of discourse. The start of a paragraph is indicated by a new line.</p>

HTML	chapter-02/paragraphs.html

```
<p>A paragraph consists of one or more sentences
   that form a self-contained unit of discourse. The
   start of a paragraph is indicated by a new
   line.</p>
<p>Text is easier to understand when it is split up
   into units of text. For example, a book may have
   chapters. Chapters can have subheadings. Under
   each heading there will be one or more
   paragraphs.</p>
```

To create a paragraph, surround the words that make up the paragraph with an opening <p> tag and closing </p> tag.

By default, a browser will show each paragraph on a new line with some space between it and any subsequent paragraphs.

RESULT

A paragraph consists of one or more sentences that form a self-contained unit of discourse. The start of a paragraph is indicated by a new line.

Text is easier to understand when it is split up into units of text. For example, a book may have chapters. Chapters can have subheadings. Under each heading there will be one or more paragraphs.

BOLD & ITALIC

<b>

By enclosing words in the tags <b> and </b> we can make characters appear bold.

The <b> element also represents a section of text that would be presented in a visually different way (for example key words in a paragraph) although the use of the <b> element does not imply any additional meaning.

See also page 51 for the <strong> element.

See also page 51 for the <strong> element.

```
chapter-02/bold.html                    HTML

<p>This is how we make a word appear <b>bold.</b>
    </p>
<p>Inside a product description you might see some
    <b>key features</b> in bold.</p>
```

RESULT

This is how we make a word appear **bold.**

Inside a product description you might see some **key features** in bold.

<i>

By enclosing words in the tags <i> and </i> we can make characters appear italic.

The <i> element also represents a section of text that would be said in a different way from surrounding content — such as technical terms, names of ships, foreign words, thoughts, or other terms that would usually be italicized.

See also page 51 for the <em> element.

```
chapter-02/italic.html                  HTML

<p>This is how we make a word appear <i>italic</i>.
    </p>
<p>It's a potato <i>Solanum teberosum</i>.</p>
<p>Captain Cook sailed to Australia on the
    <i>Endeavour</i>.</p>
```

RESULT

This is how we make a word appear *italic*.

It's a potato *Solanum teberosum*.

Captain Cook sailed to Australia on the *Endeavour*.

SUPERSCRIPT & SUBSCRIPT

```
<p>On the 4<sup>th</sup> of September you will learn
   about E=MC<sup>2</sup>.</p>
<p>The amount of CO<sub>2</sub> in the atmosphere
   grew by 2ppm in 2009<sub>1</sub>.</p>
```

RESULT

On the 4th of September you will learn about E=MC^2.

The amount of CO$_2$ in the atmosphere grew by 2ppm in 2009$_1$.

$\langle sup \rangle$

The $\langle sup \rangle$ element is used to contain characters that should be superscript such as the suffixes of dates or mathematical concepts like raising a number to a power such as 2^2.

$\langle sub \rangle$

The $\langle sub \rangle$ element is used to contain characters that should be subscript. It is commonly used with foot notes or chemical formulas such as H$_2$O.

WHITE SPACE

In order to make code easier to read, web page authors often add extra spaces or start some elements on new lines.

When the browser comes across two or more spaces next to each other, it only displays one space. Similarly if it comes across a line break, it treats that as a single space too. This is known as **white space collapsing**.

You will often see that web page authors take advantage of white space collapsing to indent their code in order to make it easier to follow.

chapter-02/white-space.html `HTML`

```
<p>The moon is drifting away from Earth.</p>
<p>The moon          is drifting away from Earth.</p>
<p>The moon is drifting away from

     Earth.</p>
```

`RESULT`

The moon is drifting away from Earth.

The moon is drifting away from Earth.

The moon is drifting away from Earth.

LINE BREAKS & HORIZONTAL RULES

HTML   chapter-02/line-breaks.html

```
<p>The Earth<br />gets one hundred tons heavier
   every day<br />due to falling space dust.</p>
```

RESULT

The Earth
gets one hundred tons heavier every day
due to falling space dust.

`<br />`

As you have already seen, the browser will automatically show each new paragraph or heading on a new line. But if you wanted to add a line break inside the middle of a paragraph you can use the line break tag `<br />`.

`<hr />`

HTML   chapter-02/horizontal-rules.html

```
<p>Venus is the only planet that rotates
   clockwise.</p>
<hr />
<p>Jupiter is bigger than all the other planets
   combined.</p>
```

RESULT

Venus is the only planet that rotates clockwise.

Jupiter is bigger than all the other planets combined.

To create a break between themes — such as a change of topic in a book or a new scene in a play — you can add a horizontal rule between sections using the `<hr />` tag.

There are a few elements that do not have any words between an opening and closing tag. They are known as **empty elements** and they are written differently.

An empty element usually has only one tag. Before the closing angled bracket of an empty element there will often be a space and a forward slash character. Some web page authors miss this out but it is a good habit to get into.

VISUAL EDITORS & THEIR CODE VIEWS

Content management systems and HTML editors such as Dreamweaver usually have two views of the page you are creating: a visual editor and a code view.

Visual editors often resemble word processors. Although each editor will differ slightly, there are some features that are common to most editors that allow you to control the presentation of text.

- Headings are created by highlighting text then using a drop-down box to select a heading.

- Bold and italic text are created by highlighting some text and pressing a **b** or *i* button.

- New paragraphs are created using the return or the enter key.

- Line breaks are created by pressing the shift key and the return key at the same time.

- Horizontal rules are created using a button with a straight line on it.

If you copy and paste text from a program that allows you to format text (such as Word) into a visual editor, it may add extra markup. To prevent this, copy the text into a plain text editor first (such as Notepad on a PC or TextEdit on a Mac) and then copy it from that program and paste it into the visual editor.

Code views show you the code created by the visual editor so you can manually edit it, or so you can just enter new code yourself. It is often activated using a button with an icon that says HTML or has angled brackets. White space may be added to the code by the editor to make the code easier to read.

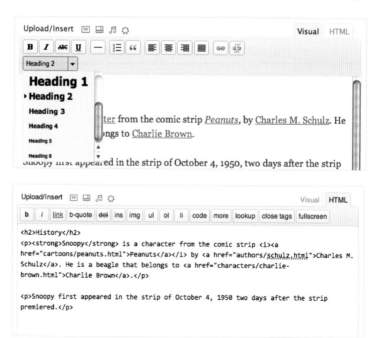

SEMANTIC MARKUP

There are some text elements that are not intended to affect the structure of your web pages, but they do add extra information to the pages — they are known as semantic markup.

In the rest of the chapter you will meet some more elements that will help you when you are adding text to web pages. For example, you are going to meet the <em> element that allows you to indicate where emphasis should be placed on selected words and the <blockquote> element which indicates that a block of text is a quotation.

Browsers often display the contents of these elements in a different way. For example, the content of the <em> element is shown in italics, and a <blockquote> is usually indented. But you should not use them to change the way that your text looks; their purpose is to describe the content of your web pages more accurately.

The reason for using these elements is that other programs, such as screen readers or search engines, can use this extra information. For example, the voice of a screen reader may add emphasis to the words inside the <em> element, or a search engine might register that your page features a quote if you use the <blockquote> element.

STRONG & EMPHASIS

<strong>

The use of the <strong> element indicates that its content has strong importance. For example, the words contained in this element might be said with strong emphasis.

By default, browsers will show the contents of a <strong> element in bold.

```
<p><strong>Beware:</strong> Pickpockets operate in
    this area.</p>
<p>This toy has many small pieces and is <strong>not
    suitable for children under five years old.
    </strong></p>
```

RESULT

Beware: Pickpockets operate in this area.

This toy has many small pieces and is **not suitable for children under five years old.**

<em>

The <em> element indicates emphasis that subtly changes the meaning of a sentence.

By default, browsers will show the contents of an <em> element in italic.

```
<p>I <em>think</em> Ivy was the first.</p>
<p>I think <em>Ivy</em> was the first.</p>
<p>I think Ivy was the <em>first</em>.</p>
```

RESULT

I *think* Ivy was the first.

I think *Ivy* was the first.

I think Ivy was the *first*.

QUOTATIONS

HTML

HTML   chapter-02/quotations.html

```html
<blockquote cite="http://en.wikipedia.org/wiki/
  Winnie-the-Pooh">
  <p>Did you ever stop to think, and forget to start
    again?</p>
</blockquote>
<p>As A.A. Milne said, <q>Some people talk to
  animals. Not many listen though. That's the
  problem.</q></p>
```

RESULT

Did you ever stop to think, and forget
to start again?

As A.A. Milne said, "Some people talk to animals.
Not many listen though. That's the problem."

There are two elements commonly used for marking up quotations:

<blockquote>

The <blockquote> element is used for longer quotes that take up an entire paragraph. Note how the <p> element is still used inside the <blockquote> element.

Browsers tend to indent the contents of the <blockquote> element, however you should not use this element just to indent a piece of text — rather you should achieve this effect using CSS.

<q>

The <q> element is used for shorter quotes that sit within a paragraph. Browsers are supposed to put quotes around the <q> element, however Internet Explorer does not — therefore many people avoid using the <q> element.

Both elements may use the cite attribute to indicate where the quote is from. Its value should be a URL that will have more information about the source of the quotation.

ABBREVIATIONS & ACRONYMS

<abbr>

If you use an abbreviation or an acronym, then the <abbr> element can be used. A title attribute on the opening tag is used to specify the full term.

In HTML 4 there was a separate <acronym> element for acronyms. To spell out the full form of the acronym, the title attribute was used (as with the <abbr> element above). HTML5 just uses the <abbr> element for both abbreviations and acronyms.

```
chapter-02/abbreviations.html                    HTML
<p><abbr title="Professor">Prof</abbr> Stephen
   Hawking is a theoretical physicist and
   cosmologist.</p>
<p><acronym title="National Aeronautics and Space
   Administration">NASA</acronym> do some crazy
   space stuff.</p>
```

RESULT

Prof Stephen Hawking is a theoretical physicist and cosmologist.

NASA do some crazy space stuff.

National Aeronautics and Space Administration

CITATIONS & DEFINITIONS

HTML
chapter-02/citations.html

```
<p><cite>A Brief History of Time</cite> by Stephen
    Hawking has sold over ten million copies
    worldwide.</p>
```

RESULT

A Brief History of Time by Stephen Hawking has sold over ten million copies worldwide.

HTML
chapter-02/definitions.html

```
<p>A <dfn>black hole</dfn> is a region of space from
    which nothing, not even light, can escape.</p>
```

RESULT

A black hole is a region of space from which nothing, not even light, can escape.

<cite>

When you are referencing a piece of work such as a book, film or research paper, the <cite> element can be used to indicate where the citation is from.

In HTML5, <cite> should not really be used for a person's name — but it was allowed in HTML 4, so most people are likely to continue to use it.

Browsers will render the content of a <cite> element in italics.

<dfn>

The first time you explain some new terminology (perhaps an academic concept or some jargon) in a document, it is known as the defining instance of it.

The <dfn> element is used to indicate the defining instance of a new term.

Some browsers show the content of the <dfn> element in italics. Safari and Chrome do not change its appearance.

AUTHOR DETAILS

<address>

The <address> element has quite a specific use: to contain contact details for the author of the page.

It can contain a physical address, but it does not have to. For example, it may also contain a phone number or email address.

Browsers often display the content of the <address> element in italics.

You may also be interested in something called the hCard microformat for adding physical address information to your markup.

ONLINE EXTRA:
You can find out more about hCards on the website accompanying this book.

chapter-02/address.html · HTML

```html
<address>
  <p><a href="mailto:homer@example.org">
     homer@example.org</a></p>
  <p>742 Evergreen Terrace, Springfield.</p>
</address>
```

RESULT

homer@example.org

742 Evergreen Terrace, Springfield.

CHANGES TO CONTENT

```
<p>It was the <del>worst</del> <ins>best</ins> idea
   she had ever had.</p>
```

RESULT

It was the ~~worst~~ <u>best</u> idea she had ever had.

```
<p>Laptop computer:</p>
<p><s>Was $995</s></p>
<p>Now only $375</p>
```

RESULT

Laptop computer:

~~Was $995~~

Now only $375

The `<ins>` element can be used to show content that has been inserted into a document, while the `<del>` element can show text that has been deleted from it.

The content of an `<ins>` element is usually underlined, while the content of a `<del>` element usually has a line through it.

The `<s>` element indicates something that is no longer accurate or relevant (but that should not be deleted).

Visually the content of an `<s>` element will usually be displayed with a line through the center.

Older versions of HTML had a `<u>` element for content that was underlined, but this is being phased out.

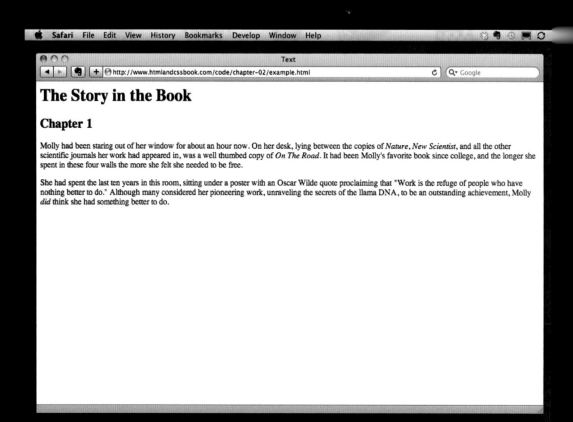

The Story in the Book

Chapter 1

Molly had been staring out of her window for about an hour now. On her desk, lying between the copies of *Nature*, *New Scientist*, and all the other scientific journals her work had appeared in, was a well thumbed copy of *On The Road*. It had been Molly's favorite book since college, and the longer she spent in these four walls the more she felt she needed to be free.

She had spent the last ten years in this room, sitting under a poster with an Oscar Wilde quote proclaiming that "Work is the refuge of people who have nothing better to do." Although many considered her pioneering work, unraveling the secrets of the llama DNA, to be an outstanding achievement, Molly *did* think she had something better to do.

EXAMPLE
TEXT

This is a very simple HTML page that demonstrates text markup.

Structural markup includes elements such as <h1>, <h2>, and <p>. Semantic information is carried in elements such as <cite> and <em>.

```html
<html>
  <head>
    <title>Text</title>
  </head>
  <body>
    <h1>The Story in the Book</h1>
    <h2>Chapter 1</h2>
    <p>Molly had been staring out of her window for about
       an hour now. On her desk, lying between the copies
       of <i>Nature</i>, <i>New Scientist</i>, and all
       the other scientific journals her work had
       appeared in, was a well thumbed copy of <cite>On
       The Road</cite>. It had been Molly's favorite book
       since college, and the longer she spent in these
       four walls the more she felt she needed to be
       free.</p>
    <p>She had spent the last ten years in this room,
       sitting under a poster with an Oscar Wilde quote
       proclaiming that <q>Work is the refuge of
       people who have nothing better to do.</q> Although
       many considered her pioneering work, unraveling
       the secrets of the llama <abbr
       title="Deoxyribonucleic acid">DNA</abbr>, to be an
       outstanding achievement, Molly <em>did</em> think
       she had something better to do.</p>
  </body>
</html>
```

- HTML elements are used to describe the structure of the page (e.g. headings, subheadings, paragraphs).

- They also provide semantic information (e.g. where emphasis should be placed, the definition of any acronyms used, when given text is a quotation).

3
LISTS

- ▸ Numbered lists
- ▸ Bullet lists
- ▸ Definition lists

There are lots of occasions when we need to use lists. HTML provides us with three different types:

- **Ordered lists** are lists where each item in the list is numbered. For example, the list might be a set of steps for a recipe that must be performed in order, or a legal contract where each point needs to be identified by a section number.

- **Unordered lists** are lists that begin with a bullet point (rather than characters that indicate order).

- **Definition lists** are made up of a set of terms along with the definitions for each of those terms.

ORDERED LISTS

`<ol>`

The ordered list is created with the `<ol>` element.

`<li>`

Each item in the list is placed between an opening `<li>` tag and a closing `</li>` tag. (The li stands for list item.)

Browsers indent lists by default.

Sometimes you may see a `type` attribute used with the `<ol>` element to specify the type of numbering (numbers, letters, roman numerals and so on). It is better to use the CSS `list-style-type` property covered on pages 333-335.

chapter-03/ordered-lists.html `HTML`

```
<ol>
  <li>Chop potatoes into quarters</li>
  <li>Simmer in salted water for 15-20
    minutes until tender</li>
  <li>Heat milk, butter and nutmeg</li>
  <li>Drain potatoes and mash</li>
  <li>Mix in the milk mixture</li>
</ol>
```

`RESULT`

1. Chop potatoes into quarters
2. Simmer in salted water for 15-20 minutes until tender
3. Heat milk, butter and nutmeg
4. Drain potatoes and mash
5. Mix in the milk mixture

UNORDERED LISTS

<ul>

```
<ul>
  <li>1kg King Edward potatoes</li>
  <li>100ml milk</li>
  <li>50g salted butter</li>
  <li>Freshly grated nutmeg</li>
  <li>Salt and pepper to taste</li>
</ul>
```

The unordered list is created with the <ul> element.

<li>

RESULT

- 1kg King Edward potatoes
- 100ml milk
- 50g salted butter
- Freshly grated nutmeg
- Salt and pepper to taste

Each item in the list is placed between an opening <li> tag and a closing </li> tag. (The li stands for list item.)

Browsers indent lists by default.

Sometimes you may see a type attribute used with the <ul> element to specify the type of bullet point (circles, squares, diamonds and so on). It is better to use the CSS list-style-type property covered on pages 333-335.

DEFINITION LISTS

`<dl>`

The definition list is created with the `<dl>` element and usually consists of a series of terms and their definitions.

Inside the `<dl>` element you will usually see pairs of `<dt>` and `<dd>` elements.

`<dt>`

This is used to contain the term being defined (the definition term).

`<dd>`

This is used to contain the definition.

Sometimes you might see a list where there are two terms used for the same definition or two different definitions for the same term.

chapter-03/definition-lists.html `HTML`

```
<dl>
  <dt>Sashimi</dt>
  <dd>Sliced raw fish that is served with
      condiments such as shredded daikon radish or
      ginger root, wasabi and soy sauce</dd>
  <dt>Scale</dt>
  <dd>A device used to accurately measure the
      weight of ingredients</dd>
  <dd>A technique by which the scales are removed
      from the skin of a fish</dd>
  <dt>Scamorze</dt>
  <dt>Scamorzo</dt>
  <dd>An Italian cheese usually made from whole
      cow's milk (although it was traditionally made
      from buffalo milk)</dd>
</dl>
```

`RESULT`

Sashimi
  Sliced raw fish that is served with condiments such as shredded daikon radish or ginger root, wasabi and soy sauce
Scale
  A device used to accurately measure the weight of ingredients
  A technique by which the scales are removed from the skin of a fish
Scamorze
Scamorzo
  An Italian cheese usually made from whole cow's milk (although it was traditionally made from buffalo milk)

NESTED LISTS

chapter-03/nested-lists.html

```html
<ul>
  <li>Mousses</li>
  <li>Pastries
    <ul>
      <li>Croissant</li>
      <li>Mille-feuille</li>
      <li>Palmier</li>
      <li>Profiterole</li>
    </ul>
  </li>
  <li>Tarts</li>
</ul>
```

RESULT

- Mousses
- Pastries
  - Croissant
  - Mille-feuille
  - Palmier
  - Profiterole
- Tarts

You can put a second list inside an `<li>` element to create a sub-list or nested list.

Browsers display nested lists indented further than the parent list. In nested unordered lists, the browser will usually change the style of the bullet point too.

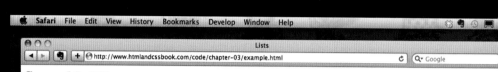

Scrambled Eggs

Eggs are one of my favorite foods. Here is a recipe for deliciously rich scrambled eggs.

Ingredients

- 2 eggs
- 1tbs butter
- 2tbs cream

Method

1. Melt butter in a frying pan over a medium heat
2. Gently mix the eggs and cream in a bowl
3. Once butter has melted add cream and eggs
4. Using a spatula fold the eggs from the edge of the pan to the center every 20 seconds (as if you are making an omelette)
5. When the eggs are still moist remove from the heat (it will continue to cook on the plate until served)

EXAMPLE
LISTS

Here you can see a main heading followed by an introductory paragraph. An unordered list is used to outline the ingredients and an ordered list is used to describe the steps.

```
<html>
  <head>
    <title>Lists</title>
  </head>
  <body>
    <h1>Scrambled Eggs</h1>
    <p>Eggs are one of my favourite foods. Here is a
       recipe for deliciously rich scrambled eggs.</p>
    <h2>Ingredients</h2>
    <ul>
      <li>2 eggs</li>
      <li>1tbs butter</li>
      <li>2tbs cream</li>
    </ul>
    <h2>Method</h2>
    <ol>
      <li>Melt butter in a frying pan over a medium
          heat</li>
      <li>Gently mix the eggs and cream in a bowl</li>
      <li>Once butter has melted add cream and eggs</li>
      <li>Using a spatula fold the eggs from the edge of
          the pan to the center every 20 seconds (as if
          you are making an omelette)</li>
      <li>When the eggs are still moist remove from the
          heat (it will continue to cook on the plate
          until served)</li>
    </ol>
  </body>
</html>
```

▸ There are three types of HTML lists: ordered, unordered, and definition.

▸ Ordered lists use numbers.

▸ Unordered lists use bullets.

▸ Definition lists are used to define terminology.

▸ Lists can be nested inside one another.

4

LINKS

- ‣ Creating links between pages
- ‣ Linking to other sites
- ‣ Email links

Links are the defining feature of the web because they allow you to move from one web page to another — enabling the very idea of browsing or surfing.

You will commonly come across the following types of links:

- Links from one website to another
- Links from one page to another on the same website
- Links from one part of a web page to another part of the same page
- Links that open in a new browser window
- Links that start up your email program and address a new email to someone

WRITING LINKS

Links are created using the <a> element. Users can click on anything between the opening <a> tag and the closing </a> tag. You specify which page you want to link to using the href attribute.

THIS IS THE PAGE THE LINK TAKES YOU TO

THIS IS THE TEXT THE USER CLICKS ON

`<a href="http://www.imdb.com">IMDB</a>`

OPENING LINK TAG

CLOSING LINK TAG

The text between the opening <a> tag and closing </a> tag is known as link text. Where possible, your link text should explain where visitors will be taken if they click on it (rather than just saying "click here"). Below you can see the link to IMDB that was created on the previous page.

Many people navigate websites by scanning the text for links. Clear link text can help visitors find what they want. This will give them a more positive impression of your site and may encourage them to visit it for longer. (It also helps people using screen reader software.)

To write good link text, you can think of words people might use when searching for the page that you are linking to. (For example, rather than write "places to stay" you could use something more specific such as "hotels in New York.")

[IMDB](#)

LINKING TO OTHER SITES

`<a>`

Links are created using the `<a>` element which has an attribute called `href`. The value of the `href` attribute is the page that you want people to go to when they click on the link.

Users can click on anything that appears between the opening `<a>` tag and the closing `</a>` tag and will be taken to the page specified in the `href` attribute.

When you link to a different website, the value of the `href` attribute will be the full web address for the site, which is known as an **absolute** URL.

Browsers show links in blue with an underline by default.

chapter-04/linking-to-other-sites.html `HTML`

```html
<p>Movie Reviews:
  <ul>
    <li><a href="http://www.empireonline.com">
        Empire</a></li>
    <li><a href="http://www.metacritic.com">
        Metacritic</a></li>
    <li><a href="http://www.rottentomatoes.com">
        Rotten Tomatoes</a></li>
    <li><a href="http://www.variety.com">
        Variety</a></li>
  </ul>
</p>
```

`RESULT`

Movie Reviews:

- Empire
- Metacritic
- Rotten Tomatoes
- Variety

ABSOLUTE URLS

URL stands for Uniform Resource Locator. Every web page has its own URL. This is the web address that you would type into a browser if you wanted to visit that specific page.

An absolute URL starts with the domain name for that site, and can be followed by the path to a specific page. If no page is specified, the site will display the homepage.

LINKING TO OTHER PAGES ON THE SAME SITE

`<a>`

```
<p>
  <ul>
    <li><a href="index.html">Home</a></li>
    <li><a href="about-us.html">About</a></li>
    <li><a href="movies.html">Movies</a></li>
    <li><a href="contact.html">Contact</a></li>
  </ul>
</p>
```

RESULT

- Home
- About
- Movies
- Contact

When you are linking to other pages within the same site, you do not need to specify the domain name in the URL. You can use a shorthand known as a **relative** URL.

If all the pages of the site are in the same folder, then the value of the href attribute is just the name of the file.

If you have different pages of a site in different folders, then you can use a slightly more complex syntax to indicate where the page is in relation to the current page. You will learn more about these on the pages 81-84.

If you look at the download code for each chapter, you will see that the index.html file contains links that use relative URLs.

RELATIVE URLS

When linking to other pages within the same site, you can use relative URLs. These are like a shorthand version of absolute URLs because you do not need to specify the domain name.

We will take a closer look at relative URLs on pages 83-84 as there are several helpful shortcuts you can use to write links to other pages on your own website.

Relative URLs help when building a site on your computer because you can create links between pages without having to set up your domain name or hosting.

DIRECTORY STRUCTURE

On larger websites it's a good idea to organize your code by placing the pages for each different section of the site into a new folder. Folders on a website are sometimes referred to as directories.

STRUCTURE

The diagram on the right shows the directory structure for a fictional entertainment listings website called ExampleArts.

The top-level folder is known as the **root** folder. (In this example, the root folder is called *examplearts*.) The root folder contains all of the other files and folders for a website.

Each section of the site is placed in a separate folder; this helps organize the files.

If you are working with a content management system, blogging software, or an e-commerce system, you might not have individual files for each page of the website.

RELATIONSHIPS

The relationship between files and folders on a website is described using the same terminology as a family tree.

In the diagram on the right, you can see some relationships have been drawn in.

The *examplearts* folder is a parent of the *movies*, *music* and *theater* folders. And the the *movies*, *music* and *theater* folders are children of the *examplearts* folder.

Instead, these systems often use one template file for each different type of page (such as news articles, blog posts, or products).

HOMEPAGES

The main homepage of a site written in HTML (and the homepages of each section in a child folder) is called *index.html*.

Web servers are usually set up to return the *index.html* file if no file name is specified.

Therefore, if you enter examplearts.com it will return examplearts.com/index .html, and examplearts.com/ music will return examplearts .com/music/index.html.

Editing the template file would change all of the pages that use that template. Do not change any code that is not HTML or you may break the page.

PARENT

The *examplearts* folder is a parent of the *music* folder.

GRANDPARENT

The *examplearts* folder is a grandparent of the *dvd* folder.

```
▼ 📁 examplearts
    📄 index.html
  ▼ 📁 images
      🖼 logo.gif
  ▼ 📁 movies
    ▼ 📁 cinema
        📄 index.html
        📄 listings.html
        📄 reviews.html
    ▼ 📁 dvd
        📄 index.html
        📄 reviews.html
  ▼ 📁 music
      📄 index.html
      📄 listings.html
      📄 reviews.html
  ▼ 📁 theater
      📄 index.html
      📄 listings.html
      📄 reviews.html
```

GRANDCHILD

The *dvd* folder is a grandchild of the *examplearts* folder.

CHILD

The *music* folder is a child of the *examplearts* folder.

Every page and every image on a website has a **URL** (or Uniform Resource Locator). The URL is made up of the domain name followed by the **path** to that page or image.

The path to the homepage of this site is `www.examplearts .com/index.html`. The path to the logo for the site is `examplearts.com/images/ logo.gif`.

You use URLs when linking to other web pages and when including images in your own site. On the next page, you will meet a shorthand way to link to files on your own site.

The root folder contains:

- A file called *index.html* which is the homepage for the entire site

- Individual folders for the movies, music and theatre sections of the site

Each sub-directory contains:

- A file called *index.html* which is the homepage for that section

- A reviews page called *reviews .html*

- A listings page called *listings .html* (except for the DVD section)

The movies section contains:

- A folder called *cinema*

- A folder called *DVD*.

RELATIVE URLS

Relative URLs can be used when linking to pages within your own website. They provide a shorthand way of telling the browser where to find your files.

When you are linking to a page on your own website, you do not need to specify the domain name. You can use **relative URLs** which are a shorthand way to tell the browser where a page is in relation to the current page.

This is especially helpful when creating a new website or learning about HTML because you can create links between pages when they are only on your personal computer (before you have got a domain name and uploaded them to the web).

Because you do not need to repeat the domain name in each link, they are also quicker to write.

If all of the files in your site are in one folder, you simply use the file name for that page.

If your site is organized into separate folders (or directories), you need to tell the browser how to get from the page it is *currently on* to the page that you are *linking to*.

If you link to the same page from two different pages you might, therefore, need to write two different relative URLs.

These links make use of the same terminology (borrowed from that of family trees) you met on the previous page which introduces directory structure.

RELATIVE LINK TYPE	EXAMPLE (from diagram on previous page)
SAME FOLDER To link to a file in the same folder, just use the file name. (Nothing else is needed.)	To link to music reviews from the music homepage: `<a href="reviews.html">Reviews</a>`
CHILD FOLDER For a child folder, use the name of the child folder, followed by a forward slash, then the file name.	To link to music listings from the homepage: `<a href="music/listings.html">Listings</a>`

GRANDCHILD FOLDER
Use the name of the child folder, followed by a forward slash, then the name of the grandchild folder, followed by another forward slash, then the file name.
	To link to DVD reviews from the homepage:
	`<a href="movies/dvd/reviews.html">`
	`Reviews</a>`

PARENT FOLDER Use `../` to indicate the folder above the current one, then follow it with the file name.	To link to the homepage from the music reviews: `<a href="../index.html">Home</a>`
GRANDPARENT FOLDER Repeat the `../` to indicate that you want to go up two folders (rather than one), then follow it with the file name.	To link to the homepage from the DVD reviews: `<a href="../../index.html">Home</a>`

When a website is live (that is, uploaded to a web server) you may see a couple of other techniques used that do not work when the files are on your local computer.

For example, you may see the name of a child folder without the name of a file. In this case the web server will usually try to show the homepage for that section.

A forward slash will return the homepage for the entire site, and a forward slash followed by a file name will return that file providing it is in the root directory.

EMAIL LINKS

mailto:

To create a link that starts up the user's email program and addresses an email to a specified email address, you use the `<a>` element. However, this time the value of the `href` attribute starts with `mailto:` and is followed by the email address you want the email to be sent to.

On the right you can see that an email link looks just like any other link but, when it is clicked on, the user's email program will open a new email message and address it to the person specified in the link.

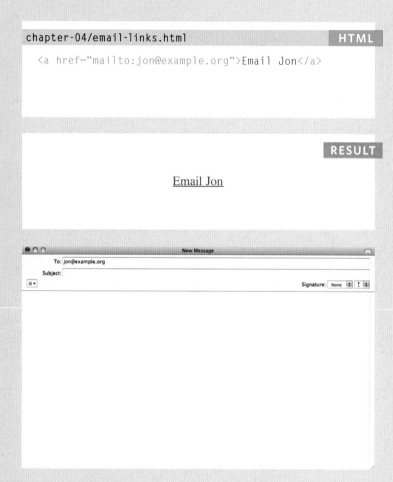

chapter-04/email-links.html   HTML

```
<a href="mailto:jon@example.org">Email Jon</a>
```

RESULT

Email Jon

OPENING LINKS IN A NEW WINDOW

HTML chapter-04/opening-links-in-a-new-window.html

```
<a href="http://www.imdb.com" target="_blank">
Internet Movie Database</a> (opens in new window)
```

RESULT

<u>Internet Movie Database</u> (opens in new window)

target

If you want a link to open in a new window, you can use the target attribute on the opening `<a>` tag. The value of this attribute should be _blank.

One of the most common reasons a web page author might want a link to be opened in a new window is if it points to another website. In such cases, they hope the user will return to the window containing their site after finishing looking at the other one.

Generally you should avoid opening links in a new window, but if you do, it is considered good practice to inform users that the link will open a new window before they click on it.

LINKING TO A SPECIFIC PART OF THE SAME PAGE

At the top of a long page you might want to add a list of contents that links to the corresponding sections lower down. Or you might want to add a link from part way down the page back to the top of it to save users from having to scroll back to the top.

Before you can link to a specific part of a page, you need to identify the points in the page that the link will go to. You do this using the id attribute (which can be used on every HTML element). You can see that the <h1> and <h2> elements in this example have been given id attributes that identify those sections of the page.

The value of the id attribute should start with a letter or an underscore (not a number or any other character) and, on a single page, no two id attributes should have the same value.

To link to an element that uses an id attribute you use the <a> element again, but the value of the href attribute starts with the # symbol, followed by the value of the id attribute of the element you want to link to. In this example, <a href="#top"> links to the <h1> element at the top of the page whose id attribute has a value of top.

chapter-04/linking-to-a-specific-part.html `HTML`

```
<h1 id="top">Film-Making Terms</h1>
<a href="#arc_shot">Arc Shot</a><br />
<a href="#interlude">Interlude</a><br />
<a href="#prologue">Prologue</a><br /><br />
<h2 id="arc_shot">Arc Shot</h2>
<p>A shot in which the subject is photographed by an
    encircling or moving camera</p>
<h2 id="interlude">Interlude</h2>
<p>A brief, intervening film scene or sequence, not
    specifically tied to the plot, that appears
    within a film</p>
<h2 id="prologue">Prologue</h2>
<p>A speech, preface, introduction, or brief scene
    preceding the main action or plot of a film;
    contrast to epilogue</p>
<p><a href="#top">Top</a></p>
```

LINKING TO A SPECIFIC PART OF ANOTHER PAGE

Film-Making Terms

Arc Shot
Interlude
Prologue

Arc Shot

A shot in which the subject is photographed by an encircling or moving camera

Interlude

A brief, intervening film scene or sequence, not specifically tied to the plot, that appears within a film

Prologue

A speech, preface, introduction, or brief scene preceding the main action or plot of a film; contrast to epilogue

Top

If you want to link to a specific part of a different page (whether on your own site or a different website) you can use a similar technique.

As long as the page you are linking to has id attributes that identify specific parts of the page, you can simply add the same syntax to the end of the link for that page.

Therefore, the href attribute will contain the address for the page (either an absolute URL or a relative URL), followed by the # symbol, followed by the value of the id attribute that is used on the element you are linking to.

For example, to link to the bottom of the homepage of the website that accompanies this book, you would write:

```
<a href="http:/www.
htmlandcssbook.com/
#bottom">
```

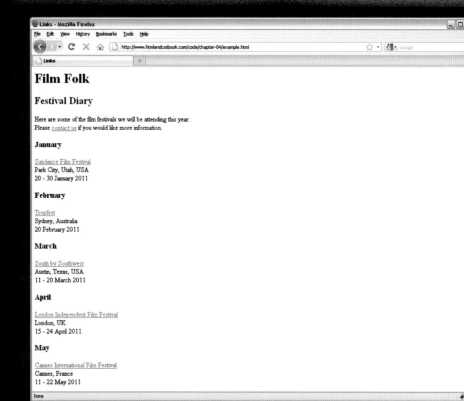

Film Folk

Festival Diary

Here are some of the film festivals we will be attending this year.
Please contact us if you would like more information.

January

Sundance Film Festival
Park City, Utah, USA
20 - 30 January 2011

February

Tropfest
Sydney, Australia
20 February 2011

March

South by Southwest
Austin, Texas, USA
11 - 20 March 2011

April

London Independent Film Festival
London, UK
15 - 24 April 2011

May

Cannes International Film Festival
Cannes, France
11 - 22 May 2011

This example is of a web page about film.

The <h1> element is used with an id attribute at the top of the page so that a link can be added to take readers from the bottom of the page to the top. There is an email link to allow readers to contact the author of the web page. There are also a number of links to qualified URLs. These link to various film festivals. Below this list is a link to a relative URL which is an "about" page that lives in the same directory.

```html
<html>
  <head>
    <title>Links</title>
  </head>
  <body>
    <h1 id="top">Film Folk</h1>
    <h2>Festival Diary</h2>
    <p>Here are some of the film festivals we
        will be attending this year.<br />Please
        <a href="mailto:filmfolk@example.org">
        contact us</a> if you would like more
        information.</p>
    <h3>January</h3>
    <p><a href="http://www.sundance.org">
        Sundance Film Festival</a><br />
        Park City, Utah, USA<br />
        20 - 30 January 2011</p>
    <h3>February</h3>
    <p><a href="http://www.tropfest.com">
        Tropfest</a><br />
        Sydney, Australia<br />
        20 February 2011</p>
    <!-- additional content -->
    <p><a href="about.html">About Film Folk</a></p>
    <p><a href="#top">Top of page</a></p>
  </body>
</html>
```

‣ Links are created using the `<a>` element.

‣ The `<a>` element uses the `href` attribute to indicate the page you are linking to.

‣ If you are linking to a page within your own site, it is best to use relative links rather than qualified URLs.

‣ You can create links to open email programs with an email address in the "to" field.

‣ You can use the `id` attribute to target elements within a page that can be linked to.

5

IMAGES

- ▸ How to add images to pages
- ▸ Choosing the right format
- ▸ Optimizing images for the web

There are many reasons why you might want to add an image to a web page: you might want to include a logo, photograph, illustration, diagram, or chart.

There are several things to consider when selecting and preparing images for your site, but taking time to get them right will make it look more attractive and professional. In this chapter you will learn how to:

- Include an image in your web pages using HTML

- Pick which image format to use

- Show an image at the right size

- Optimize an image for use on the web to make pages load faster

You can also use CSS to include images in your pages using the background-image property, which you will meet on pages 413-420.

CHOOSING IMAGES FOR YOUR SITE

A picture can say a thousand words, and great images help make the difference between an average-looking site and a really engaging one.

Images can be used to set the tone for a site in less time than it takes to read a description. If you do not have photographs to use on your website, there are companies who sell **stock images**; these are images you pay to use (there is a list of stock photography websites below). Remember that all images are subject to copyright, and you can get into trouble for simply taking photographs from another website.

If you have a page that shows several images (such as product photographs or members of a team) then putting them on a simple, consistent background helps them look better as a group.

IMAGES SHOULD...

✔ Be relevant
✔ Convey information
✔ Convey the right mood
✔ Be instantly recognisable
✔ Fit the color palette

STOCK PHOTOS

www.istockphoto.com
www.gettyimages.com
www.veer.com
www.sxc.hu
www.fotolia.com

ONLINE EXTRA

We have provided an online gallery that helps you choose the right image for your website. You can find it in the tools section of the site accompanying this book.

STORING IMAGES ON YOUR SITE

If you are building a site from scratch, it is good practice to create a folder for all of the images the site uses.

As a website grows, keeping images in a separate folder helps you understand how the site is organized. Here you can see an example of the files for a website; all of the images are stored in a folder called *images*.

On a big site you might like to add subfolders inside the *images* folder. For example, images such as logos and buttons might sit in a folder called *interface*, product photographs might sit in a page called *products*, and images related to news might live in a folder called *news*.

If you are using a content management system or blogging platform, there are usually tools built into the admin site that allow you to upload images, and the program will probably already have a separate folder for image files and any other uploads.

ADDING IMAGES

<img>

To add an image into the page you need to use an <img> element. This is an empty element (which means there is no closing tag). It must carry the following two attributes:

src

This tells the browser where it can find the image file. This will usually be a relative URL pointing to an image on your own site. (Here you can see that the images are in a child folder called *images* — relative URLs were covered on pages 83-84).

alt

This provides a text description of the image which describes the image if you cannot see it.

title

You can also use the title attribute with the <img> element to provide additional information about the image. Most browsers will display the content of this attribute in a tooltip when the user hovers over the image.

chapter-05/adding-images.html

`HTML`

```
<img src="images/quokka.jpg" alt="A family of
    quokka" title="The quokka is an Australian
    marsupial that is similar in size to the
    domestic cat." />
```

`RESULT`

The text used in the alt attribute is often referred to as **alt text**. It should give an accurate description of the image content so it can be understood by screen reader software (used by people with visual impairments) and search engines.

If the image is just to make a page look more attractive (and it has no meaning, such as a graphic dividing line), then the alt attribute should still be used but the quotes should be left empty.

HEIGHT & WIDTH OF IMAGES

HTML

```
HTML            chapter-05/height-and-width-of-images.html
<img src="images/quokka.jpg" alt="A family of
    quokka" width="600" height="450" />
```

RESULT

You will also often see an `<img>` element use two other attributes that specify its size:

height
This specifies the height of the image in pixels.

width
This specifies the width of the image in pixels.

Images often take longer to load than the HTML code that makes up the rest of the page. It is, therefore, a good idea to specify the size of the image so that the browser can render the rest of the text on the page while leaving the right amount of space for the image that is still loading.

The size of images is increasingly being specified using CSS rather than HTML — see pages 409-410 for more information about this.

WHERE TO PLACE IMAGES IN YOUR CODE

Where an image is placed in the code will affect how it is displayed. Here are three examples of image placement that produce different results:

1: BEFORE A PARAGRAPH

The paragraph starts on a new line after the image.

2: INSIDE THE START OF A PARAGRAPH

The first row of text aligns with the bottom of the image.

3: IN THE MIDDLE OF A PARAGRAPH

The image is placed between the words of the paragraph that it appears in.

chapter-05/where-to-place-images.html `HTML`

```html
<img src="images/bird.gif" alt="Bird" width="100"
    height="100" />
<p>There are around 10,000 living species of birds
    that inhabit different ecosystems from the
    Arctic to the Antarctic. Many species undertake
    long distance annual migrations, and many more
    perform shorter irregular journeys.</p>
<hr />
<p><img src="images/bird.gif" alt="Bird" width="100"
    height="100" />There are around 10,000 living
    species of birds that inhabit different
    ecosystems from the Arctic to the Antarctic. Many
    species undertake long distance annual
    migrations, and many more perform shorter
    irregular journeys.</p>
<hr />
<p>There are around 10,000 living species of birds
    that inhabit different ecosystems from the
    Arctic to the Antarctic.<img
    src="images/bird.gif" alt="Bird" width="100"
    height="100" />Many species undertake long
    distance annual migrations, and many more perform
    shorter irregular journeys.</p>
```

There are around 10,000 living species of birds that inhabit different ecosystems from the Arctic to the Antarctic. Many species undertake long distance annual migrations, and many more perform shorter irregular journeys.

There are around 10,000 living species of birds that inhabit different ecosystems from the Arctic to the Antarctic. Many species undertake long distance annual migrations, and many more perform shorter irregular journeys.

There are around 10,000 living species of birds that inhabit different ecosystems from the Arctic to the Antarctic. Many species undertake long distance annual migrations, and many more perform shorter irregular journeys.

Where you place the image in the code is important because browsers show HTML elements in one of two ways:

Block elements always appear on a new line. Examples of block elements include the `<h1>` and `<p>` elements.

If the `<img>` is followed by a block level element (such as a paragraph) then the block level element will sit on a new line after the image as shown in the first example on this page.

Inline elements sit within a block level element and do not start on a new line. Examples of inline elements include the `<b>`, `<em>`, and `<img>` elements.

If the `<img>` element is inside a block level element, any text or other inline elements will flow around the image, as shown in the second and third examples on this page.

Block and inline elements are discussed in greater depth on pages 185-186.

OLD CODE: ALIGNING IMAGES HORIZONTALLY

align

The align attribute was commonly used to indicate how the other parts of a page should flow around an image. It has been removed from HTML5 and new websites should use CSS to control the alignment of images (as you will see on pages 411-412).

I have discussed it here because you are likely to come across it if you look at older code, and because some visual editors still insert this attribute when you indicate how an image should be aligned.

The align attribute can take these horizontal values:

left

This aligns the image to the left (allowing text to flow around its right-hand side).

right

This aligns the image to the right (allowing text to flow around its left-hand side).

chapter-05/aligning-images-horizontally.html `HTML`

```html
<p><img src="images/bird.gif" alt="Bird" width="100"
    height="100" align="left" />There are around
    10,000 living species of birds that inhabit
    different ecosystems from the Arctic to the
    Antarctic. Many species undertake long distance
    annual migrations, and many more perform shorter
    irregular journeys.</p>
<hr />
<p><img src="images/bird.gif" alt="Bird" width="100"
    height="100" align="right" />There are around
    10,000 living species of birds that inhabit
    different ecosystems from the Arctic to the
    Antarctic. Many species undertake long distance
    annual migrations, and many more perform shorter
    irregular journeys.</p>
```

There are around 10,000 living species of birds that inhabit different ecosystems from the Arctic to the Antarctic. Many species undertake long distance annual migrations, and many more perform shorter irregular journeys.

There are around 10,000 living species of birds that inhabit different ecosystems from the Arctic to the Antarctic. Many species undertake long distance annual migrations, and many more perform shorter irregular journeys.

This looks a lot neater than having one line of text next to the image (as shown on the previous example).

When you give the align attribute a value of left, the image is placed on the left and text flows around it.

When you give the align attribute a value of right, the image is placed on the right and the text flows around it.

When text flows right up to the edge of an image it can make it harder to read. You will learn how to add a gap between text and images on pages 313-314 using the CSS padding and margin properties.

OLD CODE: ALIGNING IMAGES VERTICALLY

As you saw on the last page, the align attribute is no longer used in HTML5, but it is covered here because you may see it used in older websites and it is still used in the code created by some visual editors.

You can see how to use CSS to achieve the same effects on pages 285-286.

There are three values that the align attribute can take that control how the image should align vertically with the text that surrounds it:

top
This aligns the first line of the surrounding text with the top of the image.

middle
This aligns the first line of the surrounding text with the middle of the image.

bottom
This aligns the first line of the surrounding text with the bottom of the image.

chapter-05/aligning-images-vertically.html `HTML`

```
<p><img src="images/bird.gif" alt="Bird" width="100"
   height="100" align="top" />There are around
   10,000 living species of birds that inhabit
   different ecosystems from the Arctic to the
   Antarctic. Many species undertake long distance
   annual migrations, and many more perform shorter
   irregular journeys.</p>
<hr />
<p><img src="images/bird.gif" alt="Bird" width="100"
   height="100" align="middle" />There are around
   10,000 living species of birds that inhabit
   different ecosystems from the Arctic to the
   Antarctic. Many species undertake long distance
   annual migrations, and many more perform shorter
   irregular journeys.</p>
<hr />
<p><img src="images/bird.gif" alt="Bird" width="100"
   height="100" align="bottom" />There are around
   10,000 living species of birds that inhabit
   different ecosystems from the Arctic to the
   Antarctic. Many species undertake long distance
   annual migrations, and many more perform shorter
   irregular journeys.</p>
```

There are around 10,000 living species of birds that inhabit different ecosystems from the Arctic to the Antarctic. Many species undertake long distance annual migrations, and many more perform shorter irregular journeys.

There are around 10,000 living species of birds that inhabit different ecosystems from the Arctic to the Antarctic. Many species undertake long distance annual migrations, and many more perform shorter irregular journeys.

There are around 10,000 living species of birds that inhabit different ecosystems from the Arctic to the Antarctic. Many species undertake long distance annual migrations, and many more perform shorter irregular journeys.

The value of top places the first line of text near the top of the image and subsequent lines of text appear under the image.

The value of middle places the first line of text near the vertical middle of the image and subsequent lines of text appear under the image.

The value of bottom places the first line of text near the bottom of the image and subsequent lines of text under the image.

When text flows right up to the edge of an image it can make it harder to read. You will learn how to add a gap between text and images on pages 313-314 using the CSS padding and margin properties.

If you would like all of the text to wrap around the image (rather than just one line of text), you should use the CSS float property discussed on pages 370-372.

In older code, you may see the align attribute used with the values left or right to achieve the same effect (as described on the previous page), although its use is no longer recommended.

THREE RULES FOR CREATING IMAGES

There are three rules to remember when you are creating images for your website which are summarized below. We go into greater detail on each topic over the next nine pages.

1

SAVE IMAGES IN THE RIGHT FORMAT

Websites mainly use images in jpeg, gif, or png format. If you choose the wrong image format then your image might not look as sharp as it should and can make the web page slower to load.

2

SAVE IMAGES AT THE RIGHT SIZE

You should save the image at the same width and height it will appear on the website (measured in pixels). If the image is smaller than the width or height that you have specified, the image can be distorted and stretched. If the image is larger than the width and height you have specified, the image will take longer to display on the page.

3

MEASURE IMAGES IN PIXELS

Computer screens are made up of tiny squares known as pixels. The number of pixels shown per inch of screen can vary if the user increases or decreases the resolution. Therefore, when you are saving images at the right size for use on the web, you should always measure the image in terms of the width and height in pixels (and not in centimeters or inches).

TOOLS TO EDIT & SAVE IMAGES

There are several tools you can use to edit and save images to ensure that they are the right size, format, and resolution.

The most popular tool amongst web professionals is **Adobe Photoshop**. (In fact, professional web designers often use this software to design entire sites.) The full version of Photoshop is expensive, but there is a cheaper version called Photoshop Elements which would suit the needs of most beginners.

OTHER SOFTWARE
Adobe Fireworks
Pixelmator
PaintShop Pro
Paint.net

ONLINE EDITORS
www.photoshop.com
www.pixlr.com
www.splashup.com
www.ipiccy.com

ONLINE EXTRA
Watch videos that demonstrate how to resize images and save them in the correct format using both of these applications.

IMAGE FORMATS: JPEG

Whenever you have many different colors in a picture you should use a JPEG. A photograph that features snow or an overcast sky might look like it has large areas that are just white or gray, but the picture is usually made up of many different colors that are subtly different.

IMAGE FORMATS: GIF

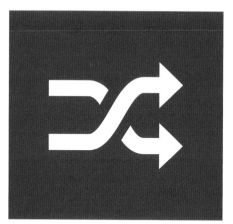

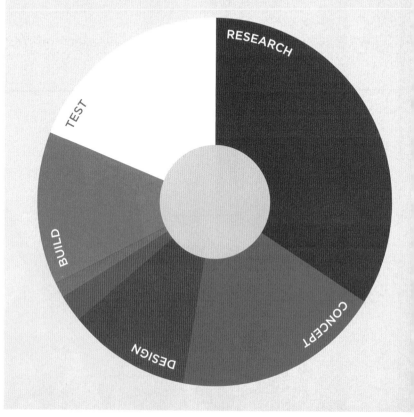

Use GIF or PNG format when saving images with few colors or large areas of the same color.

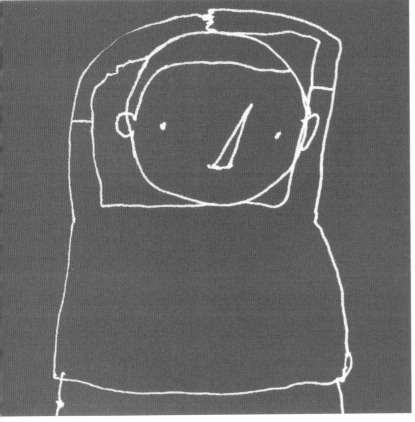

WWF

When a picture has an area that is filled with exactly the same color, it is known as flat color. Logos, illustrations, and diagrams often use flat colors. (Note that photographs of snow, sky, or grass are not flat colors, they are made up of many subtly different shades of the same color and are not as suited to GIF or PNG format.)

IMAGE DIMENSIONS

The images you use on your website should be saved at the same width and height that you want them to appear on the page.

For example, if you have designed a page to include an image that is 300 pixels wide by 150 pixels tall, the image you use should be 300 x 150 pixels. You may need to use image editing tools to resize and crop the image. When sourcing images, it is important to understand how you can alter the dimensions of an image; imagine that you had designed a web page to include an image that is 300 pixels wide by 150 pixels tall:

ONLINE EXTRA
Visit the tools section of the website accompanying this book to watch a video guide to resizing images in Photoshop and GIMP.

REDUCING IMAGE SIZE
You can reduce the size of images to create a smaller version of the image.

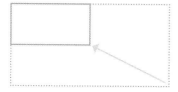

Example: If your image is 600 pixels wide and 300 pixels tall, you can reduce the size of the image by 50%.

Result: This will create an image that is quicker to download.

INCREASING IMAGE SIZE
You can't increase the size of photos significantly without affecting the image quality.

Example: If your image is only 100 pixels wide by 50 pixels tall, increasing the size by 300% would result in poor quality.

Result: The image will look blurry or blocky.

CHANGING SHAPE
Only some images can be cropped without losing valuable information (see next page).

Example: If your image is 300 pixels square, you can remove parts of it, but in doing so you might lose valuable information.

Result: Only some images can be cropped and still make sense.

CROPPING IMAGES

When cropping images it is important not to lose valuable information. It is best to source images that are the correct shape if possible.

PORTRAIT

Here you can see an illustration of a giraffe that is best suited to appearing in **portrait**.

LANDSCAPE

If we **crop** this illustration to make it landscape we lose the head and feet.

If we **add extra space** to the left and right of the illustration the background is not continued.

LANDSCAPE

Here you can see an illustration of an elephant that is best suited to appearing in **landscape**.

PORTRAIT

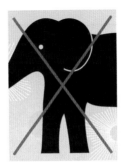

If we **crop** this illustration to make it portrait we lose the trunk and the hindquarters.

If we **add extra space** to the top and bottom of the illustration the background is not continued.

MEASURING IMAGES AND RESOLUTION

When sizing an image for use on the screen you should always set dimensions of the image in terms of pixels (not centimeters or inches).

The images on your computer screen are made up of lots of tiny squares known as **pixels**. The **resolution** of the screen is the number of pixels represented on it, and on most computers you can increase and decrease this number.

If a screen's resolution is set at 640x480 pixels, and it is then increased to 1024x768 pixels, the images and text will appear smaller because the screen is showing a lot more pixels within the same amount of space. (There are more pixels per inch.)

When creating images for print, it is best to save them at a resolution of 300 dots per inch (DPI) or higher (to ensure that they look sharp).

On the web, however, the resolution of an image is irrelevant. We only need to think of the size of the image in terms of its **dimensions** in pixels.

You may have heard that images for the web need to be 72 pixels per inch (PPI), but users can change the resolution of the screen itself (affecting the number of pixels shown per inch of the screen). Screens therefore determine the size of an image based solely on its width and height in pixels.

On a screen, an image that is 300x300 pixels at 72ppi looks exactly the same as an image that is 300x300 pixels at 500ppi. The resolution of the image only matters when the image is printed.

VECTOR IMAGES

Vector images differ from bitmap images and are resolution-independent. Vector images are commonly created in programs such as Adobe Illustrator.

When an image is a line drawing (such as a logo, illustration, or diagram), designers will often create it in vector format. Vector formatted images are very different to bitmap images.

Vector images are created by placing points on a grid, and drawing lines between those points. A color can then be added to "fill in" the lines that have been created.

The advantage of creating line drawings in vector format is that you can increase the dimensions of the image without affecting the quality of it.

The current method of using vector images for display on websites involves saving a bitmap version of the original vector image and using that.

Scalable Vector Graphics (SVG) are a relatively new format used to display vector images directly on the web (eliminating the need to create bitmap versions of them), however its use is not yet widespread.

ANIMATED GIFS

Animated GIFs show several frames of an image in sequence and therefore can be used to create simple animations.

Below you can see the individual frames that make up an animated GIF that shows an orange dot revolving around a circle — like the kind of animation you might see when a web page is loading.

Some image editing applications such as Adobe Photoshop allow you to create animated GIFs. There are several tutorials about how to do this on the web. There are also several websites that allow you to upload the graphics for the individual frames and create the animated GIF for you.

IT IS IMPORTANT TO REMEMBER:

Each extra frame of the image increases the size of the file, and can therefore add to the time it takes for an image to download (and web users do not like waiting a long time for images to download).

Because GIFs are not an ideal format for displaying photographs, animated GIFs are really only suitable for simple illustrations.

Some designers frown on animated GIFs because they remember a lot of amateur web designers overusing them in the 1990's.

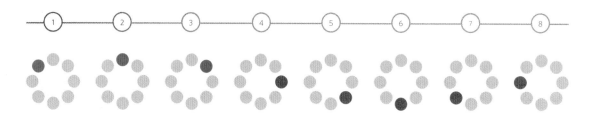

TRANSPARENCY

Creating an image that is partially transparent (or "see-through") for the web involves selecting one of two formats:

TRANSPARENT GIF

If the transparent part of the image has straight edges and it is 100% transparent (that is, not semi-opaque), you can save the image as a GIF (with the transparency option selected).

PNG

If the transparent part of the image has diagonal or rounded edges or if you want a semi-opaque transparency or a drop-shadow, then you will need to save it as a PNG.

Transparent PNGs are not fully supported in older browsers, most notably Internet Explorer 6 (IE6). There is some JavaScript you can use to get around this issue. The details of this script can be found in the tools section of the website accompanying this book.

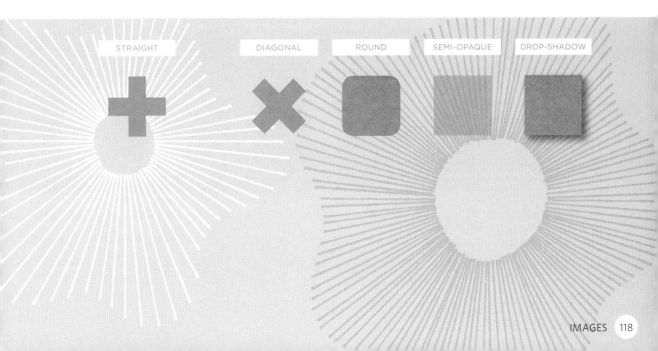

EXAMINING IMAGES ON THE WEB

CHECKING THE SIZE OF IMAGES

If you are updating a website, you might need to check the size of an existing image before creating a new one to replace it. This can be achieved by right-clicking on the image and making a selection from the pop-up menu that appears. (Mac users will need to hold down the control key and click rather than right-click.)

DOWNLOADING IMAGES

If you want to download images from a website, you can do so by accessing the same pop-up menu. (Please remember however that all images online are subject to copyright and require explicit permission to reuse.)

On the left you can see how to check the size of images and how to download them using Safari. Below is a brief overview of what to select in the pop-up menu to perform these functions in various browsers.

CHROME
Size: **_Open Image in New Tab_**
Size appears in new tab
Download: **_Save Image As_**

FIREFOX
Size: **_View Image Info_**
Size appears in pop-up window
Download: **_Save Image As_**

INTERNET EXPLORER
Size: **Properties**
Size appears in pop-up window
Download: **Save Image**

SAFARI
Size: **Open Image in New Tab**
Size appears in title bar
Download: **Save Image As**

HTML5: FIGURE AND FIGURE CAPTION

```
HTML                chapter-05/figure-and-figure-caption.html

<figure>
  <img src="images/otters.jpg" alt="Photograph of
      two sea otters floating in water" />
  <br />
  <figcaption>Sea otters hold hands when they
      sleep so they don't drift away from each
      other.</figcaption>
</figure>
```

RESULT

Sea otters hold hands when they sleep so they don't drift away from each other.

`<figure>`

Images often come with captions. HTML5 has introduced a new `<figure>` element to contain images and their caption so that the two are associated.

You can have more than one image inside the `<figure>` element as long as they all share the same caption.

Browsers sometimes indent the contents of the `<figure>` element.

`<figcaption>`

The `<figcaption>` element has been added to HTML5 in order to allow web page authors to add a caption to an image.

Before these elements were created there was no way to associate an `<img>` element with its caption.

Older browsers that do not understand HTML5 elements simply ignore the new elements and display the content of them.

In this example, the logo is a GIF because it uses flat colors, while the photographs are JPEGs. The main photo is placed inside the HTML5 `<figure>` element and has its own caption.

The `alt` attribute on each image provides a description for those using screen readers and the `title` attribute provides additional information. (This is shown in the tooltip.)

This example does not use the `height`, `width`, or `align` attributes as these are being phased out and you are encouraged to use CSS properties instead.

EXAMPLE
IMAGES

```
<html>
  <head>
    <title>Images</title>
  </head>
  <body>
    <h1>
      <img src="images/logo.gif"
           alt="From A to Zucchini" />
    </h1>
    <figure>
      <img src="images/chocolate-islands.jpg"
           alt="Chocolate Islands"
           title="Chocolate Islands Individual Cakes" />
      <p>
        <figcaption>
          This recipe for individual chocolate
          cakes is so simple and so delectable!
        </figcaption>
      </p>
    </figure>
    <h4>More Recipes:</h4>
    <p>
      <img src="images/lemon-posset.jpg"
           alt="Lemon Posset"
           title="Lemon Posset Dessert" />
      <img src="images/roasted-brussel-sprouts.jpg"
           alt="Roasted Brussel Sprouts"
           title="Roasted Brussel Sprouts Side Dish" />
      <img src="images/zucchini-cake.jpg"
           alt="Zucchini Cake"
           title="Zucchini Cake No Frosting" />
    </p>
  </body>
</html>
```

▸ The `<img>` element is used to add images to a web page.

▸ You must always specify an `src` attribute to indicate the source of an image and an `alt` attribute to describe the content of an image.

▸ You should save images at the size you will be using them on the web page and in the appropriate format.

▸ Photographs are best saved as JPEGs; illustrations or logos that use flat colors are better saved as GIFs.

6

TABLES

- ▸ How to create tables
- ▸ What information suits tables
- ▸ How to represent complex data in tables

There are several types of information that need to be displayed in a grid or table. For example: sports results, stock reports, train timetables.

When representing information in a table, you need to think in terms of a grid made up of rows and columns (a bit like a spreadsheet). In this chapter you will learn how to:

- Use the four key elements for creating tables

- Represent complex data using tables

- Add captions to tables

WHAT'S A TABLE?

A table represents information in a grid format. Examples of tables include financial reports, TV schedules, and sports results.

Grids allow us to understand complex data by referencing information on two axes.

Each block in the grid is referred to as a **table cell**. In HTML a table is written out row by row.

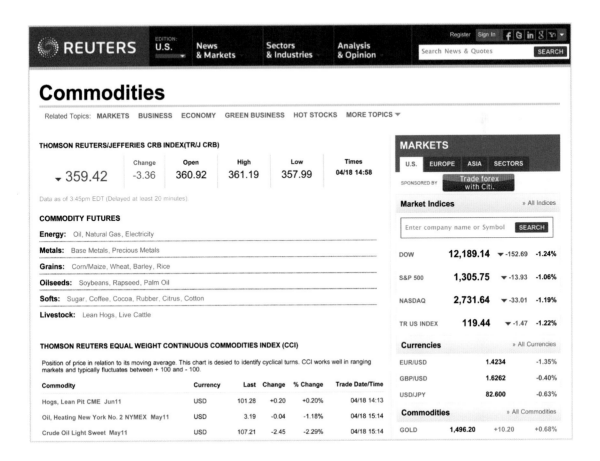

BASIC TABLE STRUCTURE

`<table>`

The `<table>` element is used to create a table. The contents of the table are written out row by row.

`<tr>`

You indicate the start of each row using the opening `<tr>` tag. (The tr stands for table row.)

It is followed by one or more `<td>` elements (one for each cell in that row).

At the end of the row you use a closing `</tr>` tag.

`<td>`

Each cell of a table is represented using a `<td>` element. (The td stands for table data.)

At the end of each cell you use a closing `</td>` tag.

Some browsers automatically draw lines around the table and/or the individual cells. You will learn how to control the borders of tables using CSS on pages 309-312 and 337-340.

chapter-06/basic-table-structure.html `HTML`

```
<table>
  <tr>
    <td>15</td>
    <td>15</td>
    <td>30</td>
  </tr>
  <tr>
    <td>45</td>
    <td>60</td>
    <td>45</td>
  </tr>
  <tr>
    <td>60</td>
    <td>90</td>
    <td>90</td>
  </tr>
</table>
```

`RESULT`

15 15 30
45 60 45
60 90 90

TABLE HEADINGS

```
HTML                    chapter-06/table-headings.html

<table>
  <tr>
    <th></th>
    <th scope="col">Saturday</th>
    <th scope="col">Sunday</th>
  </tr>
  <tr>
    <th scope="row">Tickets sold:</th>
    <td>120</td>
    <td>135</td>
  </tr>
  <tr>
    <th scope="row">Total sales:</th>
    <td>$600</td>
    <td>$675</td>
  </tr>
</table>
```

RESULT

	Saturday	**Sunday**
Tickets sold:	120	135
Total sales:	$600	$675

The `<th>` element is used just like the `<td>` element but its purpose is to represent the heading for either a column or a row. (The th stands for table heading.)

Even if a cell has no content, you should still use a `<td>` or `<th>` element to represent the presence of an empty cell otherwise the table will not render correctly. (The first cell in the first row of this example shows an empty cell.)

Using `<th>` elements for headings helps people who use screen readers, improves the ability for search engines to index your pages, and also gives you greater control over the appearance of tables when you start to use CSS.

You can use the scope attribute on the `<th>` element to indicate whether it is a heading for a column or a row. It can take the values row to indicate a heading for a row or col to indicate a heading for a column.

Browsers usually display the content of a `<th>` element in bold and in the middle of the cell.

SPANNING COLUMNS

Sometimes you may need the entries in a table to stretch across more than one column.

The colspan attribute can be used on a <th> or <td> element and indicates how many columns that cell should run across.

In the example on the right you can see a timetable with five columns; the first column contains the heading for that row (the day), the remaining four represent one hour time slots.

If you look at the table cell that contains the words 'Geography' you will see that the value of the colspan attribute is 2, which indicates that the cell should run across two columns. In the third row, 'Gym' runs across three columns.

You can see that the second and third rows have fewer <td> elements than there are columns. This is because, when a cell extends across more than one column, the <td> or <th> cells that would have been in the place of the wider cells are not included in the code.

I added some CSS styles to this example so that you can see how the cells span more than one column. You will learn how to do this on pages 250, 337-340.

chapter-06/spanning-columns.html `HTML`

```
<table>
  <tr>
    <th></th>
    <th>9am</th>
    <th>10am</th>
    <th>11am</th>
    <th>12am</th>
  </tr>
  <tr>
    <th>Monday</th>
    <td colspan="2">Geography</td>
    <td>Math</td>
    <td>Art</td>
  </tr>
  <tr>
    <th>Tuesday</th>
    <td colspan="3">Gym</td>
    <td>Home Ec</td>
  </tr>
</table>
```

`RESULT`

	9am	10am	11am	12am
Monday	Geography		Math	Art
Tuesday	Gym			Home Ec

SPANNING ROWS

```
<table>
  <tr>
    <th></th>
    <th>ABC</th>
    <th>BBC</th>
    <th>CNN</th>
  </tr>
  <tr>
    <th>6pm - 7pm</th>
    <td rowspan="2">Movie</td>
    <td>Comedy</td>
    <td>News</td>
  </tr>
  <tr>
    <th>7pm - 8pm</th>
    <td>Sport</td>
    <td>Current Affairs</td>
  </tr>
</table>
```

You may also need entries in a table to stretch down across more than one row.

The rowspan attribute can be used on a `<th>` or `<td>` element to indicate how many rows a cell should span down the table.

In the example on the left you can see that ABC is showing a movie from 6pm - 8pm, whereas the BBC and CNN channels are both showing two programs during this time period (each of which lasts one hour).

If you look at the last `<tr>` element, it only contains three elements even though there are four columns in the result below. This is because the movie in the `<tr>` element above it uses the rowspan attribute to stretch down and take over the cell below.

I have added some CSS styles to this example so that you can see how the cells span more than one row. You will learn how to apply these CSS styles to tables on pages 250, 337-340.

RESULT

	ABC	BBC	CNN
6pm - 7pm	Movie	Comedy	News
7pm - 8pm		Sport	Current Affairs

LONG TABLES

There are three elements that help distinguish between the main content of the table and the first and last rows (which can contain different content).

These elements help people who use screen readers and also allow you to style these sections in a different manner than the rest of the table (as you will see when you learn about CSS).

`<thead>`

The headings of the table should sit inside the `<thead>` element.

`<tbody>`

The body should sit inside the `<tbody>` element.

`<tfoot>`

The footer belongs inside the `<tfoot>` element.

By default, browsers rarely treat the content of these elements any differently from other elements, however designers often use CSS styles to change their appearance.

chapter-06/long-tables.html   `HTML`

```html
<table>
  <thead>
    <tr>
      <th>Date</th>
      <th>Income</th>
      <th>Expenditure</th>
    </tr>
  </thead>
  <tbody>
    <tr>
      <th>1st January</th>
      <td>250</td>
      <td>36</td>
    </tr>
    <tr>
      <th>2nd January</th>
      <td>285</td>
      <td>48</td>
    </tr>
    <!-- additional rows as above -->
    <tr>
      <th>31st January</th>
      <td>129</td>
      <td>64</td>
    </tr>
  </tbody>
  <tfoot>
    <tr>
      <td></td>
      <td>7824</td>
      <td>1241</td>
    </tr>
  </tfoot>
</table>
```

Date	Income	Expenditure
1st January	250	36
2nd January	285	48
3rd January	260	42
4th January	290	38
5th January	310	115
6th January	168	14
7th January	226	20
8th January	253	37
9th January	294	33
10th January	216	46
11th January	244	29
12th January	297	32
13th January	328	86
14th January	215	38
15th January	254	30
16th January	256	27
17th January	311	68
18th January	212	39
19th January	234	36
20th January	221	43
21st January	259	38
22nd January	246	31
23rd January	248	17
24th January	229	45
25th January	263	34
26th January	258	41
27th January	283	22
28th January	256	30
29th January	278	47
30th January	251	15
31st January	129	64
	7824	1241

Some of the HTML editors that come in content management systems offer tools to help draw tables. If the first row of your table only contains <th> elements then you may find that the editor inserts a <thead> element automatically.

Part of the reason for having separate <thead> and <tfoot> elements is so that, if you have a table that is taller than the screen (or, if printed, longer than one page) then the browser can keep the header and footer visible whilst the contents of the table scroll. This is intended to make it easier for users to see which column the data is in (however this functionality is not implemented by default in any current browser).

I have added some CSS styles to this example so that you can see the contents of the <thead> and <tfoot> being treated differently than the rest of the rows. You will learn how to apply these CSS styles to tables on pages 309-312 and 337-340.

OLD CODE: WIDTH & SPACING

There are some outdated attributes which you should not use on new websites. You may, however, come across some of them when looking at older code, so I will mention them here. All of these attributes have been replaced by the use of CSS.

The `width` attribute was used on the opening `<table>` tag to indicate how wide that table should be and on some opening `<th>` and `<td>` tags to specify the width of individual cells. The value of this attribute is the width of the table or cell in pixels.

The columns in a table need to form a straight line, so you often only see the `width` attribute on the first row (and all subsequent rows would use that setting).

The opening `<table>` tag could also use the `cellpadding` attribute to add space inside each cell of the table, and the `cellspacing` attribute to create space between each cell of the table. The values for these attributes were given in pixels.

I added CSS styles to this example so that you can see the width of the table cells more clearly. If you want to control the width or spacing of tables and cells you should use CSS as shown on pages 303, 337-340.

chapter-06/width-and-spacing.html · HTML

```html
<table width="400" cellpadding="10" cellspacing="5">
  <tr>
    <th width="150"></th>
    <th>Withdrawn</th>
    <th>Credit</th>
    <th width="150">Balance</th>
  </tr>
  <tr>
    <th>January</th>
    <td>250.00</td>
    <td>660.50</td>
    <td>410.50</td>
  </tr>
  <tr>
    <th>February</th>
    <td>135.55</td>
    <td>895.20</td>
    <td>1170.15</td>
  </tr>
</table>
```

RESULT

	Withdrawn	Credit	Balance
January	250.00	660.50	410.50
February	135.55	895.20	1170.15

OLD CODE:
BORDER & BACKGROUND

chapter-06/border-and-background.html

```html
<table border="2" bgcolor="#efefef">
  <tr>
    <th width="150"></th>
    <th>Withdrawn</th>
    <th>Credit</th>
    <th width="150" bgcolor="#cccccc">Balance</th>
  </tr>
  <tr>
    <th>January</th>
    <td>250.00</td>
    <td>660.50</td>
    <td bgcolor="#cccccc">410.50</td>
  </tr>
  <tr>
    <th>February</th>
    <td>135.55</td>
    <td>895.20</td>
    <td bgcolor="#cccccc">1170.15</td>
  </tr>
</table>
```

The border attribute was used on both the <table> and <td> elements to indicate the width of the border in pixels.

The bgcolor attribute was used to indicate background colors of either the entire table or individual table cells. The value is usually a hex code (which we discuss on pages 249-252).

This example uses the HTML border and bgcolor attributes. No CSS attributes were utilized in this example.

When building a new website you should use CSS to control the appearance of the table rather than these attributes. They are only covered here because you may come across them if you look at the code of older websites.

RESULT

	Withdrawn	Credit	Balance
January	250.00	660.50	410.50
February	135.55	895.20	1170.15

	Home starter hosting	Premium business hosting
Disk space	250mb	1gb
Bandwidth	5gb per month	50gb per month
Email accounts	3	10
Server	Shared	VPS
Support	Email	Telephone and email
Setup	Free	Free
FTP accounts	1	5
Sign up now and save 10%!		

This example shows a table for customers to compare website hosting packages. There are table headings in the first row and first column of the table.

The empty cell in the top left still has a `<th>` element to represent it. Each cell of the table must be accounted for by a `<th>` or `<td>` element. The `<th>` elements use

the `scope` attribute to indicate whether they are headings for a row or column. The final row includes the `colspan` attribute to spread across two columns.

```html
<html>
  <head>
    <title>Tables</title>
  </head>
  <body>
    <table>
      <thead>
        <tr>
          <th></th>
          <th scope="col">Home starter hosting</th>
          <th scope="col">Premium business hosting</th>
        </tr>
      </thead>
      <tbody>
        <tr>
          <th scope="row">Disk space</th>
          <td>250mb</td>
          <td>1gb</td>
        </tr>
        <tr>
          <th scope="row">Bandwidth</th>
          <td>5gb per month</td>
          <td>50gb per month</td>
        </tr>
        <!-- more rows like the two above here -->
      </tbody>
      <tfoot>
        <tr>
          <td></td>
          <td colspan="2">Sign up now and save 10%!</td>
        </tr>
      </tfoot>
    </table>
  </body>
</html>
```

▸ The `<table>` element is used to add tables to a web page.

▸ A table is drawn out row by row. Each row is created with the `<tr>` element.

▸ Inside each row there are a number of cells represented by the `<td>` element (or `<th>` if it is a header).

▸ You can make cells of a table span more than one row or column using the `rowspan` and `colspan` attributes.

▸ For long tables you can split the table into a `<thead>`, `<tbody>`, and `<tfoot>`.

7

FORMS

- ▸ How to collect information from visitors
- ▸ Different kinds of form controls
- ▸ New HTML5 form controls

Traditionally, the term 'form' has referred to a printed document that contains spaces for you to fill in information.

HTML borrows the concept of a form to refer to different elements that allow you to collect information from visitors to your site.

Whether you are adding a simple search box to your website or you need to create more complicated insurance applications, HTML forms give you a set of elements to collect data from your users. In this chapter you will learn:

- How to create a form on your website
- The different tools for collecting data
- New HTML5 form controls

WHY FORMS?

The best known form on the web is probably the search box that sits right in the middle of Google's homepage.

In addition to enabling users to search, forms also allow users to perform other functions online. You will see forms when registering as a member of a website, when shopping online, and when signing up for newsletters or mailing lists.

FORM CONTROLS

There are several types of form controls that you can use to collect information from visitors to your site.

ADDING TEXT:

Text input (single-line)
Used for a single line of text such as email addresses and names.

Ivy

Password input
Like a single line text box but it masks the characters entered.

•••••••

Text area (multi-line)
For longer areas of text, such as messages and comments.

Enter your comments...

MAKING CHOICES:

Radio buttons
For use when a user must select one of a number of options.

⦿ Rock ○ Pop ○ Jazz

Checkboxes
When a user can select and unselect one or more options.

☑ iTunes ☐ Last.fm ☐ Spotify

Drop-down boxes
When a user must pick one of a number of options from a list.

iPod ⇅

SUBMITTING FORMS:

Submit buttons
To submit data from your form to another web page.

Subscribe

Image buttons
Similar to submit buttons but they allow you to use an image.

SUBSCRIBE

UPLOADING FILES:

File upload
Allows users to upload files (e.g. images) to a website.

Browse...
Upload

HOW FORMS WORK

A user fills in a form and then presses a button to submit the information to the server.

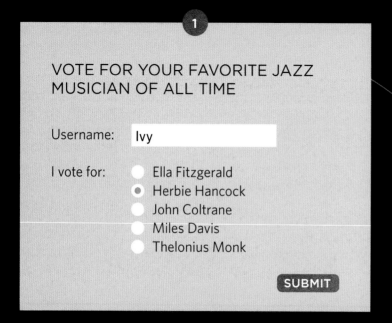

1

VOTE FOR YOUR FAVORITE JAZZ
MUSICIAN OF ALL TIME

Username: Ivy

I vote for:
○ Ella Fitzgerald
◉ Herbie Hancock
○ John Coltrane
○ Miles Davis
○ Thelonius Monk

SUBMIT

2 The name of each form control is sent to the server along with the value the user enters or selects.

3 The server processes the information using a programming language such as PHP, C#, VB.net, or Java. It may also store the information in a database.

4 The server creates a new page to send back to the browser based on the information received.

Thank you, Ivy!

You voted for Herbie Hancock.

A form may have several form controls, each gathering different information. The server needs to know which piece of inputted data corresponds with which form element.

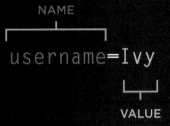

To differentiate between various pieces of inputted data, information is sent from the browser to the server using name/value pairs. In this example, the form asks for the visitor's username and also for their favorite jazz musician. The name/value pairs sent to the server are:

username=Ivy

If the form control allows the user to enter text, then the value of the form control is whatever the user has typed in.

vote=Herbie

If the form control allows you to choose from a fixed set of answers (e.g. radio buttons, checkboxes or a drop down list), the web page author will add code that gives each option an automatic value.

You should never change the name of a form control in a page unless you know that the code on the server will understand this new value.

FORM STRUCTURE

`<form>`

Form controls live inside a `<form>` element. This element should always carry the `action` attribute and will usually have a `method` and `id` attribute too.

action

Every `<form>` element requires an `action` attribute. Its `value` is the URL for the page on the server that will receive the information in the form when it is submitted.

method

Forms can be sent using one of two methods: `get` or `post`.

With the `get` method, the values from the form are added to the end of the URL specified in the `action` attribute. The `get` method is ideal for:

- short forms (such as search boxes)

- when you are just retrieving data from the web server (not sending information that should be added to or deleted from a database)

chapter-07/form-structure.html

```html
<form action="http://www.example.com/subscribe.php"
  method="get">
  <p>This is where the form controls will appear.
    </p>
</form>
```

RESULT

This is where the form controls will appear.

With the `post` method the values are sent in what are known as HTTP headers. As a rule of thumb you should use the `post` method if your form:

- allows users to upload a file

- is very long

- contains sensitive data (e.g. passwords)

- adds information to, or deletes information from, a database

If the method attribute is not used, the form data will be sent using the `get` method.

id

We look at the `id` attribute on page 183, but the value is used to identify the form distinctly from other elements on the page (and is often used by scripts — such as those that check you have entered information into fields that require values).

TEXT INPUT

```
<form action="http://www.example.com/login.php">
  <p>Username:
    <input type="text" name="username" size="15"
      maxlength="30" />
  </p>
</form>
```

RESULT

Username: [   ]

<input>

The <input> element is used to create several different form controls. The value of the type attribute determines what kind of input they will be creating.

type="text"

When the type attribute has a value of text, it creates a single-line text input.

name

When users enter information into a form, the server needs to know which form control each piece of data was entered into. (For example, in a login form, the server needs to know what has been entered as the username and what has been given as the password.) Therefore, each form control requires a name attribute. The value of this attribute identifies the form control and is sent along with the information they enter to the server.

size

The size attribute should not be used on new forms. It was used in older forms to indicate the width of the text input (measured by the number of characters that would be seen).

For example, a value of 3 would create a box wide enough to display three characters

(although a user could enter more characters if they desired).

In any new forms you write, CSS should be used to control the width of form elements. The size attribute is only mentioned here because you may come across it when looking at older code.

maxlength

You can use the maxlength attribute to limit the number of characters a user may enter into the text field. Its value is the number of characters they may enter. For example, if you were asking for a year, the maxlength attribute could have a value of 4.

PASSWORD INPUT

`<input>`

`type="password"`

When the `type` attribute has a value of `password` it creates a text box that acts just like a single-line text input, except the characters are blocked out. They are hidden in this way so that if someone is looking over the user's shoulder, they cannot see sensitive data such as passwords.

`name`

The `name` attribute indicates the name of the password input, which is sent to the server with the password the user enters.

`size, maxlength`

It can also carry the `size` and `maxlength` attributes like the the single-line text input.

chapter-07/password-input.html `HTML`

```html
<form action="http://www.example.com/login.php">
  <p>Username:
    <input type="text" name="username" size="15"
      maxlength="30" />
  </p>
  <p>Password:
    <input type="password" name="password" size="15"
      maxlength="30" />
  </p>
</form>
```

`RESULT`

Username: | Ivy

Password: | •••••••

Although the password is hidden on the screen, this does not mean that the data in a password control is sent securely to the server. You should never use these for sending sensitive data such as credit card numbers.

For full security, the server needs to be set up to communicate with users' browsers using Secure Sockets Layer (SSL). The topic of SSL is beyond the scope of this book, however there are links to learn more about it on the accompanying website.

TEXT AREA

```
<form action="http://www.example.com/comments.php">
  <p>What did you think of this gig?</p>
  <textarea name="comments" cols="20" rows="4">Enter
    your comments...</textarea>
</form>
```

RESULT

What did you think of this gig?

Enter your comments...

\<textarea\>

The \<textarea\> element is used to create a multi-line text input. Unlike other input elements this is not an empty element. It should therefore have an opening and a closing tag.

Any text that appears between the opening \<textarea\> and closing \</textarea\> tags will appear in the text box when the page loads.

If the user does not delete any text between these tags, this message will get sent to the server along with whatever the user has typed. (Some sites use JavaScript to clear this information when the user clicks in the text area.)

If you are creating a new form, you should use CSS to control the width and height of a \<textarea\>. However, if you are looking at older code, you may see the cols and rows attributes used with this element.

The cols attribute indicates how wide the text area should be (measured in numbers of characters). The rows attribute indicates how many rows the text area should take up vertically.

RADIO BUTTON

`<input>`

type="radio"

Radio buttons allow users to pick just one of a number of options.

name

The name attribute is sent to the server with the value of the option the user selects. When a question provides users with options for answers in the form of radio buttons, the value of the name attribute should be the same for all of the radio buttons used to answer that question.

value

The value attribute indicates the value that is sent to the server for the selected option. The value of each of the buttons in a group should be different (so that the server knows which option the user has selected).

checked

The checked attribute can be used to indicate which value (if any) should be selected when the page loads. The value of this attribute is checked. Only one radio button in a group should use this attribute.

HTML

```html
<form action="http://www.example.com/profile.php">
  <p>Please select your favorite genre:
  <br />
    <input type="radio" name="genre" value="rock"
      checked="checked" /> Rock
    <input type="radio" name="genre" value="pop" />
      Pop
    <input type="radio" name="genre" value="jazz" />
      Jazz
  </p>
</form>
```

RESULT

Please select your favorite genre:
◉ Rock ○ Pop ○ Jazz

Please note: Once a radio button has been selected it cannot be deselected. The user can only select a different option. If you are only allowing the user one option and want them to be able to deselect it (for example if they are indicating they agree to terms and conditions), you should use a checkbox instead.

CHECKBOX

```
<form action="http://www.example.com/profile.php">
  <p>Please select your favorite music service(s):
    <br />
    <input type="checkbox" name="service"
      value="itunes" checked="checked" /> iTunes
    <input type="checkbox" name="service"
      value="lastfm" /> Last.fm
    <input type="checkbox" name="service"
      value="spotify" /> Spotify
  </p>
</form>
```

RESULT

Please select your favorite music service(s):
☑ iTunes ☐ Last.fm ☐ Spotify

type="checkbox"
Checkboxes allow users to select (and deselect) one or more options in answer to a question.

name
The name attribute is sent to the server with the value of the option(s) the user selects. When a question provides users with options for answers in the form of checkboxes, the value of the name attribute should be the same for all of the buttons that answer that question.

value
The value attribute indicates the value sent to the server if this checkbox is checked.

checked
The checked attribute indicates that this box should be checked when the page loads. If used, its value should be checked.

DROP DOWN LIST BOX

<select>

A drop down list box (also known as a select box) allows users to select one option from a drop down list.

The <select> element is used to create a drop down list box. It contains two or more <option> elements.

name
The name attribute indicates the name of the form control being sent to the server, along with the value the user selected.

<option>

chapter-07/drop-down-list-box.html   `HTML`

```html
<form action="http://www.example.com/profile.php">
  <p>What device do you listen to music on?</p>
  <select name="devices">
    <option value="ipod">iPod</option>
    <option value="radio">Radio</option>
    <option value="computer">Computer</option>
  </select>
</form>
```

`RESULT`

What device do you listen to music on?

The <option> element is used to specify the options that the user can select from. The words between the opening <option> and closing </option> tags will be shown to the user in the drop down box.

value
The <option> element uses the value attribute to indicate the value that is sent to the server along with the name of the control if this option is selected.

selected
The selected attribute can be used to indicate the option that should be selected when the page loads. The value of this attribute should be selected.

If this attribute is not used, the first option will be shown when the page loads. If the user does not select an option, then the first item will be sent to the server as the value for this control.

The function of the drop down list box is similar to that of the radio buttons (in that only one option can be selected). There are two key factors in choosing which to use:

1. If users need to see all options at a glance, radio buttons are better suited.

2. If there is a very long list of options (such as a list of countries), drop down list boxes work better.

MULTIPLE SELECT BOX

```
<form action="http://www.example.com/profile.php">
  <p>Do you play any of the following instruments?
   (You can select more than one option by holding
   down control on a PC or command key on a Mac
   while selecting different options.)</p>
  <select name="instruments" size="3"
    multiple="multiple">
    <option value="guitar" selected="selected">
     Guitar</option>
    <option value="drums">Drums</option>
    <option value="keyboard"
      selected="selected">Keyboard</option>
    <option value="bass">Bass</option>
  </select>
</form>
```

RESULT

Do you play any of the following instruments? (You can
select more than one option by holding down control on a
PC or command key on a Mac while selecting different
options.)

Guitar
Drums
Keyboard
Bass

<select>

size

You can turn a drop down select
box into a box that shows more
than one option by adding the
size attribute. Its value should
be the number of options you
want to show at once. In the
example you can see that three
of the four options are shown.

Unfortunately, the way that
browsers have implemented this
attribute is not perfect, and it
should be tested thoroughly if
used (in particular in Firefox and
Safari on a Mac).

multiple

You can allow users to select
multiple options from this list by
adding the multiple attribute
with a value of multiple.

It is a good idea to tell users if
they can select more than one
option at a time. It is also helpful
to indicate that on a PC they
should hold down the **control** key
while selecting multiple options
and on a Mac they should use
the **command** key while selecting
options.

FILE INPUT BOX

`<input>`

If you want to allow users to upload a file (for example an image, video, mp3, or a PDF), you will need to use a file input box.

type="file"

This type of input creates a box that looks like a text input followed by a *Browse* button. (One notable exception is Safari on a Mac, which tends to display a button labelled *Choose File*, followed by the text "no file selected" or the name of the file that has been chosen by the user.) When the user clicks on the *Browse* button, a window opens up that allows them to select a file from their computer to be uploaded to the website.

When you are allowing users to upload files, the method attribute on the `<form>` element must have a value of post. (You cannot send files using the HTTP get method.)

When a user clicks on the *browse* button, the presentation of the window that allows them to browse for the file they want to upload will match the windows of the user's operating system. You cannot control the appearance of these windows.

chapter-07/file-input-box.html   HTML

```
<form action="http://www.example.com/upload.php"
  method="post">
  <p>Upload your song in MP3 format:</p>
  <input type="file" name="user-song" /><br />
  <input type="submit" value="Upload" />
</form>
```

RESULT

Upload your song in MP3 format:

_____   (Browse...)

(Upload)

SUBMIT BUTTON

<input>

HTML   chapter-07/submit-button.html

```html
<form action="http://www.example.com/subscribe.php">
  <p>Subscribe to our email list:</p>
  <input type="text" name="email" />
  <input type="submit" name="subscribe"
    value="Subscribe" />
</form>
```

RESULT

Subscribe to our email list:

[   ] (Subscribe)

type="submit"

The submit button is used to send a form to the server.

name

It can use a name attribute but it does not need to have one.

value

The value attribute is used to control the text that appears on a button. It is a good idea to specify the words you want to appear on a button because the default value of buttons on some browsers is 'Submit query' and this might not be appropriate for all kinds of forms.

Different browsers will show submit buttons in different ways and tend to fit the visual presentation of the browser. If you want to control the appearance of a submit button, you can either use CSS (as you will learn on page 343), or you can use an image for the button.

IMAGE BUTTON

`<input>`

type="image"

If you want to use an image for the submit button, you can give the type attribute a value of image. The src, width, height, and alt attributes work just like they do when used with the `<img>` element (which we saw on pages 99-100).

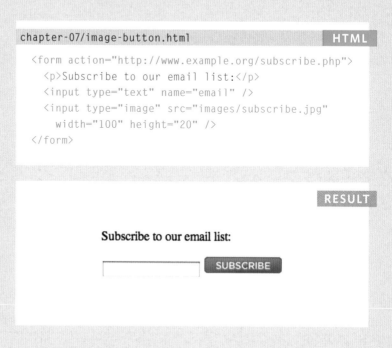

chapter-07/image-button.html   HTML

```
<form action="http://www.example.org/subscribe.php">
  <p>Subscribe to our email list:</p>
  <input type="text" name="email" />
  <input type="image" src="images/subscribe.jpg"
    width="100" height="20" />
</form>
```

RESULT

Subscribe to our email list:

SUBSCRIBE

BUTTON & HIDDEN CONTROLS

```
<form action="http://www.example.com/add.php">
  <button><img src="images/add.gif" alt="add"
    width="10" height="10" /> Add</button>
  <input type="hidden" name="bookmark"
    value="lyrics" />
</form>
```

RESULT

<button>

The <button> element was introduced to allow users more control over how their buttons appear, and to allow other elements to appear inside the button.

This means that you can combine text and images between the opening <button> tag and closing </button> tag.

<input>

type="hidden"

This example also shows a hidden form control. These form controls are not shown on the page (although you can see them if you use the *View Source* option in the browser). They allow web page authors to add values to forms that users cannot see. For example, a web page author might use a hidden field to indicate which page the user was on when they submitted a form.

LABELLING FORM CONTROLS

`<label>`

When introducing form controls, the code was kept simple by indicating the purpose of each one in text next to it. However, each form control should have its own `<label>` element as this makes the form accessible to vision-impaired users.

The `<label>` element can be used in two ways. It can:

1. Wrap around both the text description and the form input (as shown on the first line of the example to your right).

2. Be kept separate from the form control and use the `for` attribute to indicate which form control it is a label for (as shown with the radio buttons).

```
chapter-07/labelling-form-controls.html          HTML

<label>Age: <input type="text" name="age" /></label>
<br/ >
Gender:
<input id="female" type="radio" name="gender"
  value="f">
<label for="female">Female</label>
<input id="male" type="radio" name="gender"
  value="m">
<label for="male">Male</label>
```

```
                                                 RESULT

        Age: [                    ]
        Gender: ○ Female  ○ Male
```

for

The `for` attribute states which form control the label belongs to. Note how the radio buttons use the `id` attribute. The value of the `id` attribute uniquely identifies an element from all other elements on a page. (The `id` attribute is covered on page 183.)

The value of the `for` attribute matches that of the `id` attribute on the form control it is labelling. This technique using the `for` and

`id` attributes can be used on any form control. When a `<label>` element is used with a checkbox or radio button, users can click on either the form control or the label to select. The expanded clickable area makes the form easier to use. The position of the label is very important. If users do not know where to enter information or what information to enter, they are less likely to use the form correctly.

As a rule of thumb, here are the best places to place labels on form controls.

ABOVE OR TO THE LEFT:
- Text inputs
- Text areas
- Select boxes
- File uploads

TO THE RIGHT:
- Individual checkboxes
- Individual radio buttons

GROUPING FORM ELEMENTS

```html
<fieldset>
  <legend>Contact details</legend>
  <label>Email:<br />
  <input type="text" name="email" /></label><br />
  <label>Mobile:<br />
  <input type="text" name="mobile" /></label><br />
  <label>Telephone:<br />
  <input type="text" name="telephone" /></label>
</fieldset>
```

RESULT

\<fieldset>

You can group related form controls together inside the `<fieldset>` element. This is particularly helpful for longer forms.

Most browsers will show the `fieldset` with a line around the edge to show how they are related. The appearance of these lines can be adjusted using CSS.

\<legend>

The `<legend>` element can come directly after the opening `<fieldset>` tag and contains a caption which helps identify the purpose of that group of form controls.

HTML5: FORM VALIDATION

You have probably seen forms on the web that give users messages if the form control has not been filled in correctly; this is known as **form validation**.

Traditionally, form validation has been performed using JavaScript (which is beyond the scope of this book). But HTML5 is introducing validation and leaving the work to the browser.

Validation helps ensure the user enters information in a form that the server will be able to understand when the form is submitted. Validating the contents of the form before it is sent to the server helps:

● Reduce the amount of work the server has to do
● Enable users to see if there are problems with the form (faster than if validation were performed on the server)

chapter-07/html5-form-validation.html   HTML

```
<form action="http://www.example.com/login/"
    method="post">
  <label for="username">Username:</label>
  <input type="text" name="username"
    required="required" /><br />
  <label for="password">Password:</label>
  <input type="password" name="password"
    required="required" />
  <input type="submit" value="Submit" />
</form>
```

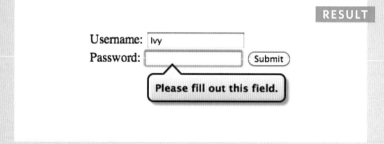

RESULT

At the time of writing, only Chrome and Opera supported HTML5 validation, although other browsers are expected to follow. In order to support older browsers (that do not understand HTML5), web page authors are likely to continue using JavaScript to validate forms.

An example of HTML5 form validation is the `required` attribute, which can be used on any form element that the user is expected to fill in. This HTML5 attribute does not need a value, but in HTML 4 all attributes must have a value. So, some people give this attribute a value of `required`.

HTML5: DATE INPUT

```
<form action="http://www.example.com/bookings/"
    method="post">
  <label for="depart">Departure date:</label>
  <input type="date" name="depart" />
  <input type="submit" value="Submit" />
</form>
```

RESULT

Departure date: `2011-06-27` (Submit)

<input>

Many forms need to gather information such as dates, email addresses, and URLs. This has traditionally been done using text inputs.

HTML5 introduces new form controls to standardize the way that some information is gathered. Older browsers that do not recognize these inputs will just treat them as a single line text box.

type="date"

If you are asking the user for a date, you can use an <input> element and give the type attribute a value of date. This will create a date input in browsers that support the new HMTL5 input types.

This example shows what the date input looks like in the Opera browser. The appearance of the date input changes across different browsers.

HTML5: EMAIL & URL INPUT

`<input>`

HTML5 has also introduced inputs that allow visitors to enter email addresses and URLs. Browsers that do not support these input types will just treat them as text boxes.

type="email"

If you ask a user for an email address, you can use the email input. Browsers that support HTML5 validation will check that the user has provided information in the correct format of an email address. Some smart phones also optimize their keyboard to display the keys you are most likely to need when entering an email address (such as the @ symbol).

type="url"

A URL input can be used when you are asking a user for a web page address. Browsers that support HTML5 validation will check that the user has provided information in the format of a URL. Some smart phones also optimize their keyboard to display the keys you are most likely to need when entering a URL.

chapter-07/html5-email-input.html `HTML`

```
<form action="http://www.example.org/subscribe.php">
  <p>Please enter your email address:</p>
  <input type="email" name="email" />
  <input type="submit" value="Submit" />
</form>
```

`RESULT`

Please enter your email address:

ivy   Submit

Please enter an email address.

chapter-07/html5-url-input.html `HTML`

```
<form action="http://www.example.org/profile.php">
  <p>Please enter your website address:</p>
  <input type="url" name="website" />
  <input type="submit" value="Submit" />
</form>
```

`RESULT`

Please enter your website address:

ivy   Submit

Please enter a URL.

HTML5: SEARCH INPUT

HTML chapter-07/html5-search-input.html

```
<form action="http://www.example.org/search.php">
  <p>Search:</p>
  <input type="search" name="search" />
  <input type="submit" value="Search" />
</form>
```

RESULT

Search:

Thelonius ⊗ (Search)

HTML chapter-07/html5-placeholder.html

```
<form action="http://www.example.org/search.php">
  <p>Search:</p>
  <input type="search" name="search"
    placeholder="Enter keyword" />
  <input type="submit" value="Search" />
</form>
```

RESULT

Search:

Enter keyword (Search)

\<input\>

If you want to create a single line text box for search queries, HTML5 provides a special type of input for that purpose.

type="search"

If you want to create a single line text box for search queries, HTML5 provides a special search input.

To create the HTML5 search box the \<input\> element should have a type attribute whose value is search. Older browsers will simply treat it like a single line text box.

Recent browsers add some features that improve usability. For example, Safari on a Mac adds a cross to clear the search box when you have started to enter information. Safari also automatically rounds the corners on the search input field.

placeholder

On any text input, you can also use an attribute called placeholder whose value is text that will be shown in the text box until the user clicks in that area. Older browsers simply ignore this attribute.

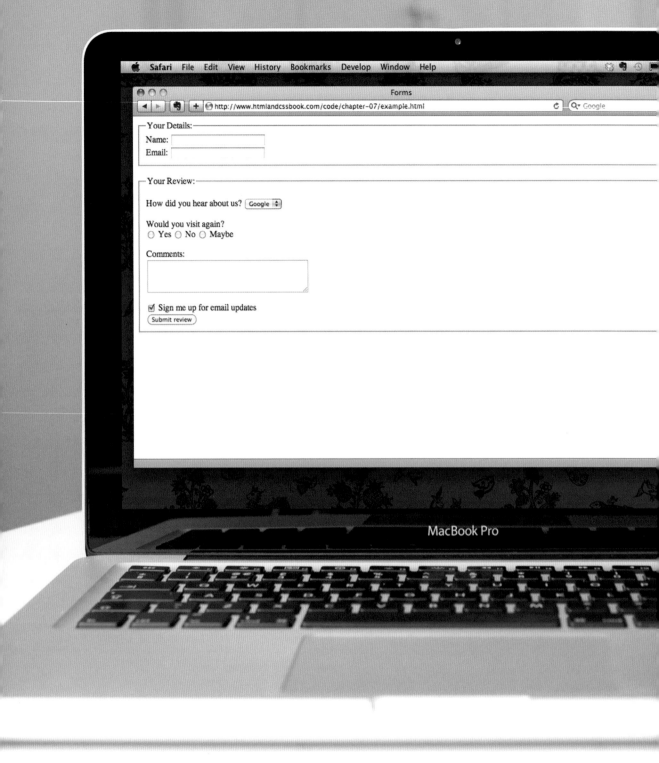

EXAMPLE
FORMS

This example shows a feedback and newsletter sign-up form. It uses a variety of form controls.

The <form> element uses the action attribute to indicate the page that the data is being sent to. Each of the form controls sits inside the <form> element. Different types of form control are suited to collecting different types of data. The <fieldset> element is used to group related questions together. The <label> element indicates the purpose of each form control.

EXAMPLE
FORMS

```
<html>
  <head>
    <title>Forms</title>
  </head>
  <body>
    <form action="http://www.example.com/review.php" method="get">
      <fieldset>
        <legend>
          Your Details:
        </legend>
        <label>
          Name:
          <input type="text" name="name" size="30" maxlength="100">
        </label>
        <br />
        <label>
          Email:
          <input type="email" name="email" size="30" maxlength="100">
        </label>
        <br />
      </fieldset>
      <br />
      <fieldset>
        <legend>
          Your Review:
        </legend>
        <p>
          <label for="hear-about">
            How did you hear about us?
          </label>
          <select name="referrer" id="hear-about">
            <option value="google">Google</option>
            <option value="friend">Friend</option>
            <option value="advert">Advert</option>
            <option value="other">Other</option>
          </select>
        </p>
        <p>
```

```
        Would you visit again?
        <br />
        <label>
          <input type="radio" name="rating" value="yes" />
          Yes
        </label>
        <label>
          <input type="radio" name="rating" value="no" />
          No
        </label>
        <label>
          <input type="radio" name="rating" value="maybe" />
          Maybe
        </label>
      </p>
      <p>
        <label for="comments">
          Comments:
        </label>
        <br />
        <textarea rows="4" cols="40" id="comments">
        </textarea>
      </p>
      <label>
        <input type="checkbox" name="subscribe" checked="checked" />
        Sign me up for email updates
      </label>
      <br />
      <input type="submit" value="Submit review" />
    </fieldset>
  </form>
 </body>
</html>
```

▸ Whenever you want to collect information from visitors you will need a form, which lives inside a `<form>` element.

▸ Information from a form is sent in name/value pairs.

▸ Each form control is given a name, and the text the user types in or the values of the options they select are sent to the server.

▸ HTML5 introduces new form elements which make it easier for visitors to fill in forms.

8

EXTRA
MARKUP

- ▸ Specifying different versions of HTML
- ▸ Identifying and grouping elements
- ▸ Comments, meta information and iframes

At this point, we have covered the main tags that fit nicely into groups and sections.

In this chapter, we will focus on some helpful topics that are not easily grouped together. You will learn about:

- The different versions of HTML and how to indicate which version you are using

- How to add comments to your code

- Global attributes, which are attributes that can be used on any element, including the `class` and `id` attributes

- Elements that are used to group together parts of the page where no other element is suitable

- How to embed a page within a page using iframes

- How to add information about the web page using the `<meta>` element

- Adding characters such as angled brackets and copyright symbols

THE EVOLUTION OF HTML

Since the web was first created, there have been several different versions of HTML.

HTML 4
RELEASED 1997

XHTML 1.0
RELEASED 2000

Each new version was designed to be an improvement on the last (with new elements and attributes added and older code removed).

There have also been several versions of each browser used to view web pages, each of which implements new code. Not all web users, however, have the latest browsers installed on their computers, which means that not everyone will be able to view all of the latest features and markup.

Where you should be particularly aware of browsers not supporting certain features, I have made a note of this (as you have seen with some of the HTML5 elements introduced in the Forms chapter — and as you will see in the CSS chapters).

With the exception of a few elements added in HTML5 (which have been highlighted), the elements you have seen in this book were all available in HTML 4.

Although HTML 4 had some presentational elements to control the appearance of pages, authors are not recommended to use them any more. (Examples include the `<center>` element for centering content on a page, `<font>` for controlling the appearance of text, and `<strike>` to put a line through the text — all of these can be achieved with CSS instead.)

In 1998, a language called XML was published. Its purpose was to allow people to write new markup languages. Since HTML was the most widely used markup language around, it was decided that HTML 4 should be reformulated to follow the rules of XML and it was renamed XHTML. This meant that authors had to follow some new, more strict rules about writing markup. For example:

- Every element needed a closing tag (except for empty elements such as `<img />`).
- Attribute names had to be in lowercase.
- All attributes required a value, and all values were to be placed in double quotes.
- Deprecated elements should no longer be used.
- Every element that was opened inside another element should be closed inside that same element.

The examples in this book all follow these strict rules of XML.

One of the key benefits of this change was that XHTML works seamlessly with other programs that are written to create and process XML documents.

It could also be used with other data formats such as Scalable Vector Graphics (SVG) — a graphical language written in XML, MathML (used to mark up mathematical formulae), and CML (used to mark up chemical formulae).

In order to help web page authors move to this new syntax, two main flavors of XHTML 1.0 were created:

- **Strict XHTML 1.0**, where authors had to follow the rules to the letter
- **Transitional XHTML 1.0**, where authors could still use presentational elements (such as `<center>` and `<font>`).

The transitional version of XHTML was created because it allowed authors to continue to follow older practices (with a less strict syntax) and use some of the elements and attributes that were going to be removed from future versions of HTML.

There was also a third version of XHTML 1.0 called **XHTML 1.0 Frameset**, which allowed web page authors to partition a browser window into several "frames," each of which would hold a different HTML page. These days, frames are very rarely used and are being phased out.

HTML5
WORK IN PROGRESS

In HTML5, web page authors do not need to close all tags, and new elements and attributes will be introduced. At the time of writing, the HTML5 specification had not been completed, but the major browser makers had started to implement many of the new features, and web page authors were rapidly adopting the new markup.

Despite the fact that HTML5 is not yet completed, you can safely take advantage of the new features of the language as long as you endeavour to ensure that users with older browsers will be able to view your pages (even though some of the extra features will not be visible to them).

DOCTYPES

Because there have been several versions of HTML, each web page should begin with a DOCTYPE declaration to tell a browser which version of HTML the page is using (although browsers usually display the page even if it is not included). We will therefore be including one in each example for the rest of the book.

As you will see when we come to look at CSS and its box model on page 316, the use of a DOCTYPE can also help the browser to render a page correctly.

Because XHTML was written in XML, you will sometimes see pages that use the XHTML strict DOCTYPE start with the optional XML declaration. Where this is used, it should be the first thing in a document. There must be nothing before it, not even a space.

HTML5 `HTML`

```
<!DOCTYPE html>
```

HTML 4

```
<!DOCTYPE html PUBLIC
  "-//W3C//DTD HTML 4.01 Transitional//EN"
  "http://www.w3.org/TR/html4/loose.dtd">
```

Transitional XHTML 1.0

```
<!DOCTYPE html PUBLIC
  "-//W3C//DTD XHTML 1.0 Transitional//EN"
  "http://www.w3.org/TR/xhtml1/DTD/
   xhtml1-transitional.dtd">
```

Strict XHTML 1.0

```
<!DOCTYPE html PUBLIC
  "-//W3C//DTD XHTML 1.0 Strict//EN"
  "http://www.w3.org/TR/xhtml1/DTD/
   xhtml1-strict.dtd">
```

XML Declaration

```
<?xml version="1.0" ?>
```

COMMENTS IN HTML

HTML   chapter-08/comments-in-html.html

```html
<!-- start of introduction -->
<h1>Current Exhibitions</h1>
<h2>Olafur Eliasson</h2>
<!-- end of introduction -->
<!-- start of main text -->
<p>Olafur Eliasson was born in Copenhagen, Denmark
   in 1967 to Icelandic parents.</p>
<p>He is known for sculptures and large-scale
   installation art employing elemental materials
   such as light, water, and air temperature to
   enhance the viewer's experience.</p>
<!-- end of main text -->
<!--
  <a href="mailto:info@example.org">Contact</a>
-->
```

RESULT

Current Exhibitions

Olafur Eliasson

Olafur Eliasson was born in Copenhagen, Denmark in 1967 to Icelandic parents.

He is known for sculptures and large-scale installation art employing elemental materials such as light, water, and air temperature to enhance the viewer's experience.

`<!-- -->`

If you want to add a comment to your code that will not be visible in the user's browser, you can add the text between these characters:

`<!-- comment goes here -->`

It is a good idea to add comments to your code because, no matter how familiar you are with the page at the time of writing it, when you come back to it later (or if someone else needs to look at the code), comments will make it much easier to understand.

Although comments are not visible to users in the main browser window, they can be viewed by anyone who looks at the source code behind the page.

On a long page, you will often see comments used to indicate where sections of the page start and end, or to contain notes that help explain the code.

Comments can also be used around blocks of code to stop that code from being displayed in the browser. In the example on the left, the email link has been commented out.

ID ATTRIBUTE

Every HTML element can carry the id attribute. It is used to uniquely identify that element from other elements on the page. Its value should start with a letter or an underscore (not a number or any other character). It is important that no two elements on the same page have the same value for their id attributes (otherwise the value is no longer unique).

As you will see when you come to look at CSS in the next section, giving an element a unique identity allows you to style it differently from any other instance of the same element on the page. For example, you might want to assign one paragraph within the page (perhaps a paragraph containing a pull quote) a different style from all of the other paragraphs. In the example on the right, the paragraph with the id attribute whose value is pullquote is made uppercase using CSS.

If you go on to learn about JavaScript (a language that allows you to add interactivity to your pages), id attributes can be used to allow the script to work with that particular element.

The id attribute is known as a **global attribute** because it can be used on any element.

`HTML`

```
<p>Water and air. So very commonplace are these
   substances, they hardly attract attention - and
   yet they vouchsafe our very existence.</p>
<p id="pullquote">Every time I view the sea I feel
   a calming sense of security, as if visiting my
   ancestral home; I embark on a voyage of seeing.
   </p>
<p>Mystery of mysteries, water and air are right
   there before us in the sea.</p>
```

`RESULT`

Water and air. So very commonplace are these substances, they hardly attract attention - and yet they vouchsafe our very existence.

EVERY TIME I VIEW THE SEA I FEEL A CALMING SENSE OF SECURITY, AS IF VISITING MY ANCESTRAL HOME; I EMBARK ON A VOYAGE OF SEEING.

Mystery of mysteries, water and air are right there before us in the sea.

CLASS ATTRIBUTE

```
<p class="important">For a one-year period from
   November 2010, the Marugame Genichiro-Inokuma
   Museum of Contemporary Art (MIMOCA) will host a
   cycle of four Hiroshi Sugimoto exhibitions.</p>
<p>Each will showcase works by the artist
   thematically contextualized under the headings
   "Science," "Architecture," "History" and
   "Religion" so as to present a comprehensive
   panorama of the artist's oeuvre.</p>
<p class="important admittance">Hours: 10:00 - 18:00
   (No admittance after 17:30)</p>
```

RESULT

FOR A ONE-YEAR PERIOD FROM NOVEMBER 2010,
THE MARUGAME GENICHIRO-INOKUMA MUSEUM
OF CONTEMPORARY ART (MIMOCA) WILL HOST A
CYCLE OF FOUR HIROSHI SUGIMOTO EXHIBITIONS.

Each will showcase works by the artist thematically
contextualized under the headings "Science," "Architecture,"
"History" and "Religion" so as to present a comprehensive
panorama of the artist's oeuvre.

HOURS: 10:00 - 18:00 (NO ADMITTANCE AFTER 17:30)

Every HTML element can also carry a class attribute. Sometimes, rather than uniquely identifying one element within a document, you will want a way to identify several elements as being different from the other elements on the page. For example, you might have some paragraphs of text that contain information that is more important than others and want to distinguish between these elements, or you might want to differentiate between links that point to other pages on your own site and links that point to external sites.

To do this you can use the class attribute. Its value should describe the class it belongs to. In the example on the left, key paragraphs have a class attribute whose value is important.

The class attribute on any element can share the same value. So, in this example, the value of important could be used on headings and links, too.

By default, using these attributes does not affect the presentation of an element. It will only change their appearance if there is a CSS rule that indicates it should be displayed differently.

In this example, CSS has been applied to make elements with a class attribute whose value is important uppercase, and elements with a class attribute whose value is admittance red.

If you would like to indicate that an element belongs to several classes, you can separate class names with a space, as you can see in the third paragraph in the example above.

BLOCK ELEMENTS

Some elements will always appear to start on a new line in the browser window. These are known as **block level** elements.

Examples of block elements are <h1>, <p>, <ul>, and <li>.

chapter-08/block-elements.html `HTML`

```
<h1>Hiroshi Sugimoto</h1>
<p>The dates for the ORIGIN OF ART exhibition are as
  follows:</p>
<ul>
  <li>Science: 21 Nov - 20 Feb 2010/11</li>
  <li>Architecture: 6 Mar - 15 May 2011</li>
  <li>History: 29 May - 21 Aug 2011</li>
  <li>Religion: 28 Aug - 6 Nov 2011</li>
</ul>
```

`RESULT`

Hiroshi Sugimoto

The dates for the ORIGIN OF ART exhibition are as follows:

- Science: 21 Nov - 20 Feb 2010/11
- Architecture: 6 Mar - 15 May 2011
- History: 29 May - 21 Aug 2011
- Religion: 28 Aug - 6 Nov 2011

INLINE ELEMENTS

```
Timed to a single revolution of the planet around
the sun at a 23.4 degrees tilt that plays out the
rhythm of the seasons, this <em>Origins of Art</em>
cycle is organized around four themes: <b>science,
architecture, history</b> and <b>religion</b>.
```

RESULT

Timed to a single revolution of the planet around the sun at a 23.4 degrees tilt that plays out the rhythm of the seasons, this *Origins of Art* cycle is organized around four themes: **science, architecture, history** and **religion**.

Some elements will always appear to continue on the same line as their neighbouring elements. These are known as **inline** elements.

Examples of inline elements are <a>, <b>, <em>, and <img>.

GROUPING TEXT & ELEMENTS IN A BLOCK

`<div>`

The `<div>` element allows you to group a set of elements together in one block-level box.

For example, you might create a `<div>` element to contain all of the elements for the header of your site (the logo and the navigation), or you might create a `<div>` element to contain comments from visitors.

In a browser, the contents of the `<div>` element will start on a new line, but other than this it will make no difference to the presentation of the page.

Using an `id` or `class` attribute on the `<div>` element, however, means that you can create CSS style rules to indicate how much space the `<div>` element should occupy on the screen and change the appearance of all the elements contained within it.

It can also make it easier to follow your code if you have used `<div>` elements to hold each section of the page.

```html
<div id="header">
  <img src="images/logo.gif" alt="Anish Kapoor" />
  <ul>
    <li><a href="index.html">Home</a></li>
    <li><a href="biography.html">Biography</a></li>
    <li><a href="works.html">Works</a></li>
    <li><a href="contact.html">Contact</a></li>
  </ul>
</div><!-- end of header -->
```

RESULT

ANISH KAPOOR

- Home
- Biography
- Works
- Contact

Since there may be several other elements inside a `<div>` element, it can be helpful to add a comment after the closing `</div>` tag.

This allows you to clearly see which opening tag it is supposed to correspond to, as shown at the end of the example here.

GROUPING TEXT & ELEMENTS INLINE

HTML   chapter-08/grouping-inline-elements.html

```
<p>Anish Kapoor won the Turner Prize in 1991 and
   exhibited at the <span class="gallery">Tate
   Modern</span> gallery in London in 2003.</p>
```

RESULT

Anish Kapoor won the Turner Prize in 1991 and exhibited at the
TATE MODERN gallery in London in 2003.

The `<span>` element acts like an inline equivalent of the `<div>` element. It is used to either:

1. Contain a section of text where there is no other suitable element to differentiate it from its surrounding text

2. Contain a number of inline elements

The most common reason why people use `<span>` elements is so that they can control the appearance of the content of these elements using CSS.

You will usually see that a `class` or `id` attribute is used with `<span>` elements:

- To explain the purpose of this `<span>` element

- So that CSS styles can be applied to elements that have specific values for these attributes

IFRAMES

<iframe>

An iframe is like a little window that has been cut into your page — and in that window you can see another page. The term iframe is an abbreviation of inline frame.

One common use of iframes (that you may have seen on various websites) is to embed a Google Map into a page. The content of the iframe can be any html page (either located on the same server or anywhere else on the web).

An iframe is created using the <iframe> element. There are a few attributes that you will need to know to use it:

src
The src attribute specifies the URL of the page to show in the frame.

height
The height attribute specifies the height of the iframe in pixels.

width
The width attribute specifies the width of the iframe in pixels.

chapter-08/iframes.html

`HTML`

```
<iframe
  width="450"
  height="350"
  src="http://maps.google.co.uk/maps?q=moma+new+york
  &amp;output=embed">
</iframe>
```

`RESULT`

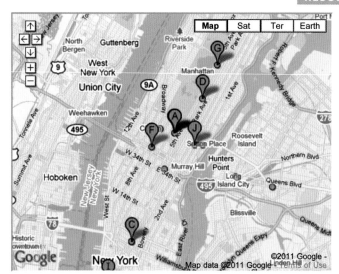

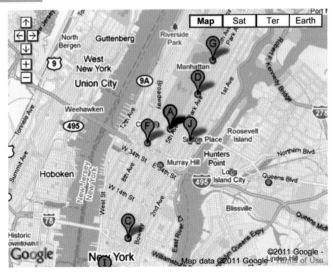

```
<iframe
  src="http://maps.google.co.uk/maps?q=moma+new+york
  &amp;output=embed"
  width="450"
  height="350"
  frameborder="0"
  scrolling="no">
</iframe>
```

RESULT

scrolling

The scrolling attribute will not be supported in HTML5. In HTML 4 and XHTML, it indicates whether the iframe should have scrollbars or not. This is important if the page inside the iframe is larger than the space you have allowed for it (using the height and width attributes). Scrollbars allow the user to move around the frame to see more content. It can take one of three values: yes (to show scrollbars), no (to hide scrollbars) and auto (to show them only if needed).

frameborder

The frameborder attribute will not be supported in HTML5. In HTML 4 and XHTML, it indicates whether the frame should have a border or not. A value of 0 indicates that no border should be shown. A value of 1 indicates that a border should be shown.

seamless

In HTML5, a new attribute called seamless can be applied to an iframe where scrollbars are not desired. The seamless attribute (like some other new HTML5 attributes) does not need a value, but you will often see authors give it a value of seamless. Older browsers do not support the seamless attribute.

INFORMATION ABOUT YOUR PAGES

`<meta>`

The `<meta>` element lives inside the `<head>` element and contains information about that web page.

It is not visible to users but fulfills a number of purposes such as telling search engines about your page, who created it, and whether or not it is time sensitive. (If the page is time sensitive, it can be set to expire.)

The `<meta>` element is an empty element so it does not have a closing tag. It uses attributes to carry the information.

The most common attributes are the `name` and `content` attributes, which tend to be used together. These attributes specify properties of the entire page. The value of the `name` attribute is the property you are setting, and the value of the `content` attribute is the value that you want to give to this property.

In the first line of the example on the opposite page, you can see a `<meta>` element where the `name` attribute indicates an intention to specify a description for the page. The `content` attribute is where this description is actually specified.

The value of the `name` attribute can be anything you want it to be. Some defined values for this attribute that are commonly used are:

description

This contains a description of the page. This description is commonly used by search engines to understand what the page is about and should be a maximum of 155 characters. Sometimes it is also displayed in search engine results.

keywords

This contains a list of comma-separated words that a user might search on to find the page. In practice, this no longer has any noticeable effect on how search engines index your site.

robots

This indicates whether search engines should add this page to their search results or not. A value of `noindex` can be used if this page should not be added. A value of `nofollow` can be used if search engines should add this page in their results but not any pages that it links to.

```html
<!DOCTYPE html>
<html>
  <head>
    <title>Information About Your Pages</title>
    <meta name="description"
      content="An Essay on Installation Art" />
    <meta name="keywords"
      content="installation, art, opinion" />
    <meta name="robots"
      content="nofollow" />
    <meta http-equiv="author"
      content="Jon Duckett" />
    <meta http-equiv="pragma"
      content="no-cache" />
    <meta http-equiv="expires"
      content="Fri, 04 Apr 2014 23:59:59 GMT" />
  </head>
  <body>
  </body>
</html>
```

The <meta> element also uses the http-equiv and content attributes in pairs. In our example, you can see three instances of the http-equiv attribute. Each one has a different purpose:

author

This defines the author of the web page.

pragma

This prevents the browser from caching the page. (That is, storing it locally to save time downloading it on subsequent visits.)

expires

Because browsers often cache the content of a page, the expires option can be used to indicate when the page should expire (and no longer be cached). Note that the date must be specified in the format shown.

ESCAPE CHARACTERS

There are some characters that are used in and reserved by HTML code. (For example, the left and right angled brackets.)

Therefore, if you want these characters to appear on your page you need to use what are termed "escape" characters (also known as escape codes or entity references). For example, to write a left angled bracket, you can use either < or <. For an ampersand, you can use either & or &.

There are also special codes that can be used to show symbols such as copyright and trademark, currency symbols, mathematical characters, and some punctuation marks. For example, if you want to include a copyright symbol on a web page you can use either © or ©.

When using escape characters, it is important to check the page in your browser to ensure that the correct symbol shows up. This is because some fonts do not support all of these characters and you might therefore need to specify a different font for these characters in your CSS code.

ONLINE EXTRA
You can find a more complete list of escape codes in the tools section of the website accompanying this book.

< **Less-than sign**
<
<

¢ **Cent sign**
¢
¢

' **Left single quote**
‘
‘

> **Greater-than sign**
>
>

£ **Pound sign**
£
£

' **Right single quote**
’
’

& **Ampersand**
&
&

¥ **Yen sign**
¥
¥

" **Left double quotes**
“
“

" **Quotation mark**
"
"

€ **Euro sign**
€
€

" **Right double quotes**
”
”

© **Copyright symbol**
©
©

× **Multiplication sign**
×
×

® **Registered trademark**
®
®

÷ **Division sign**
÷
÷

™ **Trademark**
™
™

This example starts by using a DOCTYPE to indicate that this is an HTML 4 web page. In the head, you can also see a `<meta>` tag describing the page's content. Several elements use the id and class attributes to identify their purpose. The copyright symbol has been added using an escape code.

Parts of the page have been grouped using `<div>` elements, and comments have been adde to indicate what the `</div>` elements are closing.

EXAMPLE
EXTRA MARKUP

```
<!DOCTYPE html PUBLIC
  "-//W3C//DTD HTML 4.01 Transitional//EN"
  "http://www.w3.org/TR/html4/loose.dtd">
<html>
  <head>
    <meta name="description" content="Telephone, email
      and directions for The Art Bookshop, London, UK" />
    <title>Contact The Art Bookshop, London UK</title>
  </head>
  <body>
    <div id="header">
      <h1>The Art Book Shop</h1>
      <ul>
        <li><a href="index.html">home</a></li>
        <li><a href="index.html">new publications</a>
          </li>
        <li class="current-page">
          <a href="index.html">contact</a></li>
      </ul>
    </div><!-- end header -->
    <div id="content">
      <p>Charing Cross Road, London, WC2, UK</p>
      <p><span class="contact">Telephone</span>
        0207 946 0946</p>
      <p><span class="contact">Email</span>
        <a href="mailto:books@example.com">
        books@example.com</a></p>
      <iframe width="425" height="275" frameborder="0"
        scrolling="no" marginheight="0" marginwidth="0"
        src="http://maps.google.co.uk/maps?f=q&amp;
        source=s_q&amp;hl=en&amp;geocode=&amp;
        q=charing+cross+road+london&amp;output=embed">
        </iframe>
    </div><!-- end content -->
    <p>&copy; The Art Bookshop</p>
  </body>
</html>
```

▸ `DOCTYPES` tell browsers which version of HTML you are using.

▸ You can add comments to your code between the `<!--` and `-->` markers.

▸ The `id` and `class` attributes allow you to identify particular elements.

▸ The `<div>` and `<span>` elements allow you to group block-level and inline elements together.

▸ `<iframes>` cut windows into your web pages through which other pages can be displayed.

▸ The `<meta>` tag allows you to supply all kinds of information about your web page.

▸ Escape characters are used to include special characters in your pages such as <, >, and ©.

9

FLASH, VIDEO & AUDIO

‣ How to add Flash movies into your site
‣ How to add video and audio to your site
‣ HTML5 `<video>` and `<audio>` elements

Flash is a very popular technology used to add animations, video, and audio to websites. This chapter begins by looking at how to use it in your web pages.

We then focus on how to add video and audio to your site, using either the new HTML5 <video> and <audio> elements or a hosted service (such as YouTube or SoundCloud). In this chapter you will learn:

● How to use Flash in your web pages

● How to use HTML5 `<video>` and `<audio>` elements

● When to host your own video and audio and when to use a service such as YouTube

HOW FLASH WORKS

Since the late 1990s, Flash has been a very popular tool for creating animations, and later for playing audio and video in websites.

Whether you are creating an animation or a media player in Flash, the files you put on your website are referred to as **Flash movies**.

If you want to create your own Flash movie, you need to purchase the Flash authoring environment from Adobe.

There are, however, several companies that offer Flash animations and slideshows, as well as video and audio players that you can use without purchasing this tool.

When you create a Flash file in the Flash authoring environment, it is saved with the .fla file extension. In order to use this file on a web page it has to be saved in a different format known as SWF. (It has the .swf file extension.)

When you export the movie into SWF format, Flash creates code that you can use to embed the Flash movie in your page. Traditionally, this code used the HTML <object> and <embed> tags. However, now it is more common to use JavaScript.

To view Flash, browsers need to use a plugin (an extra piece of software that runs in the browser) called the Flash Player. Statistics commonly indicate that 98% of browsers on desktop computers have the Flash plugin installed. (The percentage of mobiles and tablets with it is much less.)

There is not space in this book to teach you how to create Flash movies (there are many books devoted to that one topic), but this chapter will show you how to add Flash movies to your site.

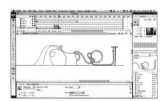

The Flash authoring environment is used to create Flash Movies.

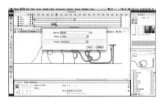

The .fla file is exported to .swf format to use in a web page.

The .swf file is included in your web page using JavaScript.

USE OF FLASH

Since 2005, a number of factors have meant that fewer websites are written in Flash or even use elements of Flash in their pages.

When Flash was first released, it was developed to create animations. The technology quickly evolved, however, and people started to use it to build media players and even entire websites.

Although Flash is still very popular, in recent years people have been more selective about when they use it (and now rarely consider building an entire website in Flash).

Despite this, Flash does have a future on the web because there are some things it does very well, such as creating animations.

There are several reasons why fewer websites are using Flash these days, including:

In 2005-6, a set of JavaScript libraries were launched (including Prototype, script.aculo.us, and JQuery) which made it easier for people to create animated effects using JavaScript.

When Apple launched the iPhone in 2007 and later the the iPad in 2010, they took the decision not to support Flash.

There have been laws introduced to ensure that websites are usable by those with visual or physical impairments — and Flash has been criticized because Flash content does not always meet accessibility requirements.

In 2008, browsers started to support HTML5 <video> and <audio> tags. At the time of writing, Flash is still a popular way of playing video and audio on the web but more and more people are switching to HTML5.

(You will see how to use these elements later in the chapter.)

TIMELINE:
FLASH, VIDEO & AUDIO

Web technologies change quickly. Here you can see some of the changes in how animation, video, and audio are created on the web.

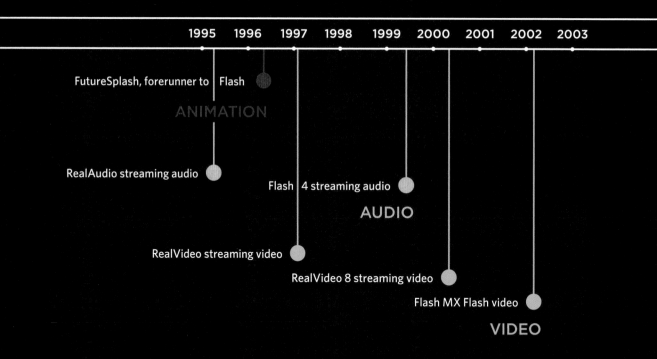

| 1995 | 1996 | 1997 | 1998 | 1999 | 2000 | 2001 | 2002 | 2003 |

FutureSplash, forerunner to Flash

ANIMATION

RealAudio streaming audio

Flash 4 streaming audio

AUDIO

RealVideo streaming video

RealVideo 8 streaming video

Flash MX Flash video

VIDEO

On this page you can see the first major players to provide web animation, audio, and video.

On the facing page, you can see some of the technologies and events replacing them.

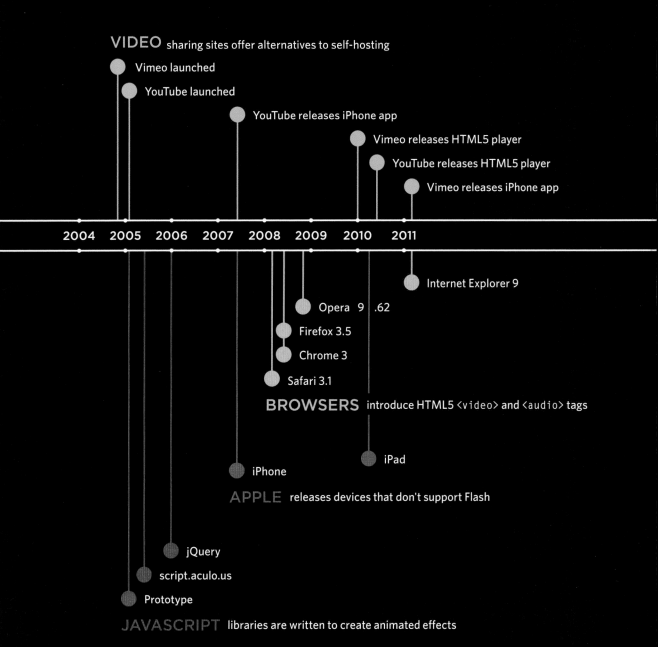

VIDEO sharing sites offer alternatives to self-hosting

Vimeo launched

YouTube launched

YouTube releases iPhone app

Vimeo releases HTML5 player

YouTube releases HTML5 player

Vimeo releases iPhone app

2004   2005   2006   2007   2008   2009   2010   2011

Internet Explorer 9

Opera 9 .62

Firefox 3.5

Chrome 3

Safari 3.1

BROWSERS introduce HTML5 <video> and <audio> tags

iPad

iPhone

APPLE releases devices that don't support Flash

jQuery

script.aculo.us

Prototype

JAVASCRIPT libraries are written to create animated effects

ADDING A FLASH MOVIE TO YOUR WEB PAGE

The most popular way of adding Flash into a web page is using JavaScript. There are several scripts that allow you to do this without an in-depth understanding of the JavaScript language.

The script we will be looking at here is called SWFObject. You can obtain a copy of it for free from Google, and you can see how we use it on the next page.

One advantage to using this technique is that it allows browsers to show alternative content for users whose browsers are not capable of showing Flash.

```html
<!DOCTYPE html>
<html>
  <head>
    <title>Adding a Flash Movie</title>
    <script type="text/javascript"
      src="http://ajax.googleapis.com/ajax/libs/
      swfobject/2.2/swfobject.js"></script>
    <script type="text/javascript">
      swfobject.embedSWF("flash/bird.swf",
      "bird", "400", "300", "8.0.0");</script>
  </head>
  <body>
    <div id="bird"><p>An animation of a bird taking
      a shower</p></div>
  </body>
</html>
```

This technique uses a `<div>` element to create a space where the Flash movie should sit. The `<div>` element has an id attribute whose value is used by the SWFObject script. In this example, the value of the id attribute is `bird`.

Inside the `<div>` element you can place the alternative content for users who are not able to play Flash.

The SWFObject script will check to see if the user's browser can play the Flash movie. If it can, the script will replace the content of the `<div>` with the `.swf` file.

For users who cannot see the Flash movie, you could show a still from the movie instead. You might also like to consider using a text description of the Flash file.

If you use a text description as alternative content, then you can achieve two further benefits:

1. The text can be accessed by those with visual and/or physical impairments who are not able to interact with the Flash file.

2. The text can be indexed by search engines (which are not as effective at indexing SWF files), increasing the chance that your content will be found.

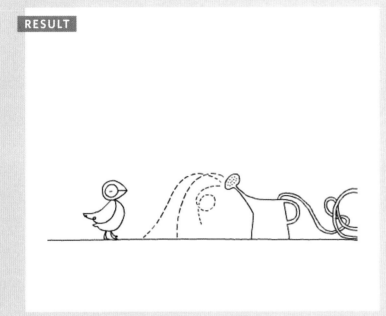

In this example, the SWFObject script is hosted on Google's servers. We **include** the script in this web page using the first of the two `<script>` elements.

The type attribute is used on the `<script>` element to indicate that the script inside is written in JavaScript. The `src` attribute tells the browser where to find the script.

The second `<script>` element is used to tell the browser about the Flash movie, as well as which element it should replace. This element is actually telling the SWFObject script **five** pieces of information, which are in the brackets:

1. The **location** of the `.swf` file:
`flash/bird.swf`

2. The element that the Flash movie should **replace**, specified by the `value` of the `id` attribute on the `<div>` element:
`bird`

3. The **width** of the Flash movie:
`400 px`

4. The **height** of the Flash movie:
`300 px`

5. The minimum **version** of the Flash player needed to view the movie:
`Flash Player 8`

UNDERSTANDING VIDEO FORMATS AND PLAYERS

To add video to your site, there are two key issues to understand: file formats and video players/plugins.

FORMATS

Movies are available in many formats (BluRay, DVD, VHS, to name a few). Online, there are even *more* video formats (including AVI, Flash Video, H264, MPEG, Ogg Theora, QuickTime, WebM, and Windows Media).

Just as your DVD player won't play a VHS cassette, browsers differ in what video formats they do and don't support.

In order for users to view your video online, you may need to convert it to another format.

The process of converting a video into another format is sometimes referred to as "encoding" the video.

There are several apps available on the web that enable you to encode videos (such as www.mirovideoconverter.com).

PLAYERS / PLUGINS

Browsers were initially designed to show text and images only. For this reason, browsers built prior to 2010 generally required another program called a player or plugin to be installed in order to play video content.

These players and plugins only supported certain video formats.

Recently browsers have evolved to support the HTML5 <video> tag (which renders players and plugins obsolete).

Unfortunately, however, you cannot rely on every visitor to your website having a recent browser that supports this new HTML5 element and the browsers that do recognize the <video> element require the video to be encoded in different formats.

APPROACH

The easiest way to add video to your site is to use a hosted service such as YouTube or Vimeo.

However, there are some cases where using these services is not appropriate (as you will see on the next page) and you will want to host the video on your own site.

At the time of writing, to ensure most people can play your video content, it is considered best practice to use the HTML5 <video> element for browsers that support it, and also Flash video for those that do not.This means you would need to upload any videos you want to show in at least two different formats: WebM and MP4.

USING HOSTED VIDEO SERVICES

The easiest way to add a video to your site is to upload the video to a site like YouTube or Vimeo and use the features provided on their site to embed the video in your page.

ADVANTAGES

Hosted video sites (such as YouTube) provide players that work with the majority of web browsers.

You do not need to worry about encoding your video since these sites allow you to upload your content in a range of formats. Once uploaded, they automatically convert your video into the various formats required by different browsers.

Web hosting companies often charge extra if you use a lot of bandwidth, and video files can be quite large. Therefore, it can cost you extra to host the videos on your own site. If your video is hosted on a site like YouTube or Vimeo, however, you do not need to pay for the bandwidth.

DISADVANTAGES

Your video will be available on the site of the hosted service, so if you want the content to be exclusively available on your site (and not visible on other sites), you need to host the video on your own server and add your own player into the page.

Some services will limit what your video is allowed to include. For example, most prohibit the use of advertising within the video you upload (which prevents you from monetizing that content).

Some hosted services will play their own adverts before your video will begin, or even overlay them over the screen as your video is playing. The quality of video on some hosted services can also be limited.

THE ALTERNATIVE

If you want to host video on your own site - rather than a hosted service - a lot more work is involved in setting up your site to play the video.

We will be looking at two different ways that you can host your own videos: using both Flash Video and the HTML5 <video> element.

In order to ensure that the maximum number of visitors to your site can see the video, you will need to use a combination of both of these techniques.

PREPARING A FLASH VIDEO FOR YOUR SITE

There are three steps you need to follow to add a Flash Video to your web page:

1

CONVERT YOUR VIDEO INTO FLV FORMAT

To play a Flash Video, you need to convert your video into FLV format. Since Flash 6, the Flash authoring environment has come with a Flash Video Encoder to convert videos into FLV format.

Some Flash video players also support a format called H264 (and some video editing programs export video in this format).

Googling "FLV or H264 converters" will allow you to find alternative encoding software.

I have provided a sample FLV file that you can use with the download code on the website (It is in a separate folder because the video files are large.)

2

FIND AN FLV PLAYER TO PLAY THE VIDEO

You'll need a **player** written in Flash to play the FLV file. Its purpose is to hold the FLV movie and add controls such as play/pause. Here are two sites that offer FLV players:

www.osflv.com
www.longtailvideo.com

You do not need the Flash authoring environment to use either of these on your website.

In the following example, we will use the OS FLV player, which is a free, open-source Flash Video player. This is included in the download code. It only supports the FLV format (not H264).

3

INCLUDE THE PLAYER & VIDEO IN YOUR PAGE

You can include the player in your page using a JavaScript technique such as SWFObject, which was mentioned earlier in this chapter.

You will also need to tell the player where it can find the video file that you want it to play. (Some players have advanced features such as the ability to create playlists of multiple videos, or add a still picture before the video plays.)

In the following example, we will also be using the SWFObject JavaScript technique mentioned on pages 207-208.

ADDING A FLASH VIDEO TO YOUR PAGES

```html
<!DOCTYPE html>
<html>
  <head>
    <title>Adding a Flash Video</title>
    <script type="text/javascript"
      src="http://ajax.googleapis.com/ajax/libs/
      swfobject/2.2/swfobject.js"></script>
    <script type="text/javascript">
      var flashvars = {};
      var params = {movie:"../video/puppy.flv"};
      swfobject.embedSWF("flash/osplayer.swf",
      "snow", "400", "320", "8.0.0",
      flashvars, params);</script>
  </head>
  <body>
    <div id="snow"><p>A video of a puppy playing in
      the snow</p></div>
  </body>
</html>
```

RESULT

This example uses the OS FLV player to display a video called puppy.flv, which has already been converted into FLV format.

You have already seen how to use SWFObject to embed a basic animation in a page, but sometimes Flash movies need information in order for them to work. In this example, the video player needs to know the path to the video it has to play, so SWFObject uses JavaScript variables to pass this information to the Flash movie. These are provided in the two lines of code that start with var.

This particular player is not expecting any information in the flashvars variable, so that is left empty.

The path to the movie is supplied in the variable called params.

```
var params = {movie:
"../videos/puppy.flv"};
```

The line after the variables is the one that tells the script to replace the HTML element with the video player. It is very similar to the one you saw in the earlier example that introduced SWFObject.

Different video players usually require information such as the path to the video in slightly different formats, but they usually come with examples and documentation to help you understand how to use them.

HTML5: PREPARING VIDEO FOR YOUR PAGES

Despite the HTML5 <video> element being a very recent addition, it is enjoying widespread use. Here are some of the key issues to be aware of:

SUPPORT

The new HTML5 <video> element is only supported by recent browsers, so you cannot just use this one technique if you want everyone to be able to see your video (you need to combine this HTML5 with Flash Video).

DIGITAL RIGHTS

At the time of writing, the <video> element does not support any type of Digital Rights Management (DRM — sometimes referred to as copy protection). But a dedicated pirate will usually find a way around DRM.

FORMATS

Not all browsers support the same video formats. Therefore, you need to supply your video in more than one format.

To reach as many browsers as possible, you should provide the video in the following formats:

H264: IE and Safari
WebM: Android, Chrome, Firefox, Opera

Chrome, Firefox, and Opera have indicated that they will support a format called WebM. (Some Flash players also support H264, and WebM - which will save on the number of conversions).

CONTROLS

The browser supplies its own controls for the player, and these can vary from browser to browser. You can control the appearance of these controls using JavaScript (but that is beyond the scope of this book).

IN THE BROWSER

One of the problems with players such as the Flash Player is that they can behave inconsistently when elements such as menus drop over them, or the window is scaled up or down. The HTML5 option solves these issues.

On page 222 you will see how to combine this HTML5 video technique with Flash Video to achieve wider reach.

I have provided a sample video in H264 and WebM format for you to try with the code downloads.

If you look at this example in Firefox and Opera you will see different controls when you hover over the video.

HTML5: ADDING VIDEO TO YOUR PAGES

chapter-09/adding-html5-video.html

```html
<!DOCTYPE html>
<html>
  <head>
    <title>Adding HTML5 Video</title>
  </head>
  <body>
    <video src="video/puppy.mp4"
      poster="images/puppy.jpg"
      width="400" height="300"
      preload
      controls
      loop>
      <p>A video of a puppy playing in the snow</p>
    </video>
  </body>
</html>
```

In HTML5 you do not need to supply values for all attributes, such as the controls, autoplay, and loop attributes used with the <video> element. These attributes are like on/off switches. If the attribute is present, it turns that option on. If the attribute is omitted, the option is turned off.

If the browser does not support the <video> element or the format of video used, it will display whatever is between the opening <video> and closing </video> tags.

preload

This attribute tells the browser what to do when the page loads. It can have one of three values:

none

The browser should not load the video until the user presses play.

auto

The browser should download the video when the page loads.

metadata

The browser should just collect information such as the size, first frame, track list, and duration.

<video>

The <video> element has a number of attributes which allow you to control video playback:

src

This attribute specifies the path to the video. (The example video is in H264 format so it will only work in IE and Safari.)

poster

This attribute allows you to specify an image to show while the video is downloading or until the user tells the video to play.

width, height

These attributes specify the size of the player in pixels.

controls

When used, this attribute indicates that the browser should supply its own controls for playback.

autoplay

When used, this attribute specifies that the file should play automatically.

loop

When used, this attribute indicates that the video should start playing again once it has ended.

HTML5: MULTIPLE VIDEO SOURCES

`<source>`

To specify the location of the file to be played, you can use the `<source>` element inside the `<video>` element. (This should replace the `src` attribute on the opening `<video>` tag.)

You can also use multiple `<source>` elements to specify that the video is available in different formats.

(Due to a bug on the iPad, you should provide the MP4 video as the first format. Otherwise, it might not play.)

src

This attribute specifies the path to the video.

type

You should use this attribute to tell the browser what format the video is in. Otherwise, it will download some of the video to see if it can play the file (which will take time and bandwidth).

codecs

The codec that was used to encode the video is supplied within the `type` attribute. Note the use of single quotes, as well as double quotes in the type attribute, when it is supplied.

```
chapter-09/multiple-video-sources.html          HTML

<!DOCTYPE html>
<html>
  <head>
    <title>Multiple Video Sources</title>
  </head>
  <body>
    <video poster="images/puppy.jpg" width="400"
      height="320" preload controls loop>
      <source src="video/puppy.mp4" type='video/
        mp4;codecs="avc1.42E01E, mp4a.40.2"' />
      <source src="video/puppy.webm" type='video/
        webm;codecs="vp8, vorbis"' />
      <p>A video of a puppy playing in the snow</p>
    </video>
  </body>
</html>
```

RESULT

If the browser does not support the `<video>` element or the format of video used, it will display whatever is between the opening `<video>` and closing `</video>` tags.

ONLINE EXTRA
We have provided links to tools that help you encode videos and audio into the correct formats in the Tools section of the website.

HTML5: COMBINING FLASH & HTML5 VIDEO

By offering your videos in both HTML5 and Flash Video formats, you will ensure that it can be viewed by the majority of users on your site.

You may choose to offer HTML5 as the first option, and Flash video as a fallback for people whose browser does not support HTML5 video. Or you may work the other way around.

Because some of the video players built in Flash support H264 encoding, if you use a player that supports this format you would only need to provide the video in H264 and WebM formats. (You would not need it in FLV format as well.) You will see this demonstrated in the example at the end of the chapter.

If you start to work with HTML5 video in depth, you can also:

- Create your own playback controls

- Provide different versions of the video for browsers that have different sized screens (so you can provide lower resolution content for handheld devices)

- Tell different parts of a page to change when the video reaches a certain point

ADDING AUDIO TO WEB PAGES

By far the most popular format for putting audio on web pages is MP3. As with video, there are three routes commonly taken:

1

USE A HOSTED SERVICE

There are several sites that allow you to upload your audio, and provide a player which you can embed in your page, such as SoundCloud.com and MySpace.com.

Some people ask how to get music to play consistently even when visitors move from one page to another on a website.

2

USE FLASH

There are several Flash movies that allow you to play MP3 files; from simple buttons that play one track to complex players that allow you to create playlists and juke boxes.

This is actually quite difficult to achieve and would rely on techniques like using AJAX to load page content or developing the entire site in Flash.

3

USE HTML5

HTML5 has introduced a new <audio> element. Browsers that support this element provide their own controls — much as they do for the video files we just looked at.

This is why some sites offer audio players in new windows, so that listeners are not interrupted when they move between pages.

ADDING A FLASH MP3 PLAYER

```html
<!DOCTYPE html>
<html>
  <head>
    <title>Adding a Flash MP3 Player</title>
    <script type="text/javascript"
      src="http://ajax.googleapis.com/ajax/libs/
      swfobject/2.2/swfobject.js"></script>
    <script type="text/javascript">
      var flashvars = {};
      var params = {mp3: "audio/test-audio.mp3"};
      swfobject.embedSWF(
        "flash/player_mp3_1.0.0.swf",
        "music-player", "200", "20", "8.0.0",
        flashvars, params);</script>
  </head>
  <body>
    <div id="music-player">
      <p>You cannot hear this track because this
        browser does not support our Flash music
        player.</p>
    </div>
  </body>
</html>
```

RESULT

There are many MP3 players that have already been written in Flash, such as:

flash-mp3-player.net
musicplayer.sourceforge.net
www.wimpyplayer.com

Each of these players has different functionality, so check their features before choosing one for your site. This example uses a free player from flash-mp3-player.net which is embedded in the page using the SWFObject technique we met on pages 207-208. The player is told the path to the MP3 file using a parameter called mp3.

After the second <script> tag, you can see that we have created two JavaScript variables; the first called flashvars, the second called params. Even though we are not using the flashvars variable, the SWFObject script expects it before the params variable so we need it there.

```
var flashvars = {};
var params = {
  mp3: "music/test-audio
       .mp3"};
```

These variables are then added at the end of the line that embeds the MP3 player in the page (just before the second closing <script> tag).

HTML5: ADDING HTML5 AUDIO TO YOUR PAGES

\<audio\>

HTML5 introduced the \<audio\> element to include audio files in your pages. As with HTML5 video, browsers expect different formats for the audio.

The \<audio\> element has a number of attributes which allow you to control audio playback:

src

This attribute specifies the path to the audio file.

controls

This attribute indicates whether or not the player should display controls. If you do not use this attribute, no controls will be shown by default. You can also specify your own controls using JavaScript.

autoplay

The presence of this attribute indicates that the audio should start playing automatically. (It is considered better practice to let visitors choose to play audio.)

```
chapter-09/adding-html5-audio.html                    HTML

<!DOCTYPE html>
<html>
  <head>
    <title>Adding HTML5 Audio</title>
  </head>
  <body>
    <audio src="audio/test-audio.ogg"
      controls autoplay>
      <p>This browser does not support our audio
      format.</p>
    </audio>
  </body>
</html>
```

RESULT

preload

This attribute indicates what the browser should do if the player is not set to autoplay. It can have the same values we saw on page 214 for the \<video\> element.

loop

This attribute specifies that the audio track should play again once it has finished.

This example only works in browsers that support the Ogg Vorbis audio format (Firefox, Chrome, and Opera). For it to work in Safari 5 and IE 9, the audio would need to be in MP3 format (or use the \<source\> element covered on the next page to offer different formats).

HTML5: MULTIPLE AUDIO SOURCES

```
<!DOCTYPE html>
<html>
  <head>
    <title>Multiple Audio Sources</title>
  </head>
  <body>
    <audio controls autoplay>
      <source src="audio/test-audio.ogg" />
      <source src="audio/test-audio.mp3" />
      <p>This browser does not support our audio
      format.</p>
    </audio>
  </body>
</html>
```

RESULT

`<source>`

It is possible to specify more than one audio file using the `<source>` element between the opening `<audio>` and closing `</audio>` tags (instead of the `src` attribute on the opening `<audio>` tag).

This is important because different browsers support different formats for audio files.

MP3: Safari 5+, Chrome 6+, IE9

Ogg Vorbis: Firefox 3.6, Chome 6, Opera 1.5

So you would need to supply two audio formats to get coverage across all recent browsers that support the `<audio>` element. You could also provide a Flash alternative for older browsers that do not support the `<audio>` element.

The HTML5 `<audio>` tag has not gained such widespread adoption as the `<video>` tag, and there have been some issues with audio quality in the first browsers to implement it.

src

The `<source>` element uses the `src` attribute to indicate where the audio file is located.

type

At the time of writing, the `type` attribute was not commonly being used on the `<source>` element in the same way it was for the `<video>` element.

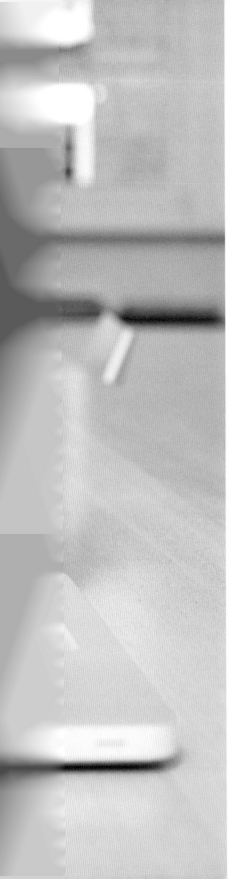

EXAMPLE
FLASH, VIDEO & AUDIO

This example uses HTML5 to show a video.

The video has been encoded in H264 and WebM formats to reach as many browsers as possible. A Flash player has been added to the page for browsers that do not support HTML5 video. The Flash player is embedded using SWFObject. If the browser does not support HTML5 video or Flash, then a plain text message will be shown to the user.

```html
<!DOCTYPE html>
<html>
  <head>
    <title>Flash, Video and Audio</title>
    <script type="text/javascript"
      src="http://ajax.googleapis.com/ajax/libs/
      swfobject/2.2/swfobject.js"></script>
    <script type="text/javascript">
      var flashvars = {};
      var params = {movie: "../video/puppy.flv"};
      swfobject.embedSWF("flash/osplayer.swf", "snow",
      "400", "320", "8.0.0", flashvars, params);</script>
  </head>
  <body>
    <video poster="images/puppy.jpg" width="400"
      height="320" controls="controls">
      <source src="video/puppy.mp4" type='video/mp4;
        codecs="avc1.42E01E, mp4a.40.2"' />
      <source src="video/puppy.webm" type='video/webm;
        codecs="vp8, vorbis"' />
      <div id="snow">
        <p>You cannot see this video of a puppy playing
          in the snow because this browser does not
          support our video formats.</p>
      </div>
    </video>
  </body>
</html>
```

SUMMARY
FLASH, VIDEO & AUDIO

▸ Flash allows you to add animations, video and audio to the web.

▸ Flash is not supported on iPhone or iPad.

▸ HTML5 introduces new `<video>` and `<audio>` elements for adding video and audio to web pages, but these are only supported in the latest browsers.

▸ Browsers that support the HTML5 elements do not all support the same video and audio formats, so you need to supply your files in different formats to ensure that everyone can see/hear them.

10

INTRODUCING CSS

- ▸ What CSS does
- ▸ How CSS works
- ▸ Rules, properties, and values

In this section, we will look at how to make your web pages more attractive, controlling the design of them using CSS.

CSS allows you to create rules that specify how the content of an element should appear. For example, you can specify that the background of the page is cream, all paragraphs should appear in gray using the Arial typeface, or that all level one headings should be in a blue, italic, Times typeface.

Once you have learned how to write a CSS rule, learning CSS mostly involves learning the different properties you can use. So this chapter will:

- Introduce you to how CSS works
- Teach you how to write CSS rules
- Show you how CSS rules apply to HTML pages

The remaining chapters in this section will look at all of the various CSS properties you can use.

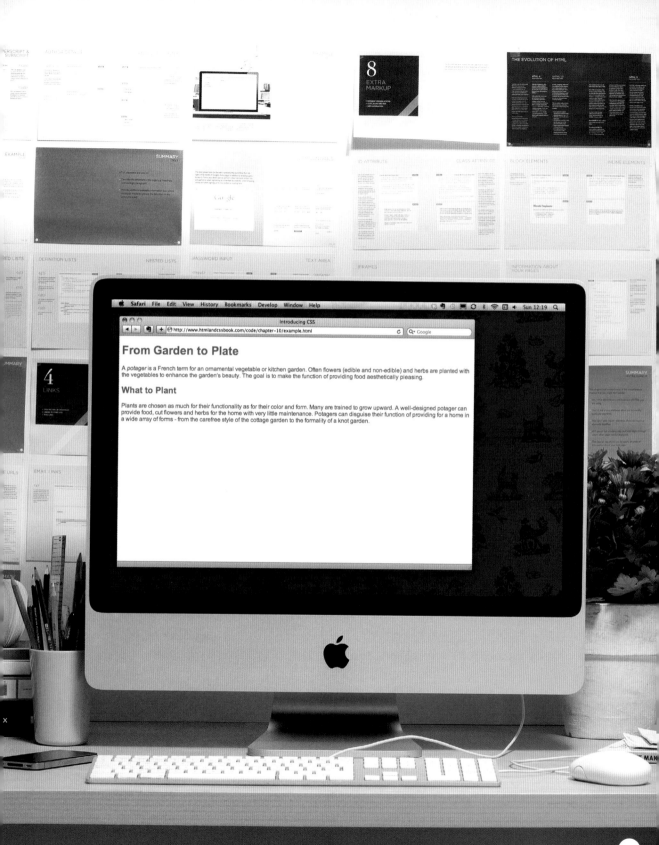

UNDERSTANDING CSS: THINKING INSIDE THE BOX

The key to understanding how CSS works is to imagine that there is an invisible box around every HTML element.

On this page, you can see a basic HTML page.

On the right hand page, you can see the same HTML page, but I have added outlines to each of the elements so that you can see how CSS will treat each element as if it lives inside its own box.

The Cottage Garden

The *cottage garden* is a distinct style of garden that uses an informal design, dense plantings, and a mixture of ornamental and edible plants.

The Cottage Garden originated in <u>England</u> and its history can be traced back for centuries, although they were re-invented in 1870's England, when stylized versions were formed as a reaction to the more structured and rigorously maintained <u>English estate gardens</u>.

The earliest cottage gardens were more practical than their modern descendants, with an emphasis on vegetables and herbs, along with some fruit trees.

BLOCK & INLINE ELEMENTS

You may remember from pages 185-186 that there is a difference between block level and inline elements and how browsers display them.

Block level elements look like they start on a new line. Examples include the <h1>-<h6>, <p> and <div> elements.

Inline elements flow within the text and do not start on a new line. Examples include <b>, <i>, <img>, <em> and <span>.

CSS allows you to create rules that control the way that each individual box (and the contents of that box) is presented.

The Cottage Garden

The *cottage garden* is a distinct style of garden that uses an informal design, dense plantings, and a mixture of ornamental and edible plants.

The Cottage Garden originated in England and its history can be traced back for centuries, although they were re-invented in 1870's England, when stylized versions were formed as a reaction to the more structured and rigorously maintained English estate gardens .

The earliest cottage gardens were more practical than their modern descendants, with an emphasis on vegetables and herbs, along with some fruit trees.

In this example, block level elements are shown with red borders, and inline elements have green borders.

The `<body>` element creates the first box, then the `<h1>`, `<h2>`, `<p>`, `<i>`, and `<a>` elements each create their own boxes within it.

Using CSS, you could add a border around any of the boxes, specify its width and height, or add a background color. You could also control text inside a box — for example, its color, size, and the typeface used.

EXAMPLE STYLES

BOXES

Width and height
Borders (color, width, and style)
Background color and images
Position in the browser window

TEXT

Typeface
Size
Color
Italics, bold, uppercase, lowercase, small-caps

SPECIFIC

There are also specific ways in which you can style certain elements such as lists, tables, and forms.

CSS ASSOCIATES STYLE RULES WITH HTML ELEMENTS

CSS works by associating rules with HTML elements. These rules govern how the content of specified elements should be displayed. A CSS rule contains two parts: a selector and a declaration.

SELECTOR

```
p {
        font-family: Arial;}
```

DECLARATION

This rule indicates that all <p> elements should be shown in the Arial typeface.

Selectors indicate which element the rule applies to. The same rule can apply to more than one element if you separate the element names with commas.

Declarations indicate how the elements referred to in the selector should be styled. Declarations are split into two parts (a property and a value), and are separated by a colon.

CSS PROPERTIES AFFECT HOW ELEMENTS ARE DISPLAYED

CSS declarations sit inside curly brackets and each is made up of two parts: a property and a value, separated by a colon. You can specify several properties in one declaration, each separated by a semi-colon.

```
h1, h2, h3 {
              font-family: Arial;
              color: yellow;}
```

PROPERTY   VALUE

This rule indicates that all <h1>, <h2> and <h3> elements should be shown in the Arial typeface, in a yellow color.

Properties indicate the aspects of the element you want to change. For example, color, font, width, height and border.

Values specify the settings you want to use for the chosen properties. For example, if you want to specify a color property then the value is the color you want the text in these elements to be.

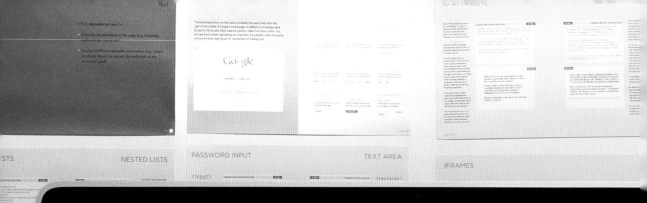

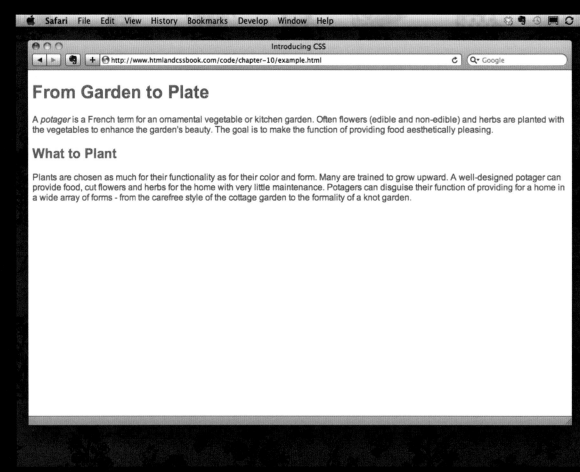

EXAMPLE
INTRODUCING CSS

Here you can see a simple web page that is styled using CSS.

This example uses two documents: the HTML file (`example.html`) and a separate CSS file (`example.css`). The fifth line of HTML uses the `<link>` element to indicate where the CSS file is located.

On the next page, you will see how CSS rules can also be placed in your HTML pages and we will discuss when you might want to do this.

```html
<!DOCTYPE html>
<html>
  <head>
    <title>Introducing CSS</title>
    <link href="css/example.css" type="text/css"
      rel="stylesheet" />
  </head>
  <body>
    <h1>From Garden to Plate</h1>
    <p>A <i>potager</i> is a French term for an
      ornamental vegetable or kitchen garden ... </p>
    <h2>What to Plant</h2>
    <p>Plants are chosen as much for their functionality
      as for their color and form ... </p>
  </body>
</html>
```

```css
body {
  font-family: Arial, Verdana, sans-serif;}
h1, h2 {
  color: #ee3e80;}
p {
  color: #665544;}
```

USING EXTERNAL CSS

`<link>`

The `<link>` element can be used in an HTML document to tell the browser where to find the CSS file used to style the page. It is an empty element (meaning it does not need a closing tag), and it lives inside the `<head>` element. It should use three attributes:

href

This specifies the path to the CSS file (which is often placed in a folder called `css` or `styles`).

type

This attribute specifies the type of document being linked to. The value should be `text/css`.

rel

This specifies the relationship between the HTML page and the file it is linked to. The value should be `stylesheet` when linking to a CSS file.

An HTML page can use more than one CSS style sheet. To do this it could have a `<link>` element for every CSS file it uses. For example, some authors use one CSS file to control the presentation (such as fonts and colors) and a second to control the layout.

chapter-10/using-external-css.html `HTML`

```
<!DOCTYPE html>
<html>
  <head>
    <title>Using External CSS</title>
    <link href="css/styles.css" type="text/css"
      rel="stylesheet" />
  </head>
  <body>
    <h1>Potatoes</h1>
    <p>There are dozens of different potato
      varieties. They are usually described as
      early, second early and maincrop.</p>
  </body>
</html>
```

chapter-10/styles.css `CSS`

```
body {
    font-family: arial;
    background-color: rgb(185,179,175);}
h1 {
    color: rgb(255,255,255);}
```

`RESULT`

Potatoes

There are dozens of different potato varieties. They are usually described as early, second early and maincrop potatoes.

USING INTERNAL CSS

```html
<!DOCTYPE html>
<html>
  <head>
    <title>Using Internal CSS</title>
    <style type="text/css">
      body {
          font-family: arial;
          background-color: rgb(185,179,175);}
      h1 {
          color: rgb(255,255,255);}
    </style>
  </head>
  <body>
    <h1>Potatoes</h1>
    <p>There are dozens of different potato
       varieties. They are usually described as
       early, second early and maincrop.</p>
  </body>
</html>
```

RESULT

Potatoes

There are dozens of different potato varieties. They are usually described as early, second early and maincrop potatoes.

<style>

You can also include CSS rules within an HTML page by placing them inside a <style> element, which usually sits inside the <head> element of the page.

The <style> element should use the type attribute to indicate that the styles are specified in CSS. The value should be text/css.

When building a site with more than one page, you should use an external CSS style sheet. This:

- Allows all pages to use the same style rules (rather than repeating them in each page).

- Keeps the content separate from how the page looks.

- Means you can change the styles used across all pages by altering just one file (rather than each individual page).

In HTML 4 and Transitional XHTML, you could also use a style attribute on most of the elements that appear in the body of a page. The CSS rules that appeared within the value of the attribute would only apply to that one element. You should avoid using this attribute in any new site but I mention it here because you may see it used in older code. Here is an example that changes the color of the text in a single paragraph to red:
<p style="color:red;">

CSS SELECTORS

There are many different types of CSS selector that allow you to target rules to specific elements in an HTML document.

The table on the opposite page introduces the most commonly used CSS selectors.

On this page, there is an HTML file to demonstrate which elements these CSS selectors would apply to.

CSS selectors are case sensitive, so they must match element names and attribute values exactly.

There are some more advanced selectors which allow you to select elements based on attributes and their values, which you will see on page 292.

IE 7 was the first version of IE to support the last two selectors in the table (the sibling selectors), so their use is less common than the other selectors shown here.

chapter-10/css-selectors.html **HTML**

```html
<!DOCTYPE html>
<html>
  <head>
    <title>CSS Selectors</title>
  </head>
  <body>
    <h1 id="top">Kitchen Garden Calendar</h1>
    <p id="introduction">Here you can read our
      handy guide about what to do when.</p>
    <h2>Spring</h2>
    <ul>
      <li><a href="mulch.html">
            Spring mulch vegetable beds</a></li>
      <li><a href="potato.html">
            Plant out early potatoes</a></li>
      <li><a href="tomato.html">
            Sow tomato seeds</a></li>
      <li><a href="beet.html">
            Sow beet seeds</a></li>
      <li><a href="zucchini.html">
            Sow zucchini seeds</a></li>
      <li><a href="rhubarb.html">
            Deadhead rhubarb flowers</a></li>
    </ul>
    <p class="note">
      This page was written by
      <a href="mailto:ivy@example.org">
        ivy@example.org</a> for
      <a href="http://www.example.org">Example</a>.
    </p>
    <p>
      <a href="#top">Top of page</a>
    </p>
  </body>
</html>
```

SELECTOR	MEANING	EXAMPLE
UNIVERSAL SELECTOR	Applies to all elements in the document	`* {}` Targets all elements on the page
TYPE SELECTOR	Matches element names	`h1, h2, h3 {}` Targets the `<h1>`, `<h2>` and `<h3>` elements

CLASS SELECTOR	Matches an element whose `class` attribute has a value that matches the one specified after the period (or full stop) symbol	`.note {}`
		Targets any element whose `class` attribute has a value of `note`
		`p.note {}`
		Targets only `<p>` elements whose `class` attribute has a value of `note`

ID SELECTOR	Matches an element whose `id` attribute has a value that matches the one specified after the pound or hash symbol	`#introduction {}` Targets the element whose `id` attribute has a value of `introduction`
CHILD SELECTOR	Matches an element that is a direct child of another	`li>a {}` Targets any `<a>` elements that are children of an `<li>` element (but not other `<a>` elements in the page)
DESCENDANT SELECTOR	Matches an element that is a descendent of another specified element (not just a direct child of that element)	`p a {}` Targets any `<a>` elements that sit inside a `<p>` element, even if there are other elements nested between them
ADJACENT SIBLING SELECTOR	Matches an element that is the next sibling of another	`h1+p {}` Targets the first `<p>` element after any `<h1>` element (but not other `<p>` elements)
GENERAL SIBLING SELECTOR	Matches an element that is a sibling of another, although it does not have to be the directly preceding element	`h1~p {}` If you had two `<p>` elements that are siblings of an `<h1>` element, this rule would apply to both

HOW CSS RULES CASCADE

If there are two or more rules that apply to the same element, it is important to understand which will take precedence.

LAST RULE
If the two selectors are identical, the latter of the two will take precedence. Here you can see the second i selector takes precedence over the first.

SPECIFICITY
If one selector is more specific than the others, the more specific rule will take precedence over more general ones. In this example:

h1 is more specific than *
p b is more specific than p
p#intro is more specific than p

IMPORTANT
You can add !important after any property value to indicate that it should be considered more important than other rules that apply to the same element.

Understanding how CSS rules cascade means you can write simpler style sheets because you can create generic rules that apply to most elements and then override the properties of individual elements that need to appear differently.

chapter-10/cascade.html **HTML**

```
<h1>Potatoes</h1>
<p id="intro">There are <i>dozens</i> of different
    <b>potato</b> varieties.</p>
<p>They are usually described as early, second early
    and maincrop potatoes.</p>
```

CSS

```
* {
  font-family: Arial, Verdana, sans-serif;}
h1 {
  font-family: "Courier New", monospace;}
i {
  color: green;}
i {
  color: red;}
b {
  color: pink;}
p b {
  color: blue !important;}
p b {
  color: violet;}
p#intro {
  font-size: 100%;}
p {
  font-size: 75%;}
```

RESULT

Potatoes

There are *dozens* of different **potato** varieties.

They are usually described as early, second early and maincrop potatoes.

INHERITANCE

```html
<div class="page">
  <h1>Potatoes</h1>
  <p>There are dozens of different potato
    varieties.</p>
  <p>They are usually described as early, second
    early and maincrop potatoes.</p>
</div>
```

CSS

```css
body {
  font-family: Arial, Verdana, sans-serif;
  color: #665544;
  padding: 10px;}
.page {
  border: 1px solid #665544;
  background-color: #efefef;
  padding: inherit;}
```

RESULT

Potatoes

There are dozens of different potato varieties.

They are usually described as early, second early and maincrop potatoes.

If you specify the font-family or color properties on the <body> element, they will apply to most child elements. This is because the value of the font-family property is **inherited** by child elements. It saves you from having to apply these properties to as many elements (and results in simpler style sheets).

You can compare this with the background-color or border properties; they are **not inherited** by child elements. If these were inherited by all child elements then the page could look quite messy.

You can force a lot of properties to inherit values from their parent elements by using inherit for the value of the properties. In this example, the <div> element with a class called page inherits the padding size from the CSS rule that applies to the <body> element.

WHY USE EXTERNAL STYLE SHEETS?

When building a website there are several advantages to placing your CSS rules in a separate style sheet.

All of your web pages can share the same style sheet. This is achieved by using the <link> element on each HTML page of your site to link to the same CSS document. This means that the same code does not need to be repeated in every page (which results in less code and smaller HTML pages).

Therefore, once the user has downloaded the CSS stylesheet, the rest of the site will load faster. If you want to make a change to how your site appears, you only need to edit the one CSS file and all of your pages will be updated. For example, you can change the style of every <h1> element by altering

the one CSS style sheet, rather than changing the CSS rules on every page. The HTML code will be easier to read and edit because it does not have lots of CSS rules in the same document. It is generally considered good practice to have the content of the site separated from the rules that determine how it appears.

Sometimes you might consider placing CSS rules in the same page as your HTML code.

If you are just creating a single page, you might decide to put the rules in the same file to keep everything in one place. (However, many authors would consider it better practice to keep the CSS in a separate file.)

If you have one page which requires a few extra rules (that are not used by the rest of the site), you might consider using CSS in the same page. (Again, most authors consider it better practice to keep all CSS rules in a separate file.)

Most of the examples in this book place the CSS rules in the <head> of the document (using the <style> element) rather than a separate document. This is simply to save you opening two files to see how the CSS examples work.

DIFFERENT VERSIONS OF CSS & BROWSER QUIRKS

CSS1 was released in 1996 and CSS2 followed two years later. Work on CSS3 has been ongoing but the major browsers have already started to implement it.

In the same way that there have been several versions of HTML, there have also been different versions of CSS.

Browsers did not implement all CSS features at once, so some older browsers do not support every property.

This is mentioned when it is likely to affect you, along with notes where CSS properties might not behave as expected.

Any seasoned user of CSS will tell you that some browsers display a few of the CSS properties in an unexpected way. But finding and squashing those bugs is easy when you know how...

Before launching any new site, it is important to test it in more than one browser, because there can be slight differences in how browsers display the pages.

You do not need lots of computers to test your site, as there are online tools to show you what a page looks like in multiple browsers:

BrowserCam.com
BrowserLab.Adobe.com
BrowserShots.org
CrossBrowserTesting.com

Using these tools, it is a good idea to check the site on different operating systems (PC, Mac, and Linux) and in older versions of the major browsers, as well as recent versions.

When you look at your site in more than one browser, you might find that some elements on your page do not look as you expect them to.

When a CSS property does not display as expected, it is generally referred to as a **browser quirk** or **CSS bug**.

Some common browser bugs are discussed in this book, but there are many smaller bugs that only occur in rare situations, or on old browsers that few people use.

If you come across a CSS bug, you can use your favorite search engine to try and find a solution. Or you can check these sites:

PositionIsEverything.net
QuirksMode.org

▸ CSS treats each HTML element as if it appears inside its own box and uses rules to indicate how that element should look.

▸ Rules are made up of selectors (that specify the elements the rule applies to) and declarations (that indicate what these elements should look like).

▸ Different types of selectors allow you to target your rules at different elements.

▸ Declarations are made up of two parts: the properties of the element that you want to change, and the values of those properties. For example, the font-family property sets the choice of font, and the value arial specifies Arial as the preferred typeface.

▸ CSS rules usually appear in a separate document, although they may appear within an HTML page.

11

COLOR

- ▸ How to specify colors
- ▸ Color terminology and contrast
- ▸ Background color

Color can really bring your pages to life.

In this chapter we will look at:

- How to specify colors, as there are three common ways in which you can indicate your choice of colors (plus extra ways made available in CSS3)

- Color terminology, as there are some terms that are very helpful to understand when it comes to picking colors

- Contrast, and ensuring that your text is readable

- Background colors for behind either your entire page or parts of a page

What you will learn about colors in this chapter will then be used in subsequent chapters when it comes to looking at colors of text and boxes in CSS.

FOREGROUND COLOR
color

The color property allows you to specify the color of text inside an element. You can specify any color in CSS in one of three ways:

RGB VALUES
These express colors in terms of how much red, green and blue are used to make it up. For example: rgb(100,100,90)

HEX CODES
These are six-digit codes that represent the amount of red, green and blue in a color, preceded by a pound or hash # sign. For example: #ee3e80

COLOR NAMES
There are 147 predefined color names that are recognized by browsers. For example: DarkCyan

We look at these three different ways of specifying colors on the next double-page spread.

CSS3 has also introduced another way to specify colors called HSLA, which you will meet near the end of this chapter on page 255-256.

chapter-11/foreground-color.html

`CSS`

```css
/* color name */
h1 {
  color: DarkCyan;}
/* hex code */
h2 {
  color: #ee3e80;}
/* rgb value */
p {
  color: rgb(100,100,90);}
```

`RESULT`

Marine Biology

The Composition of Seawater

Almost anything can be found in seawater. This includes dissolved materials from Earth's crust as well as materials released from organisms. The most important components of seawater that influence life forms are salinity, temperature, dissolved gases (mostly oxygen and carbon dioxide), nutrients, and pH. These elements vary in their composition as well as in their influence on marine life.

Above each CSS rule in this example you can see how CSS allows you to add comments to your CSS files. Anything between the /* symbols and the */ symbols will not be interpreted by the browser. They are shown in grey above.

The use of comments can help you to understand a CSS file (and organise it, by splitting a long document into sections). Here, we have used comments to indicate which method is used to specify each of the different types of colors.

BACKGROUND COLOR
background-color

chapter-11/background-color.html

```
CSS

body {
  background-color: rgb(200,200,200);}
h1 {
  background-color: DarkCyan;}
h2 {
  background-color: #ee3e80;}
p {
  background-color: white;}
```

RESULT

Marine Biology

The Composition of Seawater

Almost anything can be found in seawater. This includes dissolved materials from Earth's crust as well as materials released from organisms. The most important components of seawater that influence life forms are salinity, temperature, dissolved gases (mostly oxygen and carbon dioxide), nutrients, and pH. These elements vary in their composition as well as in their influence on marine life.

CSS treats each HTML element as if it appears in a box, and the background-color property sets the color of the background for that box.

You can specify your choice of background color in the same three ways you can specify foreground colors: RGB values, hex codes, and color names (covered on the next page).

If you do not specify a background color, then the background is transparent.

By default, most browser windows have a white background, but browser users can set a background color for their windows, so if you want to be sure that the background is white you can use the background-color property on the <body> element.

We have also used the padding property to separate the text from the edges of the boxes. This makes it easier to read and you will learn more about this property on page 313.

UNDERSTANDING COLOR

Every color on a computer screen is created by mixing amounts of red, green, and blue. To find the color you want, you can use a color picker.

Computer monitors are made up of thousands of tiny squares called pixels (if you look very closely at your monitor you should be able to see them).

When the screen is not turned on, it's black because it's not emitting any light. When it's on, each pixel can be a different color, creating a picture.

The color of every pixel on the screen is expressed in terms of a mix of red, green, and blue — just like on a television screen.

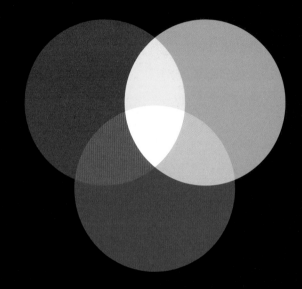

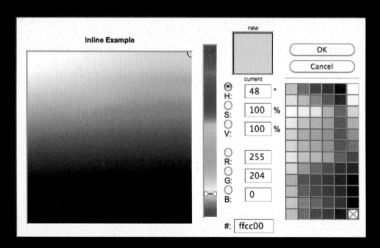

Color picking tools are available in image editing programs like Photoshop and GIMP. You can see the RGB values specified next to the radio buttons that say R, G, B.

The hex value is provided next to the pound or hash # symbol. There is also a good color picking tool at: colorschemedesigner.com

RGB VALUES

Values for red, green, and blue are expressed as numbers between 0 and 255.

`rgb(102,205,170)`

This color is made up of the following values:
102 red
205 green
170 blue

HEX CODES

Hex values represent values for red, green, and blue in hexadecimal code.

`#66cdaa`

The value of the red, 102, is expressed as 66 in hexadecimal code. The 205 of the green is expressed as cd and the 170 of the blue equates to aa. Hex values are not case sensitive. Where all the characters are the same (e.g. #ffffff), they can be abbreviated to three characters (e.g. #fff).

COLOR NAMES

Colors are represented by predefined names. However, they are very limited in number.

`MediumAquaMarine`

There are 147 color names supported by browsers (this color is MediumAquaMarine). Most consider this to be a limited color palette, and it is hard to remember the name for each of the colors so (apart from white and black) they are not commonly used.

HUE

Hue is near to the colloquial idea of color. Technically speaking however, a color can also have saturation and brightness as well as hue.

SATURATION

Saturation refers to the amount of gray in a color. At maximum saturation, there would be no gray in the color. At minimum saturation, the color would be mostly gray.

BRIGHTNESS

Brightness (or "value") refers to how much black is in a color. At maximum brightness, there would be no black in the color. At minimum brightness, the color would be very dark.

CONTRAST

When picking foreground and background colors, it is important to ensure that there is enough contrast for the text to be legible.

| LOW CONTRAST | HIGH CONTRAST | MEDIUM CONTRAST |

Text is harder to read when there is low contrast between background and foreground colors.

A lack of contrast is particularly a problem for those with visual impairments and color blindness.

It also affects those with poor monitors and sunlight on their screens (which is increasingly common as people use handheld devices outdoors).

Text is easier to read when there is higher contrast between background and foreground colors.

If you want people to read a lot of text on your page, however, then too much contrast can make it harder to read, too.

For long spans of text, reducing the contrast a little bit improves readability.

You can reduce contrast by using dark gray text on a white background or an off-white text on a dark background.

If text is reversed out (a light color on a dark background), you can increase the height between lines and the weight of the font to make it easier to read.

To check contrast there is a handy online tool at: www.snook.ca/technical/colour_contrast/colour.html

CSS3: OPACITY
opacity, rgba

```
p.one {
  background-color: rgb(0,0,0);
  opacity: 0.5;}
p.two {
  background-color: rgb(0,0,0);
  background-color: rgba(0,0,0,0.5);}
```

RESULT

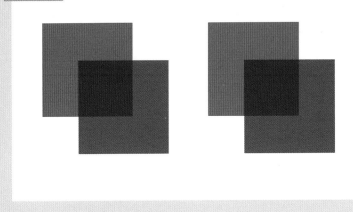

RESULT IN OLDER BROWSER

CSS3 introduces the opacity property which allows you to specify the opacity of an element and any of its child elements. The value is a number between 0.0 and 1.0 (so a value of 0.5 is 50% opacity and 0.15 is 15% opacity).

The CSS3 rgba property allows you to specify a color, just like you would with an RGB value, but adds a fourth value to indicate opacity. This value is known as an alpha value and is a number between 0.0 and 1.0 (so a value of 0.5 is 50% opacity and 0.15 is 15% opacity). The rgba value will only affect the element on which it is applied (not child elements).

Because some browsers will not recognize RGBA colors, you can offer a fallback so that they display a solid color. If there are two rules that apply to the same element, the latter of the two will take priority. To create the fallback, you can specify a color as a hex code, color name or RGB value, followed by the rule that specifies an RGBA value. If the browser understands RGBA colors it will use that rule. If it doesn't, it will use the RGB value.

At the time of writing, the opacity and rgba properties are only supported by the most recent browsers.

CSS3: HSL COLORS

CSS3 introduces an entirely new and intuitive way to specify colors using hue, saturation, and lightness values.

HUE

Hue is the colloquial idea of color. In HSL colors, hue is often represented as a color circle where the angle represents the color, although it may also be shown as a slider with values from 0 to 360.

SATURATION

Saturation is the amount of gray in a color. Saturation is represented as a percentage. 100% is full saturation and 0% is a shade of gray.

LIGHTNESS

Lightness is the amount of white (lightness) or black (darkness) in a color. Lightness is represented as a percentage. 0% lightness is black, 100% lightness is white, and 50% lightness is normal. Lightness is sometimes referred to as *luminosity*.

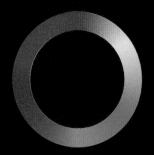

Please note that lightness is a different concept to brightness. Graphic design software (such as Photoshop and GIMP) have color pickers that use hue, saturation, and brightness — but brightness only adds black, whereas lightness offers both white and black.

CSS3: HSL & HSLA
hsl, hsla

```css
body {
  background-color: #C8C8C8;
  background-color: hsl(0,0%,78%);}
p {
  background-color: #ffffff;
  background-color: hsla(0,100%,100%,0.5);}
```

RESULT

Marine Biology

The Composition of Seawater

Almost anything can be found in seawater. This includes dissolved materials
from Earth's crust as well as materials released from organisms. The most
important components of seawater that influence life forms are salinity,
temperature, dissolved gases (mostly oxygen and carbon dioxide), nutrients,
and pH. These elements vary in their composition as well as in their influence
on marine life.

The hsl color property has been introduced in CSS3 as an alternative way to specify colors. The value of the property starts with the letters hsl, followed by individual values inside parentheses for:

HUE
This is expressed as an angle (between 0 and 360 degrees).

SATURATION
This is expressed as a percentage.

LIGHTNESS
This is expressed as a percentage with 0% being white, 50% being normal, and 100% being black.

The hsla color property allows you to specify color properties using hue, saturation, and lightness as above, and adds a fourth value which represents transparency (just like the rgba property). The a stands for:

ALPHA
This is expressed as a number between 0 and 1.0. For example, 0.5 represents 50% transparency, and 0.75 represents 75% transparency.

Because older browsers do not recognize HSL and HSLA values, it is a good idea to add an extra rule which specifies the color using a hex code, RGB value, or color name. This should appear *before* the rule that uses the HSL or HSLA value.

This provides a fallback because if there are two rules that apply to the same element in CSS, the latter of the two always takes priority. This means that if the browser understands HSL and HSLA colors, it will use that rule; and if it does not, it will use the first rule.

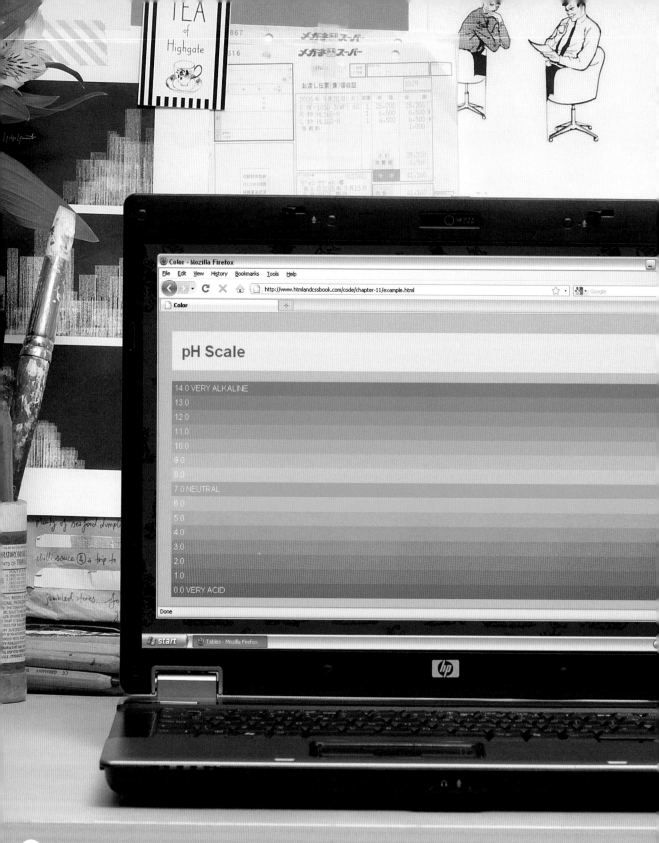

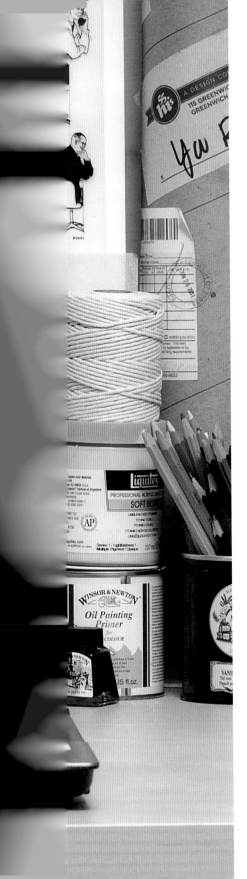

EXAMPLE
COLOR

This example shows a pH scale to demonstrate the different ways that colors can be specified using CSS (using color names, hex codes, RGB, and HSL).

The rule for the `<body>` element sets a default color for all the text as well as the default background color for the page. Both use color names.

The rule for the `<h1>` element sets the color of the heading using a hex code. There are two values for the `background-color` property of the `<h1>` element. The first provides a fallback color using a hex code and the second is an HSLA value for browsers that support this method.

Each paragraph is then shown in a different color to represent the varying levels of acidity or alkalinity, and these are specified using RGB values.

The example also uses a property called `margin` to decrease the gap between the paragraph boxes, and a property called `padding` to create a gap between the edge of the boxes and the text within them. (These properties are covered on pages 313-314.)

EXAMPLE
COLOR

```
<!DOCTYPE html>
<html>
  <head>
    <title>Color</title>
    <style type="text/css">
      body {
        background-color: silver;
        color: white;
        padding: 20px;
        font-family: Arial, Verdana, sans-serif;}
      h1 {
        background-color: #ffffff;
        background-color: hsla(0,100%,100%,0.5);
        color: #64645A;
        padding: inherit;}
      p {
        padding: 5px;
        margin: 0px;}
      p.zero {
        background-color: rgb(238,62,128);}
      p.one {
        background-color: rgb(244,90,139);}
      p.two {
        background-color: rgb(243,106,152);}
      p.three {
        background-color: rgb(244,123,166);}
      p.four {
        background-color: rgb(245,140,178);}
      p.five {
        background-color: rgb(246,159,192);}
      p.six {
        background-color: rgb(245,176,204);}
      p.seven {
        background-color: rgb(0,187,136);}
      p.eight {
        background-color: rgb(140,202,242);}
      p.nine {
        background-color: rgb(114,193,240);}
```

```
      p.ten {
        background-color: rgb(84,182,237);}
      p.eleven {
        background-color: rgb(48,170,233);}
      p.twelve {
        background-color: rgb(0,160,230);}
      p.thirteen {
        background-color: rgb(0,149,226);}
      p.fourteen {
        background-color: rgb(0,136,221);}
    </style>
  </head>
  <body>
    <h1>pH Scale</h1>
    <p class="fourteen">14.0 VERY ALKALINE</p>
    <p class="thirteen">13.0</p>
    <p class="twelve">12.0</p>
    <p class="eleven">11.0</p>
    <p class="ten">10.0</p>
    <p class="nine">9.0</p>
    <p class="eight">8.0</p>
    <p class="seven">7.0 NEUTRAL</p>
    <p class="six">6.0</p>
    <p class="five">5.0</p>
    <p class="four">4.0</p>
    <p class="three">3.0</p>
    <p class="two">2.0</p>
    <p class="one">1.0</p>
    <p class="zero">0.0 VERY ACID</p>
  </body>
</html>
```

▸ Color not only brings your site to life, but also helps convey the mood and evokes reactions.

▸ There are three ways to specify colors in CSS: RGB values, hex codes, and color names.

▸ Color pickers can help you find the color you want.

▸ It is important to ensure that there is enough contrast between any text and the background color (otherwise people will not be able to read your content).

▸ CSS3 has introduced an extra value for RGB colors to indicate opacity. It is known as RGBA.

▸ CSS3 also allows you to specify colors as HSL values, with an optional opacity value. It is known as HSLA.

12
TEXT

▸ Size and typeface of text
▸ Bold, italics, capitals, underlines
▸ Spacing between lines, words, and letters

The properties that allow you to control the appearance of text can be split into two groups:

- Those that directly affect the font and its appearance (including the typeface, whether it is regular, bold or italic, and the size of the text)

- Those that would have the same effect on text no matter what font you were using (including the color of text and the spacing between words and letters)

The formatting of your text can have a significant effect on how readable your pages are. As we look through these properties I will also give you some design tips on how to display your type.

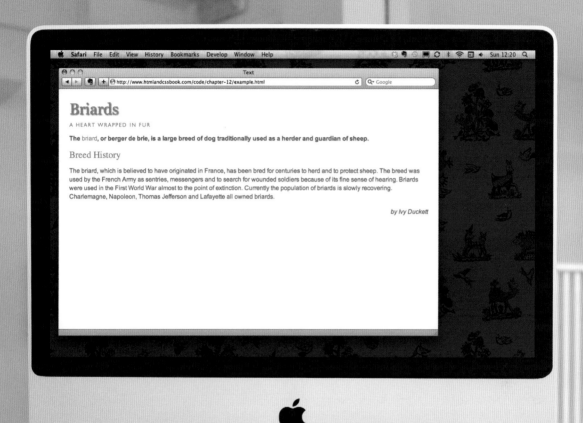

Briards

A HEART WRAPPED IN FUR

The briard**, or berger de brie, is a large breed of dog traditionally used as a herder and guardian of sheep.**

Breed History

The briard, which is believed to have originated in France, has been bred for centuries to herd and to protect sheep. The breed was used by the French Army as sentries, messengers and to search for wounded soldiers because of its fine sense of hearing. Briards were used in the First World War almost to the point of extinction. Currently the population of briards is slowly recovering. Charlemagne, Napoleon, Thomas Jefferson and Lafayette all owned briards.

by Ivy Duckett

TYPEFACE TERMINOLOGY

SERIF

Serif fonts have extra details on the ends of the main strokes of the letters. These details are known as serifs.

SANS-SERIF

Sans-serif fonts have straight ends to letters, and therefore have a much cleaner design.

MONOSPACE

Every letter in a monospace (or fixed-width) font is the same width. (Non-monospace fonts have different widths.)

In print, serif fonts were traditionally used for long passages of text because they were considered easier to read.

Screens have a lower resolution than print. So, if the text is small, sans-serif fonts can be clearer to read.

Monospace fonts are commonly used for code because they align nicely, making the text easier to follow.

ASCENDER above the cap height

CAP HEIGHT top of flat letters

X-HEIGHT height of the letter x

BASELINE line the letters sit on

DESCENDER below the baseline

WEIGHT

Light
Medium
Bold
Black

The font weight not only adds emphasis but can also affect the amount of white space and contrast on a page.

STYLE

Normal
Italic
Oblique

Italic fonts have a cursive aspect to some of the lettering. Oblique font styles take the normal style and put it on an angle.

STRETCH

Condensed
Regular
Extended

In condensed (or narrow) versions of the font, letters are thinner and closer together. In expanded versions they are thicker and further apart.

CHOOSING A TYPEFACE FOR YOUR WEBSITE

When choosing a typeface, it is important to understand that a browser will usually only display it if it's installed on that user's computer.

SERIF

Serif fonts have extra details on the end of the main strokes of the letters.

EXAMPLES:

Georgia

Times

Times New Roman

SANS-SERIF

Sans-serif fonts have straight ends to letters and therefore have a much cleaner design.

EXAMPLES:

Arial

Verdana

Helvetica

As a result, sites often use a small set of typefaces that are installed on most computers (shown above). There are some techniques to get around this limitation (which are covered on pages 271-272).

It is possible to specify more than one typeface and create an order of preference (in case the user does not have your first choice of typeface installed). This is sometimes referred to as a **font stack**.

MONOSPACE

Every letter in a monospace typeface is the same width. (Non-monospace fonts have different widths.)

EXAMPLES:

Courier

Courier New

CURSIVE

Cursive fonts either have joining strokes or other cursive characteristics, such as handwriting styles.

EXAMPLES:

Comic Sans MS

Monotype Corsiva

FANTASY

Fantasy fonts are usually decorative fonts and are often used for titles. They're not designed for long bodies of text.

EXAMPLES:

Impact

Haettenschweiler

Browsers are supposed to support at least one typeface from each of the groups above. For this reason, it is common to add the generic font name after your preferred choice of typefaces.

For example, if you wanted serif type, you could write the following:
```
font-family: Georgia, Times, serif;
```

TECHNIQUES THAT OFFER A WIDER CHOICE OF TYPEFACES

There are several ways to use fonts other than those listed on the previous page. However, typefaces are subject to copyright, so the techniques you can choose from are limited by their respective licenses.

FONT-FAMILY	FONT-FACE	SERVICE-BASED FONT-FACE
The user's computer needs the typeface installed. CSS is used to specify the typeface.	CSS specifies where a font can be downloaded from if it is not installed on the computer.	Commercial services give users access to a wider range of fonts using @font-face.
COVERED ON		
Pages 273-274	Pages 277-278	Pages 277-278
ISSUES		
There is a limited choice of typefaces that most users have installed.	The user has to download the font file, which can slow down loading of the web page.	There is an ongoing fee to cover licenses paid to font foundries.
LICENSING		
You are not distributing the typeface, so there is no licensing issue.	The license to use the font must permit its distribution using @font-face.	The service takes care of the licensing issues with the people who made the font.
CHOICE OF TYPEFACES		
There is a limited choice because the font needs to be installed on users' computers.	Choice is limited because few typefaces can be freely distributed this way.	Each service offers a different choice of fonts based on their agreements with font foundries.

SUITABLE FOR ANY LENGTH OF TEXT

If you design on a Mac, it is important to check what the typefaces look like on a PC because PCs can render type less smoothly. But if you design on a PC, then it should look fine on a Mac.

IMAGES

SIFR

CUFON

You can create a graphic that contains the text as you want it to appear in a different typeface.

The font is embedded into a Flash movie, and JavaScript replaces specified HTML text with a flash version of it.

Cufon offers similar functionality to sIFR. It uses JavaScript to create either an SVG or VML version of the text.

COVERED ON

Pages 99-100 and 109-113

See website for more details

See website for more details

ISSUES

People who use screen readers will rely on the alt text to know what is said.

This method only works if the user has Flash and JavaScript enabled on their device.

Requires JavaScript to be enabled. Also, users cannot select text, and text can't change when a user hovers over it.

LICENSING

You can use any typeface that you have a license to use on your computer (because you are not distributing the typeface).

Many commercial makers of typefaces allow this technique, although you may need to pay for an extra web-use license.

As with sIFR, some typeface makers allow use of their fonts with CUFON, but you need to check the license.

CHOICE OF TYPEFACES

Very wide choice because you can use any typeface that you have a license for.

This method provides a lot of choice because many of the major typeface manufacturers permit this kind of usage.

Slightly less choice than for sIFR, as some typeface manufacturers are not as keen on this technique.

NOT SUITABLE FOR LONG PASSAGES OF TEXT

SPECIFYING TYPEFACES
font-family

The font-family property allows you to specify the typeface that should be used for any text inside the element(s) to which a CSS rule applies.

The value of this property is the name of the typeface you want to use.

The people who are visiting your site need the typeface you have specified installed on their computer in order for it to be displayed.

You can specify a list of fonts separated by commas so that, if the user does not have your first choice of typeface installed, the browser can try to use an alternative font from the list.

It is also common to end with a generic font name for that type of font (which you saw on pages 269-270).

If a font name is made up of more than one word, it should be put in double quotes.

Designers suggest pages usually look better if they use no more than three typefaces on a page.

We will be using an extended version of the HTML shown on this page for all of the examples in this chapter.

`chapter-12/font-family.html`   HTML + CSS

```
<!DOCTYPE html>
<html>
  <head>
    <title>Font Family</title>
    <style type="text/css">
      body {
        font-family: Georgia, Times, serif;}
      h1, h2 {
        font-family: Arial, Verdana, sans-serif;}
      .credits {
        font-family: "Courier New", Courier,
          monospace;}
    </style>
  </head>
  <body>
    <h1>Briards</h1>
    <p class="credits">by Ivy Duckett</p>
    <p class="intro">The <a class="breed"
      href="http://en.wikipedia.org/wiki/
      Briard">briard</a>, or berger de brie, is
      a large breed of dog traditionally used as
      a herder and guardian of sheep...</p>
  </body>
</html>
```

RESULT

Briards

by Ivy Duckett

The briard, or berger de brie, is a large breed of dog traditionally used as a herder and guardian of sheep.

Breed History

The briard, which is believed to have originated in France, has been bred for centuries to herd and to protect sheep. The breed was used by the French Army as sentries, messengers and to search for wounded soldiers because of its fine sense of hearing. Briards were used in the First World War almost to the point of extinction. Currently the population of briards is slowly recovering. Charlemagne, Napoleon, Thomas Jefferson and Lafayette all owned briards.

SIZE OF TYPE
font-size

CSS

```css
body {
  font-family: Arial, Verdana, sans-serif;
  font-size: 12px;}
h1 {
  font-size: 200%;}
h2 {
  font-size: 1.3em;}
```

RESULT

Briards

by Ivy Duckett

The briard, or berger de brie, is a large breed of dog traditionally used as a herder and guardian of sheep.

Breed History

The briard, which is believed to have originated in France, has been bred for centuries to herd and to protect sheep. The breed was used by the French Army as sentries, messengers and to search for wounded soldiers because of its fine sense of hearing. Briards were used in the First World War almost to the point of extinction. Currently the population of briards is slowly recovering. Charlemagne, Napoleon, Thomas Jefferson and Lafayette all owned briards.

The font-size property enables you to specify a size for the font. There are several ways to specify the size of a font. The most common are:

PIXELS
Pixels are commonly used because they allow web designers very precise control over how much space their text takes up. The number of pixels is followed by the letters px.

PERCENTAGES
The default size of text in browsers is 16px. So a size of 75% would be the equivalent of 12px, and 200% would be 32px.

If you create a rule to make all text inside the <body> element to be 75% of the default size (to make it 12px), and then specify another rule that indicates the content of an element inside the <body> element should be 75% size, it will be 9px (75% of the 12px font size).

EMS
An em is equivalent to the width of a letter m.

We will look at these measurements in greater detail on the next page.

TYPE SCALES

You may have noticed that programs such as Word, Photoshop and InDesign offer the same sizes of text.

This is because they are set according to a scale or ratio that was developed by European typographers in the sixteenth century.

It is considered that this scale for type is pleasing to the eye and it has therefore changed little in the last 400 years.

For this reason, when you are designing pages, using sizes from this scale will help them look more attractive.

On the next page, you can see how to achieve this scale using pixels, percentages, and ems.

Print designers often refer to the size of text in terms of points rather than pixels (hence the use of pt in the scale on the right). A pixel roughly equates to a point because a point corresponds to 1/72 of an inch, and most computer displays have a resolution of 72 dots per inch.

The default size of text in a

browser is 16 pixels. So if you use percentages or ems, you calculate the size of text you want based on the default size of the text used in browsers. For example, you could scale down to 12 pixels for body copy and scale up to 24 pixels for headings.

Recently, some web designers have started to leave the body text at the default size of 16 pixels and adjust the other font sizes using a scale that keeps the relative proportions of this one.

When you first see body text at 16 pixels, it might seem quite large. Once you get used to the larger type, however, most people find it far easier to read; and going back to a page where main type is 12 pixels will often then look quite small.

8pt
9pt
10pt
11pt
12pt
14pt
18pt
24pt
36pt
48pt
60pt
72pt

UNITS OF TYPE SIZE

PIXELS

TWELVE PIXEL SCALE

h1	24px
h2	18px
h3	14px
body	12px

=

PERCENTAGES

h1	200%
h2	150%
h3	117%
body	75%

=

EMS

h1	1.5em
h2	1.3em
h3	0.875em
body	100%
p	0.75em

SIXTEEN PIXEL SCALE

h1	32px
h2	24px
h3	18px
body	16px

=

h1	200%
h2	150%
h3	112.5%
body	100%

=

h1	2em
h2	1.5em
h3	1.125em
body	100%
p	1em

Setting font size in pixels is the best way to ensure that the type appears at the size you intended (because percentages and ems are more likely to vary if a user has changed the default size of text in their browser).

Pixels are relative to the resolution of the screen, so the same type size will look larger when a screen has a resolution of 800x600 than it would when it is 1280x800.

You can also use pt for point sizes instead of px for pixels, but you should only do this when creating style sheets for printer-friendly versions of pages.

The default size of text in a web browser is 16 pixels. Using percentages of this amount, you can create a scale where the default text size is 12 pixels, and headings are sized in relation to this.

It is possible for users to change the default size of text in their web browsers. If they have done this, the fonts will be displayed at the same scale that the designer intended, but at a larger size.

Ems allow you to change the size of text relative to the size of the text in the parent element. Since the default size of text in web browsers is 16 pixels, you can use similar rules to those shown for percentages.

Because users can change the default size of text in their browser, the fonts could all appear larger (or smaller) than the designer intended.

The extra p rule above is to help Internet Explorer 6 and 7 display the fonts at the right size. Without this extra rule, IE6 and IE7 exaggerate the relative sizes of other text.

MORE FONT CHOICE
@font-face

@font-face allows you to use a font, even if it is not installed on the computer of the person browsing, by allowing you to specify a path to a copy of the font, which will be downloaded if it is not on the user's machine.

Because this technique allows a version of the font to be downloaded to the user's computer, it is important that the license for the font permits it to be used in this way.

You add the font to your style sheet using the @font-face rule, as shown on the right.

font-family

This specifies the name of the font. This name can then be used as a value of the font-family property in the rest of the style sheet (as shown in the rule for the <h1> and <h2> elements).

src

This specifies the path to the font. In order for this technique to work in all browsers, you will probably need to specify paths to a few different versions of the font, as shown on the next page.

format

This specifies the format that the font is supplied in. (It's discussed in detail on the next page.)

chapter-12/font-face.html `CSS`

```css
@font-face {
  font-family: 'ChunkFiveRegular';
  src: url('fonts/chunkfive.eot');}
h1, h2 {
  font-family: ChunkFiveRegular, Georgia, serif;}
```

`RESULT`

Briards

by Ivy Duckett

The briard, or berger de brie, is a large breed of dog traditionally used as a herder and guardian of sheep.

Breed History

The briard, which is believed to have originated in France, has been bred for centuries to herd and to protect sheep. The breed was used by the French Army as sentries, messengers and to search for wounded soldiers because of its fine sense of hearing. Briards were used in the First World War almost to the point of extinction. Currently the population of briards is slowly recovering. Charlemagne, Napoleon, Thomas Jefferson and Lafayette all owned briards.

Many typeface makers do not allow you to use their fonts in this way, but there are open source fonts you can use freely. You can find lists of them at:

www.fontsquirrel.com
www.fontex.org
www.openfontlibrary.org

When looking at fonts on these sites, it is still important to check the font's license agreement because some fonts are only free for personal use (that is, not for use on commercial websites).

There are some sites that give you access to use commercial fonts, because they negotiated permission to let their customers use these fonts for a fee:

www.typekit.com
www.kernest.com
www.fontspring.com

Google also provides open source fonts. Rather than adding the @font-face rule to your own style sheet, you link to a CSS file and font files on their servers:
www.google.com/webfonts

UNDERSTANDING FONT FORMATS

```
CSS        chapter-12/understanding-font-formats.html

@font-face {
  font-family: 'ChunkFiveRegular';
  src: url('fonts/chunkfive.eot');
  src: url('fonts/chunkfive.eot?#iefix')
       format('embedded-opentype'),
    url('fonts/chunkfive.woff') format('woff'),
    url('fonts/chunkfive.ttf')
     format('truetype'),
    url('fonts/chunkfive.svg#ChunkFiveRegular')
    format('svg');}
```

BROWSER	FORMAT			
	eot	woff	ttf / otf	svg
Chrome (all)				●
Chrome 6+		●	●	●
Firefox 3.5			●	
Firefox 3.6+		●	●	
IE 5 - 8	●			
IE 9+	●	●	◖	
Opera 10+			●	●
Safari 3.1+			●	●
iOS <4.2				●
iOS 4.2+			●	●

Different browsers support different formats for fonts (in the same way that they support different audio and video formats), so you will need to supply the font in several variations to reach all browsers.

If you do not have all of these formats for your font, you can upload the font to a website called FontSquirrel where they will convert it for you:

www.fontsquirrel.com/fontface/generator

Font Squirrel also provides you with the CSS code for the @font-face rule. This is very helpful because, when you are dealing with multiple font formats, the src and format properties of the @font-face rule can get rather complicated.

You can see an example of a more complicated @font-face rule on the left.

The various font formats should appear in your code in this order:

1: eot
2: woff
3: ttf/otf
4: svg

Because the browser needs to download the font file in order to show it, users might see something known as a Flash of Unstyled Content (FOUC) or Flash of Unstyled Text (FOUT). Two things you can do to try to minimize this behavior are to delete any unneccesary glyphs from the font and/or host the font on a Content Delivery Network (a special type of web hosting that offers faster delivery of files).

BOLD
font-weight

The font-weight property allows you to create bold text. There are two values that this property commonly takes:

normal
This causes text to appear at a normal weight.

bold
This causes text to appear bold.

In this example, you can see that the element whose class attribute has a value of credits has been bolded.

You might wonder why there is a normal weight. This is because if, for example, you created a rule for the <body> element indicating that all text inside the body should appear bold, you might need an option that allows the text in certain instances to appear normal weight. So it is essentially used as an "off switch."

`CSS`

```
.credits {
  font-weight: bold;}
```

`RESULT`

Briards

by Ivy Duckett

The briard, or berger de brie, is a large breed of dog traditionally used as a herder and guardian of sheep.

Breed History

The briard, which is believed to have originated in France, has been bred for centuries to herd and to protect sheep. The breed was used by the French Army as sentries, messengers and to search for wounded soldiers because of its fine sense of hearing. Briards were used in the First World War almost to the point of extinction. Currently the population of briards is slowly recovering. Charlemagne, Napoleon, Thomas Jefferson and Lafayette all owned

ITALIC
font-style

```
CSS                          chapter-12/font-style.html

.credits {
    font-style: italic;}
```

RESULT

Briards

by Ivy Duckett

The briard, or berger de brie, is a large breed of dog traditionally used as a herder and guardian of sheep.

Breed History

The briard, which is believed to have originated in France, has been bred for centuries to herd and to protect sheep. The breed was used by the French Army as sentries, messengers and to search for wounded soldiers because of its fine sense of hearing. Briards were used in the First World War almost to the point of extinction. Currently the population of briards is slowly recovering. Charlemagne, Napoleon, Thomas Jefferson and Lafayette all owned briards.

If you want to create italic text, you can use the font-style property. There are three values this property can take:

normal
This causes text to appear in a normal style (as opposed to italic or oblique).

italic
This causes text to appear italic.

oblique
This causes text to appear oblique.

In this example, you can see that the credits have been italicized.

Italic fonts were traditionally stylized versions of the font based on calligraphy, whereas an oblique version would take the normal version and put it on an angle.

It is not unusual for the browser to fail to find an italic version of a typeface, in which case it will use an algorithm to place the normal version of the type on a slant, which means that a lot of italic text online is actually oblique.

UPPERCASE & LOWERCASE

text-transform

The text-transform property is used to change the case of text giving it one of the following values:

uppercase
This causes the text to appear uppercase.

lowercase
This causes the text to appear lowercase.

capitalize
This causes the first letter of each word to appear capitalized.

In this example, the <h1> element is uppercase, the <h2> element is lowercase, and the credits are capitalized. In the HTML, the word *by* in the credits had a lowercase *b*.

If you do utilize the uppercase option, it is worth looking at the letter-spacing property to increase the gap between each letter as shown on page 284. This will help improve readability.

chapter-12/text-transform.html `CSS`

```
h1 {
  text-transform: uppercase;}
h2 {
  text-transform: lowercase;}
.credits {
  text-transform: capitalize;}
```

`RESULT`

BRIARDS

By Ivy Duckett

The briard, or berger de brie, is a large breed of dog traditionally used as a herder and guardian of sheep.

breed history

The briard, which is believed to have originated in France, has been bred for centuries to herd and to protect sheep. The breed was used by the French Army as sentries, messengers and to search for wounded soldiers because of its fine sense of hearing. Briards were used in the First World War almost to the point of extinction. Currently the population of briards is slowly recovering. Charlemagne, Napoleon, Thomas Jefferson and Lafayette all owned briards.

UNDERLINE & STRIKE
text-decoration

```
.credits {
    text-decoration: underline;}
a {
    text-decoration: none;}
```

RESULT

Briards

by Ivy Duckett

The briard, or berger de brie, is a large breed of dog traditionally used as a herder and guardian of sheep.

Breed History

The briard, which is believed to have originated in France, has been bred for centuries to herd and to protect sheep. The breed was used by the French Army as sentries, messengers and to search for wounded soldiers because of its fine sense of hearing. Briards were used in the First World War almost to the point of extinction. Currently the population of briards is slowly recovering. Charlemagne, Napoleon, Thomas Jefferson and Lafayette all owned briards.

The text-decoration property allows you to specify the following values:

none
This removes any decoration already applied to the text.

underline
This adds a line underneath the text.

overline
This adds a line over the top of the text.

line-through
This adds a line through words.

blink
This animates the text to make it flash on and off (however this is generally frowned upon, as it is considered rather annoying).

In this example, the credits have been underlined. Also, the name of the breed (which is a link) is not underlined, which it would be by default because it is a link.

This property is commonly used by designers to remove the underlines that browsers place under links. Pages 290-291 show how to add or remove an underline when a user hovers over a link.

LEADING
line-height

Leading (pronounced *ledding*) is a term typographers use for the vertical space between lines of text. In a typeface, the part of a letter that drops beneath the baseline is called a **descender**, while the highest point of a letter is called the **ascender**. Leading is measured from the bottom of the descender on one line to the top of the ascender on the next.

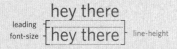

In CSS, the `line-height` property sets the height of an entire line of text, so the difference between the `font-size` and the `line-height` is equivalent to the leading (as shown in the diagram above).

Increasing the `line-height` makes the vertical gap between lines of text larger.

chapter-12/line-height.html `CSS`

```
p {
    line-height: 1.4em;}
```

`RESULT`

Briards

by Ivy Duckett

The briard, or berger de brie, is a large breed of dog traditionally used as a herder and guardian of sheep.

Breed History

The briard, which is believed to have originated in France, has been bred for centuries to herd and to protect sheep. The breed was used by the French Army as sentries, messengers and to search for wounded soldiers because of its fine sense of hearing. Briards were used in the First World War almost to the point of extinction. Currently the population of briards is slowly recovering. Charlemagne, Napoleon, Thomas Jefferson and Lafayette all owned briards.

`RESULT MINUS CSS`

Briards

by Ivy Duckett

The briard, or berger de brie, is a large breed of dog traditionally used as a herder and guardian of sheep.

Breed History

The briard, which is believed to have originated in France, has been bred for centuries to herd and to protect sheep. The breed was used by the French Army as sentries, messengers and to search for wounded soldiers because of its fine sense of hearing. Briards were used in the First World War almost to the point of extinction. Currently the population of briards is slowly recovering. Charlemagne, Napoleon, Thomas Jefferson and Lafayette all owned briards.

Increasing the default amount of leading can make text easier to read. The vertical space between lines should be larger than the space between each word as this helps the eye move along the line instead of down them. A good starter setting is around 1.4 to 1.5em. Because users can adjust the default size of text in their browser, the value of the `line-height` property is best given in ems, not pixels, so that the gap between lines is relative to the size of text the user has selected.

LETTER & WORD SPACING
letter-spacing, word-spacing

```
h1, h2 {
  text-transform: uppercase;
  letter-spacing: 0.2em;}
.credits {
  font-weight: bold;
  word-spacing: 1em;}
```

RESULT

BRIARDS

by   Ivy   Duckett

The briard, or berger de brie, is a large breed of dog traditionally used as a herder and guardian of sheep.

BREED HISTORY

The briard, which is believed to have originated in France, has been bred for centuries to herd and to protect sheep. The breed was used by the French Army as sentries, messengers and to search for wounded soldiers because of its fine sense of hearing. Briards were used in the First World War almost to the point of extinction. Currently the population of briards is slowly recovering. Charlemagne, Napoleon, Thomas Jefferson and Lafayette all owned briards.

RESULT MINUS CSS

Briards

by Ivy Duckett

The briard, or berger de brie, is a large breed of dog traditionally used as a herder and guardian of sheep.

Breed History

The briard, which is believed to have originated in France, has been bred for centuries to herd and to protect sheep. The breed was used by the French Army as sentries, messengers and to search for wounded soldiers because of its fine sense of hearing. Briards were used in the First World War almost to the point of extinction. Currently the population of briards is slowly recovering. Charlemagne, Napoleon, Thomas Jefferson and Lafayette all owned briards.

Kerning is the term typographers use for the space between each letter. You can control the space between each letter with the letter-spacing property.

It is particularly helpful to increase the kerning when your heading or sentence is all in uppercase. If your text is in sentence (or normal) case, increasing or decreasing the kerning can make it harder to read.

You can also control the gap between words using the word-spacing property.

When you specify a value for these properties, it should be given in ems, and it will be added on top of the default value specified by the font.

The default gap between words is set by the typeface (often around 0.25em), and it is unlikely that you would need to change this property regularly. If the typeface is bold or you have increased the space between letters, then a larger gap between words can increase readability.

ALIGNMENT
text-align

The `text-align` property allows you to control the alignment of text. The property can take one of four values:

left

This indicates that the text should be left-aligned.

right

This indicates that the text should be right-aligned.

center

This allows you to center text.

justify

This indicates that every line in a paragraph, except the last line, should be set to take up the full width of the containing box.

When you have several paragraphs of text, it is considered easiest to read if the text is left-aligned.

Justified text looks at the words on each individual line and creates an equal gap between those words. It can look odd if you end up with large gaps between some words and smaller gaps between others. This often happens when your lines are not very wide or when your text contains long words.

chapter-12/text-align.html `CSS`

```
h1 {
  text-align: left;}
p {
  text-align: justify;}
.credits {
  text-align: right;}
```

`RESULT`

Briards

by Ivy Duckett

The briard, or berger de brie, is a large breed of dog traditionally used as a herder and guardian of sheep.

Breed History

The briard, which is believed to have originated in France, has been bred for centuries to herd and to protect sheep. The breed was used by the French Army as sentries, messengers and to search for wounded soldiers because of its fine sense of hearing. Briards were used in the First World War almost to the point of extinction. Currently the population of briards is slowly recovering. Charlemagne, Napoleon, Thomas Jefferson and Lafayette all owned briards.

VERTICAL ALIGNMENT
vertical-align

chapter-12/vertical-align.html

```
#six-months {
   vertical-align: text-top;}
#one-year {
   vertical-align: baseline;}
#two-years {
   vertical-align: text-bottom;}
```

RESULT

Briard Life Stages

 Six months

 One year

 Two years

The vertical-align property is a common source of confusion. It is **not** intended to allow you to vertically align text in the middle of block level elements such as <p> and <div>, although it does have this effect when used with table cells (the <td> and <th> elements).

It is more commonly used with inline elements such as <img>, <em>, or <strong> elements. When used with these elements, it performs a task very similar to the HTML align attribute used on the <img> element, which you met on pages 103-106. The values it can take are:

```
baseline
sub
super
top
text-top
middle
bottom
text-bottom
```

It can also take a **length** (usually specified in pixels or ems) or a **percentage** of the line height.

INDENTING TEXT
text-indent

The `text-indent` property allows you to indent the first line of text within an element. The amount you want the line indented by can be specified in a number of ways but is usually given in pixels or ems.

It can take a negative value, which means it can be used to push text off the browser window. You can see this technique used in this example, where the `<h1>` element uses a background image to represent the heading. The text has been moved far to the left, off the screen. (Background images are covered on pages 413-418.)

We still want the heading text to be on the page (for search engines and those who cannot see the image), but we cannot have it displayed on top of the logo or it will be unreadable. By pushing it 9,999 pixels to the left, it is way out of sight but still in the HTML code.

The second rule in this example indents the credits 20 pixels to the right.

```
chapter-12/text-indent.html                      CSS

h1 {
  background-image: url("images/logo.gif");
  background-repeat: no-repeat;
  text-indent: -9999px;}
.credits {
  text-indent: 20px;}
```

RESULT

by Ivy Duckett

The briard, or berger de brie, is a large breed of dog traditionally used as a herder and guardian of sheep.

Breed History

The briard, which is believed to have originated in France, has been bred for centuries to herd and to protect sheep. The breed was used by the French Army as sentries, messengers and to search for wounded soldiers because of its fine sense of hearing. Briards were used in the First World War almost to the point of extinction. Currently the population of briards is slowly recovering. Charlemagne, Napoleon, Thomas Jefferson and Lafayette all owned

CSS3: DROP SHADOW
text-shadow

CSS

```css
p.one {
  background-color: #eeeeee;
  color: #666666;
  text-shadow: 1px 1px 0px #000000;}
p.two {
  background-color: #dddddd;
  color: #666666;
  text-shadow: 1px 1px 3px #666666;}
p.three {
  background-color: #cccccc;
  color: #ffffff;
  text-shadow: 2px 2px 7px #111111;}
p.four {
  background-color: #bbbbbb;
  color: #cccccc;
  text-shadow: -1px -2px #666666;}
p.five {
  background-color: #aaaaaa;
  color: #ffffff;
  text-shadow: -1px -1px #666666;}
```

RESULT

The briard is known as a heart wrapped in fur.

The briard is known as a heart wrapped in fur.

The briard is known as a heart wrapped in fur.

The briard is known as a heart wrapped in fur.

The briard is known as a heart wrapped in fur.

The text-shadow property has become commonly used despite lacking support in all browsers.

It is used to create a drop shadow, which is a dark version of the word just behind it and slightly offset. It can also be used to create an embossed effect by adding a shadow that is slightly lighter than the text.

The value of this property is quite complicated because it can take three lengths and a color for the drop shadow.

The first length indicates how far to the left or right the shadow should fall.

The second value indicates the distance to the top or bottom that the shadow should fall.

The third value is optional and specifies the amount of blur that should be applied to the drop shadow.

The fourth value is the color of the drop shadow.

The text-shadow property has become very popular but at the time of writing it was not supported in any versions of Internet Explorer (currently IE9). Other browser makers introduced it in Firefox 3.1, Safari 3, Chrome 2 and Opera 9.5.

FIRST LETTER OR LINE
:first-letter, :first-line

You can specify different values for the first letter or first line of text inside an element using `:first-letter` and `:first-line`.

Technically these are not properties. They are known as **pseudo-elements**.

You specify the pseudo-element at the end of the selector, and then specify the declarations as you would normally for any other element.

It is worth trying this example in your browser so that you can see how the `first-line` pseudo-element will only affect the first line of text, even if you resize your browser window and less or more words appear on each line.

```
chapter-12/first-letter-and-line.html                    CSS

p.intro:first-letter {
    font-size: 200%;}
p.intro:first-line {
    font-weight: bold;}
```

RESULT

Briards

by Ivy Duckett

The briard, or berger de brie, is a large breed of dog traditionally used as a herder and guardian of sheep.

Breed History

The briard, which is believed to have originated in France, has been bred for centuries to herd and to protect sheep. The breed was used by the French Army as sentries, messengers and to search for wounded soldiers because of its fine sense of hearing. Briards were used in the First World War almost to the point of extinction. Currently the population of briards is slowly recovering. Charlemagne, Napoleon, Thomas Jefferson and Lafayette all owned briards.

CSS introduces both pseudo-elements and pseudo-classes. A pseudo-element acts like an extra element is in the code. In the case of the `:first-letter` and `:first-line` pseudo elements, it is as if there is an extra element around the first letter or the first line which can have its own styles applied.

A pseudo-class acts like an extra value for a `class` attribute. In the case of the `:visited` pseudo-class, which you meet on the next page, it allows you to have different styles for links that have been visited. Similarly, the `:hover` pseudo-class allows you to style elements differently when a user hovers over them.

STYLING LINKS
:link, :visited

`CSS`

```
a:link {
  color: deeppink;
  text-decoration: none;}
a:visited {
  color: black;}
a:hover {
  color: deeppink;
  text-decoration: underline;}
a:active {
  color: darkcyan;}
```

`RESULT`

Dog Breeds: B

- Basset Hound
- Beagle
- Bearded Collie
- Beauceron
- Bedlington Terrier
- **Belgian Shepherd**
- Bergamasco
- Bichon Frise
- Bloodhound
- Bolognese
- Border Collie
- Border Terrier
- Borzoi
- Bouvier des Flandres
- **Briard**
- Bull Terrier
- Bulldog

Browsers tend to show links in blue with an underline by default, and they will change the color of links that have been visited to help users know which pages they have been to.

In CSS, there are two **pseudo-classes** that allow you to set different styles for links that have and have not yet been visited.

:link
This allows you to set styles for links that have not yet been visited.

:visited
This allows you to set styles for links that have been clicked on.

They are commonly used to control colors of the links and also whether they are to appear underlined or not.

On the left, you can see that visited links are shown in a different color to help visitors know what they have already seen.

Often, the :hover and :active pseudo-classes (covered on the next page) are used to alter the appearance of a link when a user hovers over or clicks on it.

RESPONDING TO USERS
:hover, :active, :focus

There are three pseudo-classes that allow you to change the appearance of elements when a user is interacting with them.

:hover

This is applied when a user hovers over an element with a pointing device such as a mouse. This has commonly been used to change the appearance of links and buttons when a user places their cursor over them. It is worth noting that such events do not work on devices that use touch screens (such as the iPad) because the screen is not able to tell when someone is hovering their finger over an element.

:active

This is applied when an element is being activated by a user; for example, when a button is being pressed or a link being clicked. Sometimes this is used to make a button or link feel more like it is being pressed by changing the style or position of the element slightly.

:focus

This is applied when an element has focus. Any element that you can interact with, such as a link you can click on or any form control can have focus.

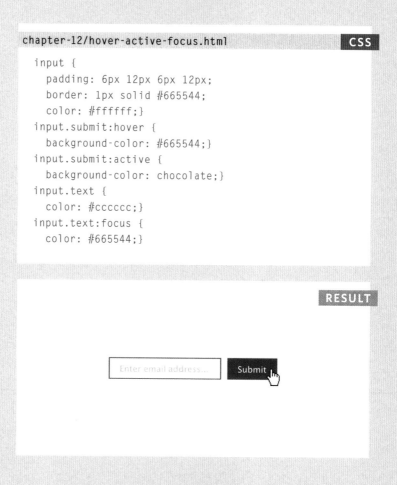

```
chapter-12/hover-active-focus.html                    CSS

input {
  padding: 6px 12px 6px 12px;
  border: 1px solid #665544;
  color: #ffffff;}
input.submit:hover {
  background-color: #665544;}
input.submit:active {
  background-color: chocolate;}
input.text {
  color: #cccccc;}
input.text:focus {
  color: #665544;}
```

Focus occurs when a browser discovers that you are ready to interact with an element on the page. For example, when your cursor is in a form input ready to accept typing, that element is said to have focus. It is also possible to use the tab key on your keyboard to move through the interactive items on a page. When pseudo-classes are used, they should appear in this order: :link, :visited, :hover, :focus, :active.

ATTRIBUTE SELECTORS

You met the most popular CSS selectors on page 238. There are also a set of attribute selectors that allow you to create rules that apply to elements that have an attribute with a specific value.

SELECTOR	MEANING	EXAMPLE
EXISTENCE	`[]` Matches a specific attribute (whatever its value)	`p[class]` Targets any `<p>` element with an attribute called `class`
EQUALITY	`[=]` Matches a specific attribute with a specific value	`p[class="dog"]` Targets any `<p>` element with an attribute called `class` whose value is `dog`
SPACE	`[~=]` Matches a specific attribute whose value appears in a space-separated list of words	`p[class~="dog"]` Targets any `<p>` element with an attribute called `class` whose value is a list of space-separated words, one of which is `dog`
PREFIX	`[^=]` Matches a specific attribute whose value begins with a specific string	`p[attr^"d"]` Targets any `<p>` element with an attribute whose value begins with the letter "d"
SUBSTRING	`[*=]` Matches a specific attribute whose value contains a specific substring	`p[attr*"do"]` Targets any `<p>` element with an attribute whose value contains the letters "do"
SUFFIX	`[$=]` Matches a specific attribute whose value ends with a specific string	`p[attr$"g"]` Targets any `<p>` element with an attribute whose value ends with the letter "g"

Briards

A HEART WRAPPED IN FUR

The briard, or berger de brie, is a large breed of dog traditionally used as a herder and guardian of sheep.

Breed History

The briard, which is believed to have originated in France, has been bred for centuries to herd and to protect sheep. The breed was used by the French Army as sentries, messengers and to search for wounded soldiers because of its fine sense of hearing. Briards were used in the First World War almost to the point of extinction. Currently the population of briards is slowly recovering. Charlemagne, Napoleon, Thomas Jefferson and Lafayette all owned briards.

by Ivy Duckett

EXAMPLE
TEXT

This example combines many of the techniques shown in this chapter.

The sizes of fonts are controlled using the `font-size` property. The headings are changed from bold to normal using the `font-weight` property. We have also specified different choices of font using the `font-family` property.

The `<h1>` element uses the CSS3 `text-shadow` property to create the drop shadow behind it. The `<h2>` element is converted to uppercase using the `text-transform` property, and to make the uppercase text easier to read, we have increased the space between each letter using the `letter-spacing` property.

For the main body text, we have increased the `line-height` property so there is a bigger gap between each line of text, thereby making it easier to read. In the first paragraph, the `first-line` pseudo-element allows us to style the first line of the introduction in bold. Finally, the credit is italicized and aligned to the right-hand side of the page.

EXAMPLE
TEXT

```
<!DOCTYPE html>
<html>
  <head>
    <title>Text</title>
    <style type="text/css">
      body {
        padding: 20px;}
      h1, h2, h3, a {
        font-weight: normal;
        color: #0088dd;
        margin: 0px;}
      h1 {
        font-family: Georgia, Times, serif;
        font-size: 250%;
        text-shadow: 2px 2px 3px #666666;
        padding-bottom: 10px;}
      h2 {
        font-family: "Gill Sans", Arial, sans-serif;
        font-size: 90%;
        text-transform: uppercase;
        letter-spacing: 0.2em;}
      h3 {
        font-size: 150%;}
      p {
        font-family: Arial, Verdana, sans-serif;
        line-height: 1.4em;
        color: #665544;}
      p.intro:first-line {
        font-weight: bold;}
      .credits {
        font-style: italic;
        text-align: right;}
      a {
        text-decoration: none;}
      a:hover {
        text-decoration: underline;}
    </style>
  </head>
```

```
<body>
  <h1>Briards</h1>
  <h2>A Heart wrapped in fur</h2>
  <p class="intro">The <a class="breed" href="http://en.wikipedia.org/wikiBriard">
    briard</a>, or berger de brie, is a large breed of dog traditionally used as a
    herder and guardian of sheep.</p>
  <h3>Breed History</h3>
  <p>The briard, which is believed to have originated in France, has been bred for
    centuries to herd and to protect sheep. The breed was used by the French Army as
    sentries, messengers and to search for wounded soldiers because of its fine sense
    of hearing. Briards were used in the First World War almost to the point of
    extinction. Currently the population of briards is slowly recovering.
    Charlemagne, Napoleon, Thomas Jefferson and Lafayette all owned briards.</p>
  <p class="credits">by Ivy Duckett</p>
</body>
</html>
```

▸ There are properties to control the choice of font, size, weight, style, and spacing.

▸ There is a limited choice of fonts that you can assume most people will have installed.

▸ If you want to use a wider range of typefaces there are several options, but you need to have the right license to use them.

▸ You can control the space between lines of text, individual letters, and words. Text can also be aligned to the left, right, center, or justified. It can also be indented.

▸ You can use pseudo-classes to change the style of an element when a user hovers over or clicks on text, or when they have visited a link.

13

BOXES

- ▸ Controlling size of boxes
- ▸ Box model for borders, margin and padding
- ▸ Displaying and hiding boxes

At the beginning of this section on CSS, you saw how CSS treats each HTML element as if it lives in its own box.

You can set several properties that affect the appearance of these boxes. In this chapter you will see how to:

- Control the dimensions of your boxes

- Create borders around boxes

- Set margins and padding for boxes

- Show and hide boxes

Once you have learned how to control the appearance of each box, you will see how to position these boxes on your pages in Chapter 15 when we look at page layout.

BOX DIMENSIONS
width, height

By default a box is sized just big enough to hold its contents. To set your own dimensions for a box you can use the `height` and `width` properties.

The most popular ways to specify the size of a box are to use pixels, percentages, or ems. Traditionally, pixels have been the most popular method because they allow designers to accurately control their size.

When you use percentages, the size of the box is relative to the size of the browser window or, if the box is encased within another box, it is a percentage of the size of the containing box.

When you use ems, the size of the box is based on the size of text within it. Designers have recently started to use percentages and ems more for measurements as they try to create designs that are flexible across devices which have different-sized screens.

In the example on the right, you can see that a containing `<div>` element is used which is 300 pixels wide by 300 pixels high. Inside of this is a paragraph that is 75% of the width and height of the containing element. This means that the size of the paragraph is 225 pixels wide by 225 pixels high.

chapter-13/width-height.html `HTML`

```html
<div>
  <p>The Moog company pioneered the commercial
     manufacture of modular voltage-controlled
     analog synthesizer systems in the early
     1950s.</p>
</div>
```

`CSS`

```css
div {
  height: 300px;
  width: 400px;
  background-color: #ee3e80;}
p {
  height: 75%;
  width: 75%;
  background-color: #e1ddda;}
```

`RESULT`

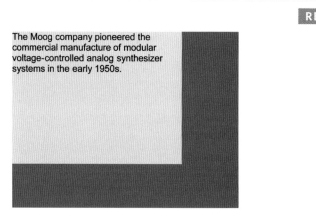

The Moog company pioneered the commercial manufacture of modular voltage-controlled analog synthesizer systems in the early 1950s.

LIMITING WIDTH
min-width, max-width

```html
<tr>
  <td><img src="images/rhodes.jpg" width="200"
      height="150" alt="Fender Rhodes" /></td>
  <td class="description">The Rhodes piano is an
      electro-mechanical piano, invented by Harold
      Rhodes during the fifties and later
      manufactured in a number of models ...</td>
  <td>$1400</td>
</tr>
```

CSS

```css
td.description {
  min-width: 450px;
  max-width: 650px;
  text-align: left;
  padding: 5px;
  margin: 0px;}
```

RESULT

Photo	Description	Price
	The Rhodes piano is an electro-mechanical piano, invented by Harold Rhodes during the fifties and later manufactured in a number of models, first in collaboration with Fender and after 1965 by CBS. It employs a piano-like keyboard with hammers that hit small metal tines, amplified by electromagnetic pickups.	$1400
	The Wurlitzer electric piano is an electro-mechanical piano, created by the Rudolph Wurlitzer Company of Mississippi. The Wurlitzer company itself never called the instrument an "electric piano", instead inventing the phrase "Electronic Piano" and using this as a trademark throughout the production of the instrument. It employs a piano-like keyboard with hammers that hit small metal tines, amplified by electromagnetic pickups.	$1600
	A Clavinet is an electronically amplified clavichord manufactured by the Hohner company. Each key uses a rubber tip to perform a hammer on a string. Its distinctive bright staccato sound is often compared to that of an electric guitar. Various models were produced over the years, including the models I, II, L, C, D6, and E7.	$1200

Some page designs expand and shrink to fit the size of the user's screen. In such designs, the min-width property specifies the smallest size a box can be displayed at when the browser window is narrow, and the max-width property indicates the maximum width a box can stretch to when the browser window is wide.

These are very helpful properties to ensure that the contents of pages are legible (especially on the smaller screens of handheld devices). For example, you can use the max-width property to ensure that lines of text do not appear too wide within a big browser window and you can use the min-width property to make sure that they do not appear too narrow.

You may find it helpful to try this example out in your browser so that you can see what happens when you increase or decrease the size of the browser window.

Please note that these properties were first supported in IE7 and Firefox 2 so they will not work in older versions of these browsers.

LIMITING HEIGHT
min-height, max-height

In the same way that you might want to limit the width of a box on a page, you may also want to limit the height of it. This is achieved using the `min-height` and `max-height` properties.

The example on this page demonstrates these properties in action. It also shows you what happens when the content of the box takes up more space than the size specified for the box.

If the box is not big enough to hold the content, and the content expands outside the box it can look very messy. To control what happens when there is not enough space for the content of a box, you can use the `overflow` property, which is discussed on the next page.

chapter-13/min-height-max-height.html `HTML`

```
<h2>Fender Mustang</h2>
<p>The Fender Mustang was introduced in 1964 as the
   basis of a major redesign of Fender's ...</p>
<h2>Fender Stratocaster</h2>
<p>The Fender Stratocaster or "Strat" is one of the
   most popular electric guitars of all time ...</p>
<h2>Gibson Les Paul</h2>
<p>The Gibson Les Paul is a solid body electric
   guitar that was first sold in 1952 ...</p>
```

`CSS`

```
h2, p {
  width: 400px;
  font-size: 90%;
  line-height: 1.2em;}
h2 {
  color: #0088dd;
  border-bottom: 1px solid #0088dd;}
p {
  min-height: 10px;
  max-height: 30px;}
```

`RESULT`

Fender Mustang

The Fender Mustang was introduced in 1964 as the basis of a major redesign of Fender's student models then consisting of the Musicmaster and Duo-Sonic. It was originally popular in **Fender Stratocaster** sixties surf music and attained cult status in the 1990s largely as a result of its use by a number of alternative rock bands. The Fender Stratocaster or "Strat" is one of the most popular electric guitars of all time, and its design has been copied by many guitar makers. It was designed by Leo Fender, George **Gibson Les Paul** Fullerton and Fredie Tavares in 1954.

The Gibson Les Paul is a solid body electric guitar that was first sold in 1952. The Les Paul was designed by Ted McCarty in collaboration with popular guitarist Les Paul, whom Gibson enlisted to endorse the new model. It is one of the most well-known electric guitar types in the world.

OVERFLOWING CONTENT
overflow

```html
<h2>Fender Stratocaster</h2>
<p class="one">The Fender Stratocaster or "Strat"
   is one of the most popular electric guitars of
   all time, and its design has been copied by many
   guitar makers. It was designed by Leo... </p>
<h2>Gibson Les Paul</h2>
<p class="two">The Gibson Les Paul is a solid body
   electric guitar that was first sold in 1952.
   The Les Paul was designed by Ted McCarty... </p>
```

CSS

```css
p.one {
  overflow: hidden;}
p.two {
  overflow: scroll;}
```

RESULT

Fender Stratocaster

The Fender Stratocaster or
"Strat" is one of the most
popular electric guitars of all
time, and its design has been
copied by many guitar makers.

Gibson Les Paul

The Gibson Les Paul is a
solid body electric guitar that
was first sold in 1952. The
Les Paul was designed by

The overflow property tells the browser what to do if the content contained within a box is larger than the box itself. It can have one of two values:

hidden

This property simply hides any extra content that does not fit in the box.

scroll

This property adds a scrollbar to the box so that users can scroll to see the missing content.

On the left, you can see two boxes whose contents expand beyond their set dimensions. The first example has the overflow property with a value of hidden. The second example has the overflow property with a value of scroll.

The overflow property is particularly handy because some browsers allow users to adjust the size of the text to appear as large or as small as they want. If the text is set too large then the page can become an unreadable mess. Hiding the overflow on such boxes helps prevent items overlapping on the page.

BORDER, MARGIN & PADDING

Every box has three available properties that can be adjusted to control its appearance:

1

BORDER

Every box has a border (even if it is not visible or is specified to be 0 pixels wide). The border separates the edge of one box from another.

2

MARGIN

Margins sit outside the edge of the border. You can set the width of a margin to create a gap between the borders of two adjacent boxes.

3

PADDING

Padding is the space between the border of a box and any content contained within it. Adding padding can increase the readability of its contents.

If you specify a width for a box, then the borders, margin, and padding are added to its width and height.

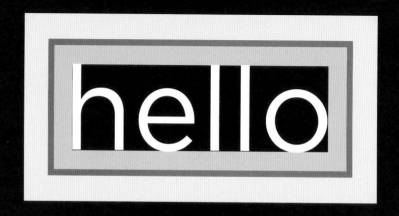

WHITE SPACE &
VERTICAL MARGIN

The `padding` and `margin` properties are very helpful in adding space between various items on the page.

WITH
MARGIN & PADDING

Moog

Moog synthesisers were created by Dr. Robert Moog under the company name Moog Music. Popular models include the Moog Modular, Minimoog, Micromoog, Moog Rogue, and Moog Source.

ARP

ARP Instruments Inc. was set up by Alan Peralman, and was the main competitor for Moog during the 1970'x. Popular models include the Arp 2600 and the ARP Odyssey.

Sequential Circuits

Sequential Circuits Inc was founded by Dave Smith, and the company was pivotal in the creation of MIDI. Famous models include the Prophet 5, Prophet 600, and Pro-One.

WITHOUT
MARGIN & PADDING

Moog

Moog synthesisers were created by Dr. Robert Moog under the company name Moog Music. Popular models include the Moog Modular, Minimoog, Micromoog, Moog Rogue, and Moog Source.

ARP

ARP Instruments Inc. was set up by Alan Peralman, and was the main competitor for Moog during the 1970'x. Popular models include the Arp 2600 and the ARP Odyssey.

Sequential Circuits

Sequential Circuits Inc was founded by Dave Smith, and the company was pivotal in the creation of MIDI. Famous models include the Prophet 5, Prophet 600, and Pro-One.

Designers refer to the space between items on a page as **white space**. Imagine you had a border around a box. You would not want the text to touch this border or it would become harder to read.

Or, imagine you had two boxes sitting side by side (each with a black border). You would not necessarily want the boxes to touch edges as this would make the line look twice as thick on the facing sides.

If the bottom margin of any box touches the top margin of another, the browser will render it differently than you might expect. It will only show the larger of the two margins. If both margins are the same size, it will only show one.

BORDER WIDTH
border-width

The border-width property is used to control the width of a border. The value of this property can either be given in pixels or using one of the following values:

thin
medium
thick

(You cannot use percentages with this property.)

You can control the individual size of borders using four separate properties:

border-top-width
border-right-width
border-bottom-width
border-left-width

You can also specify different widths for the four border values in one property, like so:

border-width: 2px 1px 1px 2px;

The values here appear in clockwise order: top, right, bottom, left.

```
<p class="one">Hohner's "Clavinet" is essentially an
   electric clavichord.</p>
<p class="two">Hohner's "Clavinet" is essentially an
   electric clavichord.</p>
<p class="three">Hohner's "Clavinet" is essentially
   an electric clavichord.</p>
```

CSS

```
p.one {
   border-width: 2px;}
p.two {
   border-width: thick;}
p.three {
   border-width: 1px 4px 12px 4px;}
```

RESULT

Hohner's "Clavinet" is essentially an electric clavichord.

Hohner's "Clavinet" is essentially an electric clavichord.

Hohner's "Clavinet" is essentially an electric clavichord.

BORDER STYLE
border-style

```html
<p class="one">Wurlitzer Electric Piano</p>
<p class="two">Wurlitzer Electric Piano</p>
<p class="three">Wurlitzer Electric Piano</p>
<p class="four">Wurlitzer Electric Piano</p>
<p class="five">Wurlitzer Electric Piano</p>
<p class="six">Wurlitzer Electric Piano</p>
<p class="seven">Wurlitzer Electric Piano</p>
<p class="eight">Wurlitzer Electric Piano</p>
```

CSS

```css
p.one {border-style: solid;}
p.two {border-style: dotted;}
p.three {border-style: dashed;}
p.four {border-style: double;}
p.five {border-style: groove;}
p.six {border-style: ridge;}
p.seven {border-style: inset;}
p.eight {border-style: outset;}
```

RESULT

Wurlitzer Electric Piano

Wurlitzer Electric Piano

Wurlitzer Electric Piano

Wurlitzer Electric Piano

Wurlitzer Electric Piano

Wurlitzer Electric Piano

Wurlitzer Electric Piano

Wurlitzer Electric Piano

You can control the style of a border using the border-style property. This property can take the following values:

solid a single solid line

dotted a series of square dots (if your border is 2px wide, then the dots are 2px squared with a 2px gap between each dot)

dashed a series of short lines

double two solid lines (the value of the border-width property creates the sum of the two lines)

groove appears to be carved into the page

ridge appears to stick out from the page

inset appears embedded into the page

outset looks like it is coming out of the screen

hidden / none no border is shown

You can individually change the styles of different borders using:
border-top-style
border-left-style
border-right-style
border-bottom-style

BORDER COLOR
border-color

You can specify the color of a border using either RGB values, hex codes or CSS color names (as you saw on pages 251-252).

It is possible to individually control the colors of the borders on different sides of a box using:

```
border-top-color
border-right-color
border-bottom-color
border-left-color
```

It is also possible to use a shorthand to control all four border colors in the one property:

```
border-color: darkcyan
deeppink darkcyan
deeppink;
```

The values here appear in clockwise order: top, right, bottom, left.

You could also use HSL values to specify the color as shown on pages 255-256. However, these were only introduced in CSS3 and will not work in older browsers.

chapter-13/border-color.html   HTML

```html
<p class="one">The ARP Odyssey was introduced in
    1972.</p>
<p class="two">The ARP Odyssey was introduced in
    1972.</p>
```

CSS

```css
p.one {
  border-color: #0088dd;}
p.two {
  border-color: #bbbbaa #111111 #ee3e80 #0088dd;}
```

RESULT

The ARP Odyssey was introduced in 1972.

The ARP Odyssey was introduced in 1972.

SHORTHAND
border

HTML	chapter-13/border-shorthand.html

```
<p>Here is a simple chord sequence played on a
   Hammond organ through a Leslie speaker.</p>
```

CSS

```
p {
   width: 250px;
   border: 3px dotted #0088dd;}
```

RESULT

Here is a simple chord sequence played on a Hammond organ through a Leslie speaker.

The border property allows you to specify the width, style and color of a border in one property (and the values should be coded in that specific order).

PADDING
padding

The padding property allows you to specify how much space should appear between the content of an element and its border.

The value of this property is most often specified in pixels (although it is also possible to use percentages or ems). If a percentage is used, the padding is a percentage of the browser window (or of the containing box if it is inside another box).

Please note: If a width is specified for a box, padding is added onto the width of the box.

As you can see, the second paragraph here is much easier to read because there is a space between the text and the border of the box. The box is also wider because it has padding.

You can specify different values for each side of a box using:

```
padding-top
padding-right
padding-bottom
padding-left
```

Or you can use a shorthand (where the values are in clockwise order: top, right, bottom, left):

```
padding: 10px 5px 3px 1px;
```

chapter-13/padding.html HTML

```
<p>Analog synths produce a wave sound, whereas the
   sounds stored on a digital synth have been
   sampled and then turned into numbers.</p>
<p class="example">Analog synths produce a wave
   sound, whereas the sounds stored on a digital
   synth have been sampled and then ... </p>
```

CSS

```
p {
  width: 275px;
  border: 2px solid #0088dd;}
p.example {
  padding: 10px;}
```

RESULT

Analog synths produce a wave sound, whereas the sounds stored on a digital synth have been sampled and then turned into numbers.

Analog synths produce a wave sound, whereas the sounds stored on a digital synth have been sampled and then turned into numbers.

The value of the padding property is not inherited by child elements in the same way that the color value of the font-family property is; so you need to specify the padding for every element that needs to use it.

Up until Internet Explorer 6, the width of the box would include the padding and margins. You can see more about this on page 316.

MARGIN
margin

```
<p>Analog synthesizers are often said to have a
   "warmer" sound than their digital counterparts.
   </p>
<p class="example">Analog synthesizers are often
   said to have a "warmer" sound than their digital
   counterparts.</p>
```

CSS

```
p {
  width: 200px;
  border: 2px solid #0088dd;
  padding: 10px;}
p.example {
  margin: 20px;}
```

RESULT

> Analog synthesizers are
> often said to have a
> "warmer" sound than their
> digital counterparts.

> Analog synthesizers are
> often said to have a
> "warmer" sound than their
> digital counterparts.

The value of the margin property is not inherited by child elements in the same way that the color value of the font-family property is, so you need to specify the margin for every element that needs to use it.

Up until Internet Explorer 6, the width of the box would include the padding and margins. You can see more about this on page 316.

The margin property controls the gap between boxes. Its value is commonly given in pixels, although you may also use percentages or ems.

If one box sits on top of another, margins are collapsed , which means the larger of the two margins will be used and the smaller will be disregarded.

Please note: If the width of a box is specified then the margin is added to the width of the box.

You can specify values for each side of a box using:

```
margin-top
margin-right
margin-bottom
margin-left
```

You can also use the shorthand (where the values are in clockwise order: top, right, bottom, left):
```
margin: 1px 2px 3px 4px;
```

Sometimes you might see the following, which means that the left and right margins should be 10 pixels and the top and bottom margins should be 20 pixels:
```
margin: 20px 10px;
```

(This same shorthand shown above can also be applied to padding.)

CENTERING CONTENT

If you want to center a box on the page (or center it inside the element that it sits in), you can set the left-margin and right-margin to auto.

In order to center a box on the page, you need to set a width for the box (otherwise it will take up the full width of the page).

Once you have specified the width of the box, setting the left and right margins to auto will make the browser put an equal gap on each side of the box. This centers the box on the page (or within the element that the box sits inside).

In order for this to work in older browsers (particularly IE6), the element that the box sits inside should have a text-align property with its value set to center.

The text-align property is inherited by child elements. You therefore also need to specify the text-align property on the centered box if you do not want the text inside it to be centered.

```
chapter-13/centering-content.html                    HTML
<body>
  <p>Analog synthesizers are often said to have a
    "warmer" sound than their digital
    counterparts.</p>
  <p class="example">Analog synthesizers are often
    said to have a "warmer" sound than their
    digital counterparts.</p>
</body>
```

```
                                                      CSS
body {
  text-align: center;}
p {
  width: 300px;
  padding: 50px;
  border: 20px solid #0088dd;}
p.example {
  margin: 10px auto 10px auto;
  text-align: left;}
```

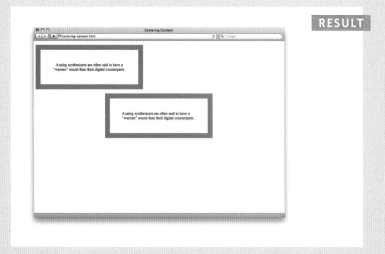

IE6 BOX MODEL

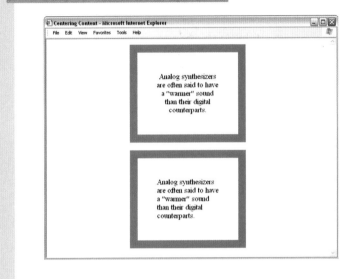

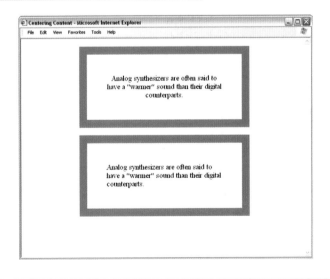

When you specify the width of a box, any padding or margin should be added to the width of it. Internet Explorer 6, however, has a quirk whereby it includes the padding and margins in the width of the box.

The way around this is to ensure that you provide a DOCTYPE declaration for the HTML page. (DOCTYPE declarations were covered on page 181.) You can use either the HTML5, HTML 4 strict, or HTML 4 transitional DOCTYPE declarations to ensure that IE6 follows the correct box model.

To demonstrate this, you can see the example from the left hand page shown in IE6, first without a DOCTYPE declaration and then again with the HTML5 DOCTYPE declaration.

CHANGE INLINE/BLOCK
display

The display property allows you to turn an inline element into a block-level element or vice versa, and can also be used to hide an element from the page.

The values this property can take are:

inline

This causes a block-level element to act like an inline element.

block

This causes an inline element to act like a block-level element.

inline-block

This causes a block-level element to flow like an inline element, while retaining other features of a block-level element.

none

This hides an element from the page. In this case, the element acts as though it is not on the page at all (although a user could still see the content of the box if they used the **view source** option in their browser).

If you use this property, it is important to note that inline boxes are **not** supposed to create block-level elements.

`HTML`

```
<ul>
  <li>Home</li>
  <li>Products</li>
  <li class="coming-soon">Services</li>
  <li>About</li>
  <li>Contact</li>
</ul>
```

`CSS`

```
li {
  display: inline;
  margin-right: 10px;}
li.coming-soon {
  display: none;}
```

`RESULT`

Home   Products   About   Contact

In this example you can see a list. Each item in the list is usually treated as a block-level element, but the rule for the <li> elements indicates that they should be treated as inline elements, which means they will sit alongside each other rather than appearing on new lines.

This technique is often used to create navigation for a site, and in this example a margin has been added to the right of each of the items to separate them out. The rule that applies to the <li> element whose class is coming-soon has been hidden as if it were not in the page at all.

HIDING BOXES
visibility

HTML

```
<ul>
  <li>Home</li>
  <li>Products</li>
  <li class="coming-soon">Services</li>
  <li>About</li>
  <li>Contact</li>
</ul>
```

CSS

```
li {
  display: inline;
  margin-right: 10px;}
li.coming-soon {
  visibility: hidden;}
```

RESULT

Home   Products   About   Contact

The visibility property allows you to hide boxes from users but It leaves a space where the element would have been.

This property can take two values:

hidden
This hides the element.

visible
This shows the element.

If the visibility of an element is set to hidden, a blank space will appear in its place.

If you do not want a blank space to appear, then you should use the display property with a value of none instead (as covered on the previous page).

Please note that anyone can view the contents of any elements whose visibility property has been set to hidden by viewing the source in their browser.

CSS3: BORDER IMAGES
border-image

The border-image property applies an image to the border of any box. It takes a background image and slices it into nine pieces.

Here is the image. I have added marks where it is sliced in the example, taking 18 pixels from each corner to place an entire circle in each corner. The corner slices are always placed in the four corners of the box, but we have a choice whether the sides are stretched or repeated.

This property requires three pieces of information:

1: The URL of the image
2: Where to slice the image
3: What to do with the straight edges; the possible values are:
  stretch stretches the image
  repeat repeats the image
  round like repeat but if the tiles do not fit exactly, scales the tile image so they will

The box must also have a border width for the image to be shown.

The -moz-border-image and -webkit-border-image properties are not in the CSS specification but help earlier versions of Chrome, Firefox, and Safari display this effect.

```
chapter-13/border-image.html                    HTML

<p class="one"></p>
<p class="two"></p>
```

```
                                                 CSS

p.one {
  -moz-border-image: url("images/dots.gif")
    11 11 11 11 stretch;
  -webkit-border-image: url("images/dots.gif")
    11 11 11 11 stretch;
  border-image: url("images/dots.gif")
    11 11 11 11 stretch;}
p.two {
  -moz-border-image: url("images/dots.gif")
    11 11 11 11 round;
  -webkit-border-image: url("images/dots.gif")
    11 11 11 11 round;
  border-image: url("images/dots.gif")
    11 11 11 11 round;}
```

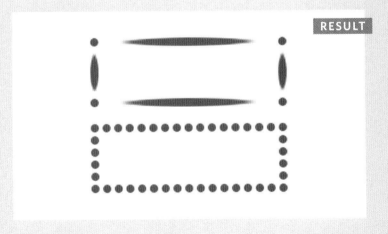

RESULT

CSS3: BOX SHADOWS
box-shadow

```css
p.one {
  -moz-box-shadow: -5px -5px #777777;
  -webkit-box-shadow: -5px -5px #777777;
  box-shadow: -5px -5px #777777;}
p.two {
  -moz-box-shadow: 5px 5px 5px #777777;
  -webkit-box-shadow: 5px 5px 5px #777777;
  box-shadow: 5px 5px 5px #777777;}
p.three {
  -moz-box-shadow: 5px 5px 5px 5px #777777;
  -webkit-box-shadow: 5px 5px 5px 5px #777777;
  box-shadow: 5px 5px 5px 5px #777777;}
p.four {
  -moz-box-shadow: 0 0 10px #777777;
  -webkit-box-shadow: 0 0 10px #777777;
  box-shadow: 0 0 10px #777777;}
p.five {
  -moz-box-shadow: inset 0 0 10px #777777;
  -webkit-box-shadow: inset 0 0 10px #777777;
  box-shadow: inset 0 0 10px #777777;}
```

RESULT

The box-shadow property allows you to add a drop shadow around a box. It works just like the text-shadow property that you met on page 288. It must use at least the first of these two values as well as a color:

HORIZONTAL OFFSET
Negative values position the shadow to the left of the box.

VERTICAL OFFSET
Negative values position the shadow to the top of the box.

BLUR DISTANCE
If omitted, the shadow is a solid line like a border.

SPREAD OF SHADOW
If used, a positive value will cause the shadow to expand in all directions, and a negative value will make it contract.

The inset keyword can also be used before these values to create an inner-shadow.

Chrome, Firefox, and Safari were quick to support this property using the -moz-box-shadow and -webkit-box-shadow properties. These are not in the CSS specification but using them can help this style to work in these browsers.

CSS3: ROUNDED CORNERS
border-radius

CSS3 introduces the ability to create rounded corners on any box, using a property called border-radius. The value indicates the size of the radius in pixels.

Older browsers that do not support this property will show a box with right-angled corners.

The -moz-border-radius and -webkit-border-radius properties are not in the CSS specification. However, they are used in some versions of Chrome, Firefox, and Safari to offer early support for this style (and therefore can be used to achieve this effect in more browsers).

You can specify individual values for each corner of a box using:

border-top-right-radius
border-bottom-right-radius
border-bottom-left-radius
border-top-left-radius

You can also use a shorthand of these four properties (in clockwise order: top, right, bottom, left). For example:

border-radius: 5px, 10px, 5px, 10px;

chapter-13/border-radius.html `HTML`

```
<p>Pet Sounds featured a number of unconventional
   instruments such as bicycle bells, buzzing
   organs, harpsichords, flutes, Electro-Theremin,
   dog whistles, trains, Hawaiian-sounding string
   instruments, Coca-Cola cans and barking dogs.</p>
```

`CSS`

```
p {
   border: 5px solid #ee3e80;
   padding: 20px;
   width: 275px;
   border-radius: 10px;
   -moz-border-radius: 10px;
   -webkit-border-radius: 10px;}
```

`RESULT`

Pet Sounds featured a number of unconventional instruments such as bicycle bells, buzzing organs, harpsichords, flutes, Electro-Theremin, dog whistles, trains, Hawaiian-sounding string instruments, Coca-Cola cans and barking dogs.

CSS3: ELLIPTICAL SHAPES
border-radius

```
<p class="one"></p>
<p class="two"></p>
<p class="three"></p>
```

CSS

```
p.one {
  border-top-left-radius: 80px 50px;
  -moz-border-radius-top-left: 80px 50px;
  -webkit-border-radius-top-left: 80px 50px;}
p.two {
  border-radius: 1em 4em 1em 4em / 2em 1em 2em 1em;
  -moz-border-radius: 1em 4em 1em 4em
    / 2em 1em 2em 1em;
  -webkit-border-radius:  1em 4em 1em 4em
    / 2em 1em 2em 1em;}
p.three {
  padding: 0px;
  border-radius: 100px;
  -moz-border-radius: 100px;
  -webkit-border-radius: 100px;}
```

RESULT

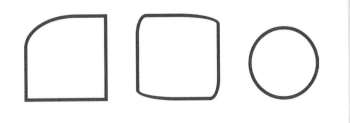

To create more complex shapes, you can specify different distances for the horizontal and the vertical parts of the rounded corners.

For example, this will create a radius that is wider than it is tall:

```
border-radius: 80px 50px;
```

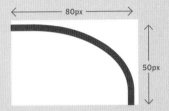

You can target just one corner using the individual properties for that corner:

```
border-top-left-radius:
80px 50px;
```

There is also a shorthand for targetting all four corners at once; first you specify the four horizontal values, then the four vertical values, as shown in the second shape on the left.

You can even create a circle by taking a square box and making the border-radius the same height as the square, as shown in the third shape on the left.

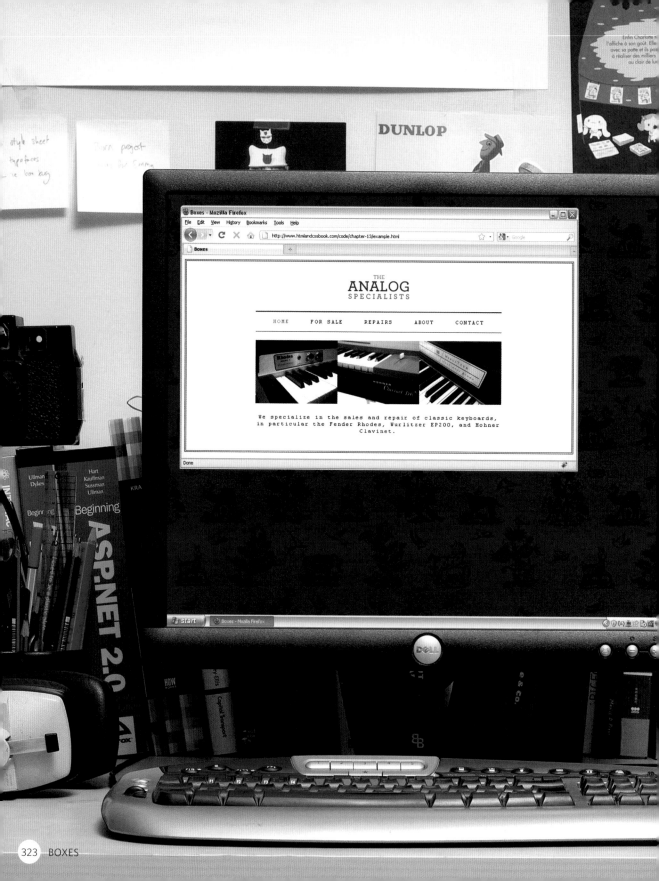

EXAMPLE
BOXES

In this example, you can see a simple homepage for a music shop.

The whole page sits inside a `<div>` element with an `id` of `page`. This is centered using the `margin` property, with a value of `auto` for the left and right margins. The logo and other content are centered using this same technique.

The main `<div>` has a double-lined border around it, and the size of this box will expand and contract if the browser window is resized. To prevent the page from becoming too narrow or too wide, the `min-width` and `max-width` properties are used.

The navigation is created using an unordered list. There are borders set to the top and bottom of this list to make it stand out. The `display` property has been applied to each of the items in the list so they behave like inline (rather than block-level) elements. This enables the navigation links to sit next to each other horizontally. The `padding` property has been used to create space between each of the links.

The `width` property for the `<ul>` element is set to 570 pixels, and the `width` property for the `<p>` elements beneath them is set to 600 pixels. They actually end up the same width as each other because the `<ul>` element also uses padding to create a gap between the border of the box it creates and the links inside it, and any padding, borders, or margins are added to the width and height of the box.

If we had not included a `DOCTYPE` declaration at the start of this page, the sizes of the boxes would be different from each other in Internet Explorer 6 because this browser did not implement the box model in the correct way.

EXAMPLE
BOXES

```
<!DOCTYPE html>
<html>
  <head>
    <title>Boxes</title>
    <style type="text/css">
      body {
        font-size: 80%;
        font-family: "Courier New", Courier, monospace;
        letter-spacing: 0.15em;
        background-color: #efefef;}
      #page {
        max-width: 940px;
        min-width: 720px;
        margin: 10px auto 10px auto;
        padding: 20px;
        border: 4px double #000;
        background-color: #ffffff;}
      #logo {
        width: 150px;
        margin: 10px auto 25px auto;}
      ul {
        width: 570px;
        padding: 15px;
        margin: 0px auto 0px auto;
        border-top: 2px solid #000;
        border-bottom: 1px solid #000;
        text-align: center;}
      li {
        display: inline;
        margin: 0px 3px;}
      p {
        text-align: center;
        width: 600px;
        margin: 20px auto 20px auto;
        font-weight: normal;}
```

```
    a {
      color: #000000;
      text-transform: uppercase;
      text-decoration: none;
      padding: 6px 18px 5px 18px;}
    a:hover, a.on {
      color: #cc3333;
      background-color: #ffffff;}
    </style>
  </head>
<body>
  <div id="page">
    <div id="logo">
      <img src="images/logo.gif" alt="The Analog Specialists" />
    </div>
    <ul id="navigation">
      <li><a href="#" class="on">Home</a></li>
      <li><a href="#">For Sale</a></li>
      <li><a href="#">Repairs</a></li>
      <li><a href="#">About</a></li>
      <li><a href="#">Contact</a></li>
    </ul>
    <p>
      <img src="images/keys.jpg" alt="Fender Rhodes, Hohner Clavinet,
          and Wurlitzer EP200" />
    </p>
    <p>
      We specialize in the sales and repair of classic keyboards, in particular
      the Fender Rhodes, Wurlitzer EP200, and Hohner Clavinet.
    </p>
  </div>
</body>
</html>
```

- ▸ CSS treats each HTML element as if it has its own box.

- ▸ You can use CSS to control the dimensions of a box.

- ▸ You can also control the borders, margins and padding for each box with CSS.

- ▸ It is possible to hide elements using the display and visibility properties.

- ▸ Block-level boxes can be made into inline boxes, and inline boxes made into block-level boxes.

- ▸ Legibility can be improved by controlling the width of boxes containing text and the leading.

- ▸ CSS3 has introduced the ability to create image borders and rounded borders.

14

LISTS, TABLES AND FORMS

▸ Specifying bullet point styles
▸ Adding borders and backgrounds to tables
▸ Changing the appearance of form elements

There are several CSS properties that were created to work with specific types of HTML elements, such as lists, tables, and forms.

In this chapter you will learn how to:

- Specify the type of bullet point or numbering on lists
- Add borders and backgrounds to table cells
- Control the appearance of form controls

Together, these properties allow you to take finer control over specific parts of your pages.

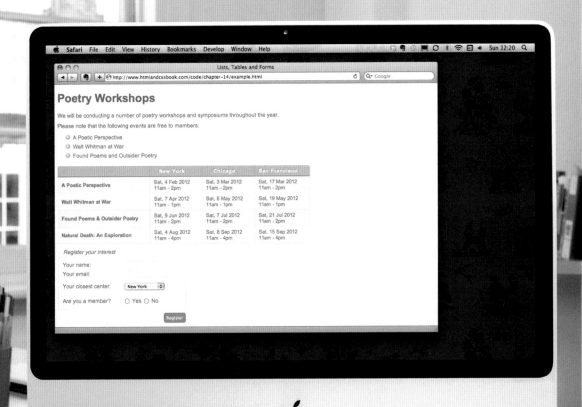

BULLET POINT STYLES
list-style-type

The list-style-type property allows you to control the shape or style of a bullet point (also known as a **marker**).

It can be used on rules that apply to the `<ol>`, `<ul>`, and `<li>` elements.

UNORDERED LISTS

For an unordered list you can use the following values:

```
  none
● disc
○ circle
■ square
```

ORDERED LISTS

For an ordered (numbered) list you can use the following values:

```
decimal
1 2 3
```

```
decimal-leading-zero
01 02 03
```

```
lower-alpha
a b c
```

```
upper-alpha
A B C
```

```
lower-roman
i. ii. iii.
```

```
upper-roman
I II III
```

chapter-14/list-style-type.html `HTML`

```html
<h1>The Complete Poems</h1>
<h2>Emily Dickinson</h2>
<ol>
  <li>Life</li>
  <li>Nature</li>
  <li>Love</li>
  <li>Time and Eternity</li>
  <li>The Single Hound</li>
</ol>
```

`CSS`

```css
ol {
  list-style-type: lower-roman;}
```

`RESULT`

The Complete Poems

Emily Dickinson

   i. Life
  ii. Nature
 iii. Love
 iv. Time and Eternity
  v. The Single Hound

IMAGES FOR BULLETS
list-style-image

```
<h1>Index of Translated Poems</h1>
<h2>Arthur Rimbaud</h2>
<ul>
  <li>Ophelia</li>
  <li>To Music</li>
  <li>A Dream for Winter</li>
  <li>Vowels</li>
  <li>The Drunken Boat</li>
</ul>
```

CSS

```
ul {
  list-style-image: url("images/star.png");}
li {
  margin: 10px 0px 0px 0px;}
```

RESULT

Index of Translated Poems

Arthur Rimbaud

- ☆ Ophelia
- ☆ To Music
- ☆ A Dream for Winter
- ☆ Vowels
- ☆ The Drunken Boat

You can specify an image to act as a bullet point using the list-style-image property.

The value starts with the letters url and is followed by a pair of parentheses. Inside the parentheses, the path to the image is given inside double quotes.

This property can be used on rules that apply to the <ul> and <li> elements.

The example on this page also shows the use of the margin property to increase the vertical gap between each item in the list.

POSITIONING THE MARKER
list-style-position

Lists are indented into the page by default and the list-style-position property indicates whether the marker should appear on the inside or the outside of the box containing the main points.

This property can take one of two values:

outside

The marker sits to the left of the block of text. (This is the default behaviour if this property is not used.)

inside

The marker sits inside the box of text (which is indented).

In the example shown, the width of the list has been limited to 250 pixels. This ensures that the text wraps onto a new line so you can see how the value of inside sits the bullet inside the first line of text.

A margin has been added to each list item so that there is a clear gap between each.

chapter-14/list-style-position.html `HTML`

```
<ul class="illuminations">
  <li>That idol, black eyes and ...</li>
  <li>Gracious son of Pan! ...</li>
  <li>When the world is reduced ...</li>
</ul>
<ul class="season">
  <li>Once, if my memory serves ...</li>
  <li>Hadn't I once a youth ...</li>
  <li>Autumn already! ...</li>
</ul>
```

`CSS`

```
ul {
  width: 250px;}
li {
  margin: 10px;}
ul.illuminations {
  list-style-position: outside;}
ul.season {
  list-style-position: inside;}
```

`RESULT`

- That idol, black eyes and yellow mop, without parents or court ...
- Gracious son of Pan! Around your forehead crowned with flowerets ...
- When the world is reduced to a single dark wood for our four ...

`RESULT`

- Once, if my memory serves me well, my life was a banquet ...
- Hadn't I once a youth that was lovely, heroic, fabulous ...
- Autumn already! - But why regret the everlasting sun if we are

LIST SHORTHAND
list-style

```html
<h1>Quotes from Edgar Allan Poe</h1>
<ul>
  <li> I have great faith in fools; self-confidence
  my friends call it.</li>
  <li>All that we see or seem is but a dream within
  a dream.</li>
  <li>I would define, in brief, the poetry of words
  as the rhythmical creation of Beauty.</li>
</ul>
```

As with several of the other CSS properties, there is a property that acts as a shorthand for list styles. It is called list-style, and it allows you to express the markers' style, image and position properties in any order.

CSS

```css
ul {
  list-style: inside circle;
  width: 300px;}
li {
  margin: 10px 0px 0px 0px;}
```

RESULT

Quotes from Edgar Allan Poe

- I have great faith in fools; self-confidence my friends call it.

- All that we see or seem is but a dream within a dream.

- I would define, in brief, the poetry of words as the rhythmical creation of Beauty.

TABLE PROPERTIES

You have already met several properties that are commonly used with tables. Here we will put them together in a single example using the following:

`width` to set the width of the table

`padding` to set the space between the border of each table cell and its content

`text-transform` to convert the content of the table headers to uppercase

`letter-spacing`, `font-size` to add additional styling to the content of the table headers

`border-top`, `border-bottom` to set borders above and below the table headers

`text-align` to align the writing to the left of some table cells and to the right of the others

`background-color` to change the background color of the alternating table rows

`:hover` to highlight a table row when a user's mouse goes over it

chapter-14/table-properties.html

`HTML`

```
<h1>First Edition Auctions</h1>
<table>
  <tr>
    <th>Author</th>
    <th>Title</th>
    <th class="money">Reserve Price</th>
    <th class="money">Current Bid</th>
  </tr>
  <tr>
    <td>E.E. Cummings</td>
    <td>Tulips & Chimneys</td>
    <td class="money">$2,000.00</td>
    <td class="money">$2,642.50</td>
  </tr>
  <tr class="even">
    <td>Charles d'Orleans</td>
    <td>Poemes</td>
    <td class="money"></td>
    <td class="money">$5,866.00</td>
  </tr>
  <tr>
    <td>T.S. Eliot</td>
    <td>Poems 1909 - 1925</td>
    <td class="money">$1,250.00</td>
    <td class="money">$8,499.35</td>
  </tr>
  <tr class="even">
    <td>Sylvia Plath</td>
    <td>The Colossus</td>
    <td class="money"></td>
    <td class="money">$1031.72</td>
  </tr>
</table>
```

```css
body {
  font-family: Arial, Verdana, sans-serif;
  color: #111111;}
table {
  width: 600px;}
th, td {
  padding: 7px 10px 10px 10px;}
th {
  text-transform: uppercase;
  letter-spacing: 0.1em;
  font-size: 90%;
  border-bottom: 2px solid #111111;
  border-top: 1px solid #999;
  text-align: left;}
tr.even {
  background-color: #efefef;}
tr:hover {
  background-color: #c3e6e5;}
.money {
  text-align: right;}
```

First Edition Auctions

AUTHOR	TITLE	RESERVE PRICE	CURRENT BID
E.E. Cummings	Tulips & Chimneys	$2,000.00	$2,642.50
Charles d'Orleans	Poemes		$5,866.00
T.S. Eliot	Poems 1909 - 1925	$1,250.00	$8,499.35
Sylvia Plath	The Colossus		$1031.72

Here are some tips for styling tables to ensure they are clean and easy to follow:

GIVE CELLS PADDING
If the text in a table cell either touches a border (or another cell), it becomes much harder to read. Adding padding helps to improve readability.

DISTINGUISH HEADINGS
Putting all table headings in bold (the default style for the `<th>` element) makes them easier to read. You can also make headings uppercase and then either add a background color or an underline to clearly distinguish them from content.

SHADE ALTERNATE ROWS
Shading every other row can help users follow along the lines. Use a subtle distinction from the normal color of the rows to keep the table looking clean.

ALIGN NUMERALS
You can use the `text-align` property to align the content of any column that contains numbers to the right, so that large numbers are clearly distinguished from smaller ones.

ONLINE EXTRA
There are more examples of using CSS to style tables in the tools section of the website.

BORDER ON EMPTY CELLS
empty-cells

If you have empty cells in your table, then you can use the empty-cells property to specify whether or not their borders should be shown.

Since browsers treat empty cells in different ways, if you want to explicitly show or hide borders on any empty cells then you should use this property.

It can take one of three values:

show
This shows the borders of any empty cells.

hide
This hides the borders of any empty cells.

inherit
If you have one table nested inside another, the inherit value instructs the table cells to obey the rules of the containing table.

In the first table on the left, you can see that the border of the empty cell is showing. In the second table, it is hidden.

```
chapter-14/empty-cells.html          HTML

<table class="one">
  <tr>
    <td>1</td>
    <td>2</td>
  </tr>
  <tr>
    <td>3</td>
    <td></td>
  </tr>
</table>
```

```
                                      CSS

td {
  border: 1px solid #0088dd;
  padding: 15px;}
table.one {
  empty-cells: show;}
table.two {
  empty-cells: hide;}
```

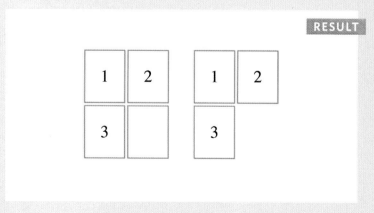

GAPS BETWEEN CELLS
border-spacing, border-collapse

chapter-14/gaps-between-cells.html

```html
<table class="one">
  <tr>
    <td>1</td>
    <td>2</td>
  </tr>
  <tr>
    <td>3</td>
    <td>4</td>
  </tr>
</table>
```

CSS

```css
td {
  background-color: #0088dd;
  padding: 15px;
  border: 2px solid #000000;}
table.one {
  border-spacing: 5px 15px;}
table.two {
  border-collapse: collapse;}
```

RESULT

The border-spacing property allows you to control the distance between adjacent cells. By default, browsers often leave a small gap between each table cell, so if you want to increase or decrease this space then the border-spacing property allows you to control the gap.

The value of this property is usually specified in pixels. You can specify two values if desired to specify separate numbers for horizontal and vertical spacing.

When a border has been used on table cells, where two cells meet, the width of lines would be twice that of the outside edges. It is possible to collapse adjacent borders to prevent this by using the border-collapse property. Possible values are:

collapse
Borders are collapsed into a single border where possible. (border-spacing will be ignored and cells pushed together, and empty-cells properties will be ignored.)

separate
Borders are detached from each other. (border-spacing and empty-cells will be obeyed.)

STYLING FORMS

Nobody I know enjoys filling in forms, so if you can make yours look more attractive and easier to use, more people are likely to fill them in. Also, when you come to look at a form in a few different browsers (as shown on the right), you will see that each browser displays it differently.

CSS is commonly used to control the appearance of form elements. This is both to make them more attractive and to make them more consistent across different browsers

It is most common to style:

- Text inputs and text areas
- Submit buttons
- Labels on forms, to get the form controls to align nicely

In the coming pages you will see how to control these with CSS.

Styling text inputs and submit buttons is fairly easy. It is harder to get select boxes, radio buttons, and checkboxes to look consistent across all browsers.

To achieve this, you might like to download the CSS files available at http://formalize.me. The author of this website has done the hard work of making

forms look consistent across browsers. Although the solution incorporates JavaScript, no prior knowledge of this is needed in order to implement the code.

STYLING TEXT INPUTS

```css
input {
  font-size: 120%;
  color: #5a5854;
  background-color: #f2f2f2;
  border: 1px solid #bdbdbd;
  border-radius: 5px;
  padding: 5px 5px 5px 30px;
  background-repeat: no-repeat;
  background-position: 8px 9px;
  display: block;
  margin-bottom: 10px;}
input:focus, input:hover {
  background-color: #ffffff;
  border: 1px solid #b1e1e4;}
input#email {
  background-image: url("images/email.png");}
input#twitter {
  background-image: url("images/twitter.png");}
input#web {
  background-image: url("images/web.png");}
```

This example demonstrates the CSS properties commonly used with text inputs, most of which you have already met.

`font-size` sets the size of the text entered by the user.

`color` sets the text color, and `background-color` sets the background color of the input.

`border` adds a border around the edge of the input box, and `border-radius` can be used to create rounded corners (for browsers that support this property).

The `:focus` pseudo-class is used to change the background color of the text input when it is being used, and the `:hover` psuedo-class applies the same styles when the user hovers over them.

`background-image` adds a background image to the box. Because there is a different image for each input, we are using an attribute selector looking for the value of the `id` attribute on each input.

You will learn more about background images and how to position them in Chapter 16.

RESULT

STYLING SUBMIT BUTTONS

Here are some properties that can be used to style submit buttons. This example builds on the one in the previous page, and the submit button inherits the styles set for the `<input>` element on the last page.

`color` is used to change the color of the text on the button.

`text-shadow` can give a 3D look to the text in browsers that support this property.

`border-bottom` has been used to make the bottom border of the button slightly thicker, which gives it a more 3D feel.

`background-color` can make the submit button stand out from other items around it. (Creating a consistent style for all buttons helps users understand how they should interact with the site.) A gradient background has been added for browsers that support gradients. Gradients are covered on page 419.

The `:hover` pseudo-class has been used to change the appearance of the button when the user hovers over it. In this case, the background changes, the text gets darker, and the thicker border is applied to the top of the button.

chapter-14/styling-submit-buttons.html CSS

```css
input#submit {
  color: #444444;
  text-shadow: 0px 1px 1px #ffffff;
  border-bottom: 2px solid #b2b2b2;
  background-color: #b9e4e3;
  background: -webkit-gradient(linear, left top,
    left bottom, from(#beeae9), to(#a8cfce));
  background:
    -moz-linear-gradient(top, #beeae9, #a8cfce);
  background:
    -o-linear-gradient(top, #beeae9, #a8cfce);
  background:
    -ms-linear-gradient(top, #beeae9, #a8cfce);}
input#submit:hover {
  color: #333333;
  border: 1px solid #a4a4a4;
  border-top: 2px solid #b2b2b2;
  background-color: #a0dbc4;
  background: -webkit-gradient(linear, left top,
    left bottom, from(#a8cfce), to(#beeae9));
  background:
    -moz-linear-gradient(top, #a8cfce, #beeae9);
  background:
    -o-linear-gradient(top, #a8cfce, #beeae9);
  background:
    -ms-linear-gradient(top, #a8cfce, #beeae9);}
```

RESULT

Register

STYLING FIELDSETS & LEGENDS

chapter-14/styling-fieldsets-and-legends.html

```
fieldset {
  width: 350px;
  border: 1px solid #dcdcdc;
  border-radius: 10px;
  padding: 20px;
  text-align: right;}
legend {
  background-color: #efefef;
  border: 1px solid #dcdcdc;
  border-radius: 10px;
  padding: 10px 20px;
  text-align: left;
  text-transform: uppercase;}
```

RESULT

NEWSLETTER

Name:

Email:

Subscribe

Fieldsets are particularly helpful in determining the edges of a form. In a long form they can help group together related information within it.

The legend is used to indicate what information is required in the fieldset.

Properties commonly used with these two elements include:

width is used to control the width of the fieldset. In this example, the width of the fieldset forces the form elements to wrap onto a new line in the correct place. (If it were wider, the items might sit on one line.)

color is used to control the color of text.

background-color is used to change the color behind these items.

border is used to control the appearance of the border around the fieldset and/or legend.

border-radius is used to soften the edges of these elements in browsers that support this property.

padding can be used to add space inside these elements.

ALIGNING FORM CONTROLS: PROBLEM

Labels for form elements are often different lengths, which means that the form controls will not appear in a straight line. This is demonstrated in the example on the right (without CSS applied to the form controls).

In this form, each topic we ask the user about is placed inside a `<div>` element to ensure that each question appears on a new line. It is easier for users to fill in a form if the form controls are aligned in a straight vertical line. The CSS on the opposite page addresses this.

If you look at where we ask users their gender, the two radio buttons each have their own `<label>` (one saying male and another saying female). A `<span>` element has been added to the title which will help align these controls.

On the previous page we saw another technique to align form elements. When the form only contains text inputs, by setting all of the text inputs to be the same width, as well as aligning all of the form content to the right, the fields line up and the labels are in a consistent place. For more complex forms, you will need a solution more like the one shown on these pages.

chapter-14/aligning-form-controls-problem.html `HTML`

```html
<form action="example.php" method="post">
  <div>
    <label for="name" class="title">Name:</label>
    <input type="text" id="name" name="name" />
  </div>
  <div>
    <label for="email" class="title">Email:</label>
    <input type="email" id="email" name="email" />
  </div>
  <div class="radio-buttons">
    <span class="title">Gender:</span>
    <input type="radio" name="gender" id="male"
      value="M" />
    <label for="male">M</label>
    <input type="radio" name="gender" id="female"
      value="F" />
    <label for="female">F</label><br />
  </div>
  <div class="submit">
    <input type="submit" value="Register"
      id="submit" />
  </div>
</form>
```

`RESULT WITHOUT CSS`

Name:
Email:
Gender: ○ M ○ F
Register

ALIGNING FORM CONTROLS: SOLUTION

chapter-14/aligning-form-controls-solution.html

```css
div {
  border-bottom: 1px solid #efefef;
  margin: 10px;
  padding-bottom: 10px;
  width: 260px;}
.title {
  float: left;
  width: 100px;
  text-align: right;
  padding-right: 10px;}
.submit {
  text-align: right;}
```

Each row of the form has a title telling users what they need to enter. For the text inputs, the title is in the `<label>` element. For the radio buttons, the title is in a `<span>` element. Both have a `class` attribute with a value of `title`.

We can use a property called `float` to move the titles to the left of the page. (The `float` property is covered in greater detail on pages 370-376.)

By setting the `width` property on those elements, we know that the titles will each take up the same width. Therefore, the form controls next to them will line up.

The `text-align` property is used to align the titles to the right, and `padding` is used to make sure there is a gap between the text in the title boxes and the form controls.

Styles are also applied to the `<div>` elements that contain each row of the form (fixing their width and creating vertical space between each row). The submit button is also aligned to the right.

RESULT

Name:

Email:

Gender: ○ M ○ F

Register

CURSOR STYLES
cursor

The cursor property allows you to control the type of mouse cursor that should be displayed to users.

For example, on a form you might set the cursor to be a hand when the user hovers over it.

Here are the most commonly used values for this property:

```
auto
crosshair
default
pointer
move
text
wait
help
url("cursor.gif");
```

You should only use these values to add helpful information for users in places they would expect to see that cursor. (For example, using a crosshair on a link might confuse users because they are not used to seeing it.)

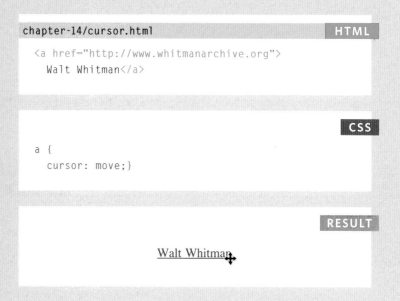

```
chapter-14/cursor.html                          HTML

<a href="http://www.whitmanarchive.org">
   Walt Whitman</a>
```

```
                                                 CSS

a {
   cursor: move;}
```

```
                                              RESULT

                    Walt Whitman
```

WEB DEVELOPER TOOLBAR

This helpful extension for Firefox and Chrome provides tools to show you the CSS styles that apply to an element when you hover over it, along with the structure of the HTML.

Download this tool from:
www.chrispederick.com/work/web-developer

To see the CSS styles and HTML structure of a web page, go to the CSS menu of the Web Developer Toolbar and pick **View Style Information**.

1: OUTLINES

When you hover over an element, a red outline will be drawn around it, showing you how much space the element takes up.

2: STRUCTURE

While you are hovering over an element, the structure will be shown at the top of the window. Here you can see the `<li>` element has a class of completed, inside a `<ul>` with a class called to-do. The list is inside a `<div>` element with an id of page, and this sits inside the `<body>` and `<html>` elements.

This can be very helpful when writing CSS selectors to help you target the right element.

3: CSS STYLES

When hovering over an element, click with your mouse to display the CSS. You will be shown the rules that apply to that element (and the line they are on). Above the rules, you can see the name of the style sheet (and the path to it).

This helps check which styles are being applied to an element. You can use it on code for your own site or when you want to see what styles someone else is using on their site.

This tool also allows you to change the screen size, validate your HTML and CSS code, and turn off images.

EXAMPLE
LISTS, TABLES AND FORMS

This example demonstrates several of the CSS properties we have met in this chapter to control the presentation of lists, tables, and forms.

For the list of free poetry events near the start of the page, the bullet points are styled with an image. The space between each list item is increased using the line-height property.

For the table, the gaps between cells are removed using the border-spacing property. Font size is set for the <td> and <th> elements as they do not inherit their size from parent elements.

The head of the table has a darker background, light text, and a dark 2-pixel line between it and the table content. Rounded corners on the table header are created using the :first-child and :last-child pseudo classes (for browsers that support rounded corners).

Alternate rows of the table have different shading, and texture is added with different borders on each side of the cell.

For the form, the related form controls are put in a <fieldset> element. The labels of the form controls on the left also use the float property to ensure the form controls are vertically aligned.

When the text boxes of the form receive focus, or the user hovers over it, the background color and border colors change. The submit button has also been styled to make it clear where people should submit the form.

EXAMPLE
LISTS, TABLES AND FORMS

```html
<!DOCTYPE html>
<html>
  <head>
    <title>Lists, Tables and Forms</title>
    <style type="text/css">
      body {
        font-family: Arial, Verdana, sans-serif;
        font-size: 90%;
        color: #666666;
        background-color: #f8f8f8;}
      li {
        list-style-image: url("images/icon-plus.png");
        line-height: 1.6em;}
      table {
        border-spacing: 0px;}
      th, td {
        padding: 5px 30px 5px 10px;
        border-spacing: 0px;
        font-size: 90%;
        margin: 0px;}
      th, td {
        text-align: left;
        background-color: #e0e9f0;
        border-top: 1px solid #f1f8fe;
        border-bottom: 1px solid #cbd2d8;
        border-right: 1px solid #cbd2d8;}
      tr.head th {
        color: #ffffff;
        background-color: #90b4d6;
        border-bottom: 2px solid #547ca0;
        border-right: 1px solid #749abe;
        border-top: 1px solid #90b4d6;
        text-align: center;
        text-shadow: -1px -1px 1px #666666;
        letter-spacing: 0.15em;}
      td {
        text-shadow: 1px 1px 1px #ffffff;}
```

```css
tr.even td, tr.even th {
  background-color: #e8eff5;}
tr.head th:first-child {
  -webkit-border-top-left-radius: 5px;
  -moz-border-radius-topleft: 5px;
  border-top-left-radius: 5px;}
tr.head th:last-child {
  -webkit-border-top-right-radius: 5px;
  -moz-border-radius-topright: 5px;
  border-top-right-radius: 5px;}
fieldset {
  width: 310px;
  margin-top: 20px;
  border: 1px solid #d6d6d6;
  background-color: #ffffff;
  line-height: 1.6em;}
legend {
  font-style: italic;
  color: #666666;}
input[type="text"] {
  width: 120px;
  border: 1px solid #d6d6d6;
  padding: 2px;
  outline: none;}
input[type="text"]:focus,
input[type="text"]:hover {
  background-color: #d0e2f0;
  border: 1px solid #999999;}
input[type="submit"] {
  border: 1px solid #006633;
  background-color: #009966;
  color: #ffffff;
  border-radius: 5px;
  padding: 5px;
  margin-top: 10px;}
input[type="submit"]:hover {
  border: 1px solid #006633;
```

EXAMPLE
LISTS, TABLES AND FORMS

```
      background-color: #00cc33;
      color: #ffffff;
      cursor: pointer;}
    .title {
      float: left;
      width: 160px;
      clear: left;}
    .submit {
      width: 310px;
      text-align: right;}
  </style>
</head>
<body>
  <h1>Poetry Workshops</h1>
  <p>We will be conducting a number of poetry workshops
    and symposiums throughout the year.</p>
  <p>Please note that the following events are free to
    members:</p>
  <ul>
    <li>A Poetic Perspective</li>
    <li>Walt Whitman at War</li>
    <li>Found Poems and Outsider Poetry</li>
  </ul>
  <table>
    <tr class="head">
      <th></th>
      <th>New York</th>
      <th>Chicago</th>
      <th>San Francisco</th>
    </tr>
    <tr>
      <th>A Poetic Perspective</th>
      <td>Sat, 4 Feb 2012<br />11am - 2pm</td>
      <td>Sat, 3 Mar 2012<br />11am - 2pm</td>
      <td>Sat, 17 Mar 2012<br />11am - 2pm</td>
    </tr>
    <tr class="even">
      <th>Walt Whitman at War</th>
```

```
          <td>Sat, 7 Apr 2012<br />11am - 1pm</td>
          <td>Sat, 5 May 2012<br />11am - 1pm</td>
          <td>Sat, 19 May 2012<br />11am - 1pm</td>
      </tr>
      <tr>
          <th>Found Poems &amp; Outsider Poetry</th>
          <td>Sat, 9 Jun 2012<br />11am - 2pm</td>
          <td>Sat, 7 Jul 2012<br />11am - 2pm</td>
          <td>Sat, 21 Jul 2012<br />11am - 2pm</td>
      </tr>
      <tr class="even">
          <th>Natural Death: An Exploration</th>
          <td>Sat, 4 Aug 2012<br />11am - 4pm</td>
          <td>Sat, 8 Sep 2012<br />11am - 4pm</td>
          <td>Sat, 15 Sep 2012<br />11am - 4pm</td>
      </tr>
    </table>
    <form action="http://www.example.com/form.php" method="get">
      <fieldset>
        <legend>Register your interest</legend>
        <p><label class="title" for="name">Your name:</label>
          <input type="text" name="name" id="name"><br />
          <label class="title" for="email">Your email:</label>
          <input type="text" name="email" id="email"></p>
        <p><label for="location" class="title">Your closest center:</label>
          <select name="location" id="location">
            <option value="ny">New York</option>
            <option value="il">Chicago</option>
            <option value="ca">San Francisco</option>
          </select></p>
        <span class="title">Are you a member?</span>
        <label><input type="radio" name="member" value="yes" /> Yes</label>
        <label><input type="radio" name="member" value="no" /> No</label>
      </fieldset>
      <div class="submit"><input type="submit" value="Register" /></div>
    </form>
  </body>
</html>
```

‣ In addition to the CSS properties covered in other chapters which work with the contents of all elements, there are several others that are specifically used to control the appearance of lists, tables, and forms.

‣ List markers can be given different appearances using the `list-style-type` and `list-style` image properties.

‣ Table cells can have different borders and spacing in different browsers, but there are properties you can use to control them and make them more consistent.

‣ Forms are easier to use if the form controls are vertically aligned using CSS.

‣ Forms benefit from styles that make them feel more interactive.

15

LAYOUT

- ▸ Controlling the position of elements
- ▸ Creating site layouts
- ▸ Designing for different sized screens

In this chapter we are going to look at how to control where each element sits on a page and how to create attractive page layouts.

This involves learning about how designing for a screen can be different from designing for other mediums (such as print). In this chapter we will:

- Explore different ways to position elements using normal flow, relative positioning, absolute positioning and floats.

- Discover how various devices have different screen sizes and resolutions, and how this affects the design process.

- Learn the difference between fixed width and liquid layouts, and how they are created.

- Find out how designers use grids to make their page designs look more professional.

KEY CONCEPTS IN POSITIONING ELEMENTS

BUILDING BLOCKS

CSS treats each HTML element as if it is in its own box. This box will either be a **block-level** box or an **inline** box.

Block-level boxes start on a new line and act as the main building blocks of any layout, while inline boxes flow between surrounding text. You can control how much space each box takes up by setting the width of the boxes (and sometimes the height, too). To separate boxes, you can use borders, margins, padding, and background colors.

BLOCK-LEVEL ELEMENTS
START ON A NEW LINE
Examples include:
`<h1> <p> <ul> <li>`

Lorem Ipsum

Lorem ipsum dolor sit amet, consectetur adipisicing elit, sed do eiusmod tempor incididunt ut labore et dolore magna aliqua. Ut enim ad minim veniam, quis nostrud exercitation ullamco laboris nisi ut aliquip ex ea commodo consequat. Duis aute irure dolor in reprehenderit in voluptate velit.

- Lorem ipsum dolor sit
- Consectetur adipisicing
- Elit, sed do eiusmod

INLINE ELEMENTS
FLOW IN BETWEEN
SURROUNDING TEXT
Examples include:
`<img> <b> <i>`

Lorem ipsum dolor sit amet, consectetur adipisicing elit, sed do eiusmod tempor incididunt ut **labore et dolore** magna aliqua. Ut enim ad minim veniam, quis nostrud exercitation ullamco laboris nisi ut aliquip ex ea commodo consequat.

Duis aute irure dolor in reprehenderit in voluptate velit esse cillum dolore eu fugiat nulla pariatur. Excepteur sint occaecat cupidatat non proident, sunt in culpa qui officia deserunt mollit anim id est laborum. Lorem ipsum dolor sit amet, consectetur adipisicing elit, sed do eiusmod tempor incididunt ut labore et dolore magna aliqua.

CONTAINING ELEMENTS

If one block-level element sits inside another block-level element then the outer box is known as the **containing** or **parent** element.

It is common to group a number of elements together inside a `<div>` (or other block-level) element. For example, you might group together all of the elements that form the header of a site (such as the logo and the main navigation). The `<div>` element that contains this group of elements is then referred to as the **containing** element.

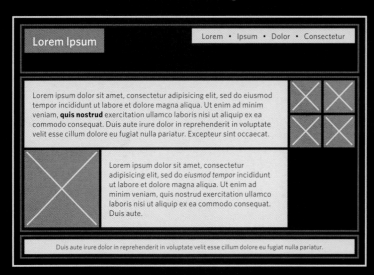

A box may be nested inside several other block-level elements. The containing element is always the **direct parent** of that element.

The orange lines in this diagram represent `<div>` elements. The header (containing the logo and navigation) are in one `<div>` element, the main content of the page is in another, and the footer is in a third. The `<body>` element is the containing element for these three `<div>` elements. The second `<div>` element is the containing element for two paragraphs of Latin text and images (represented by crossed squares).

CONTROLLING THE POSITION OF ELEMENTS

CSS has the following positioning schemes that allow you to control the layout of a page: normal flow, relative positioning, and absolute positioning. You specify the positioning scheme using the `position` property in CSS. You can also float elements using the `float` property.

NORMAL FLOW

Every block-level element appears on a new line, causing each item to appear lower down the page than the previous one. Even if you specify the width of the boxes and there is space for two elements to sit side-by-side, they will not appear next to each other. This is the default behavior (unless you tell the browser to do something else).

RELATIVE POSITIONING

This moves an element from the position it would be in normal flow, shifting it to the top, right, bottom, or left of where it would have been placed. This does not affect the position of surrounding elements; they stay in the position they would be in in normal flow.

ABSOLUTE POSITIONING

This positions the element in relation to its containing element. It is taken out of normal flow, meaning that it does not affect the position of any surrounding elements (as they simply ignore the space it would have taken up). Absolutely positioned elements move as users scroll up and down the page.

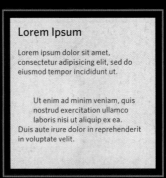

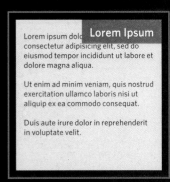

The paragraphs appear one after the other, vertically down the page.

The second paragraph has been pushed down and right from where it would otherwise have been in normal flow.

The heading is positioned to the top right, and the paragraphs start at the top of the screen (as if the heading were not there).

See page 365

See page 366

See page 367

To indicate where a box should be positioned, you may also need to use box offset properties to tell the browser how far from the top or bottom and left or right it should be placed. (You will meet these when we introduce the positioning schemes on the following pages.)

FIXED POSITIONING

This is a form of absolute positioning that positions the element in relation to the browser window, as opposed to the containing element. Elements with fixed positioning do not affect the position of surrounding elements and they do not move when the user scrolls up or down the page.

FLOATING ELEMENTS

Floating an element allows you to take that element out of normal flow and position it to the far left or right of a containing box. The floated element becomes a block-level element around which other content can flow.

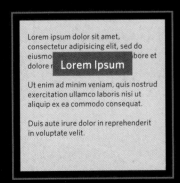

The heading has been placed in the center of the page and 25% from the top of the screen. (The rest appears in normal flow.)

See page 368

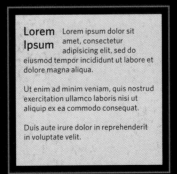

The heading has been floated to the left, allowing the paragraphs of text to flow around it.

See page 370-376

When you move any element from normal flow, boxes can overlap. The z-index property allows you to control which box appears on top.

NORMAL FLOW
position:static

In normal flow, each block-level element sits on top of the next one. Since this is the default way in which browsers treat HTML elements, you do not need a CSS property to indicate that elements should appear in normal flow, but the syntax would be:

position: static;

I have not specified a `width` property for the heading element, so you can see how it stretches the width of the entire browser window by default.

The paragraphs are restricted to 450 pixels wide. This shows how the elements in normal flow start on a new line even if they do not take up the full width of the browser window.

All of the examples that demonstrate positioning will use a similar HTML structure.

chapter-15/normal-flow.html `HTML`

```
<body>
  <h1>The Evolution of the Bicycle</h1>
  <p>In 1817 Baron von Drais invented a walking
     machine that would help him get around the
     royal gardens faster...</p>
</body>
```

`CSS`

```
body {
  width: 750px;
  font-family: Arial, Verdana, sans-serif;
  color: #665544;}
h1 {
  background-color: #efefef;
  padding: 10px;}
p {
  width: 450px;}
```

`RESULT`

The Evolution of the Bicycle

In 1817 Baron von Drais invented a walking machine that would help him get around the royal gardens faster: two same-size in-line wheels, the front one steerable, mounted in a frame upon which you straddled. The device was propelled by pushing your feet against the ground, thus rolling yourself and the device forward in a sort of gliding walk.

The machine became known as the Draisienne (or "hobby horse"). It was made entirely of wood. This enjoyed a short lived popularity as a fad, not being practical for transportation in any other place than a well maintained pathway such as in a park or garden.

The next appearance of a two-wheeled riding machine was in 1865, when pedals were applied directly to the front wheel. This machine was known as the velocipede (meaning "fast foot") as well as the "bone shaker," since its wooden structure combined with the cobblestone roads of the day made for an extremely uncomfortable ride. They also became a fad and indoor riding academies, similar to roller rinks, could be found in large cities.

RELATIVE POSITIONING
position:relative

HTML

```
<body>
  <h1>The Evolution of the Bicycle</h1>
  <p>In 1817 Baron von Drais invented a walking
     machine that would help him get around the
     royal gardens faster...</p>
</body>
```

CSS

```
p.example {
  position: relative;
  top: 10px;
  left: 100px;}
```

RESULT

The Evolution of the Bicycle

In 1817 Baron von Drais invented a walking machine that
would help him get around the royal gardens faster: two same-
size in-line wheels, the front one steerable, mounted in a frame
upon which you straddled. The device was propelled by
pushing your feet against the ground, thus rolling yourself and
the device forward in a sort of gliding walk.

The machine became known as the Draisienne (or "hobby
horse"). It was made entirely of wood. This enjoyed a short
lived popularity as a fad, not being practical for transportation in
any other place than a well maintained pathway such as in a
park or garden.

The next appearance of a two-wheeled riding machine was in
1865, when pedals were applied directly to the front wheel.
This machine was known as the velocipede (meaning "fast
foot") as well as the "bone shaker," since its wooden structure
combined with the cobblestone roads of the day made for an
extremely uncomfortable ride. They also became a fad and
indoor riding academies, similar to roller rinks, could be found
in large cities.

Relative positioning moves an element in relation to where it would have been in normal flow.

For example, you can move it 10 pixels lower than it would have been in normal flow or 20% to the right.

You can indicate that an element should be relatively positioned using the position property with a value of relative.

You then use the offset properties (top or bottom and left or right) to indicate how far to move the element from where it would have been in normal flow.

To move the box up or down, you can use either the top or bottom properties.

To move the box horizontally, you can use either the left or right properties.

The values of the box offset properties are usually given in pixels, percentages or ems.

ABSOLUTE POSITIONING
position:absolute

When the position property is given a value of absolute, the box is taken out of normal flow and no longer affects the position of other elements on the page. (They act like it is not there.)

The box offset properties (top or bottom and left or right) specify where the element should appear in relation to its containing element.

In this example, the heading has been positioned at the top of the page and 500 pixels from its left edge. The width of the heading is set to be 250 pixels wide.

The width property has also been applied to the <p> elements in this example to prevent the text from overlapping and becoming unreadable.

By default, most browsers add a margin to the top of the <h1> element. This is why there is a gap between the top of the browser and the box containing the <h1> element. If you wanted to remove this margin, you could add the following code to the <h1> element's style rules:
margin: 0px;

chapter-15/position-absolute.html `HTML`

```
<body>
  <h1>The Evolution of the Bicycle</h1>
  <p>In 1817 Baron von Drais invented a walking
    machine that would help him get around the
    royal gardens faster...</p>
</body>
```

`CSS`

```
h1 {
  position: absolute;
  top: 0px;
  left: 500px;
  width: 250px;}
p {
  width: 450px;}
```

`RESULT`

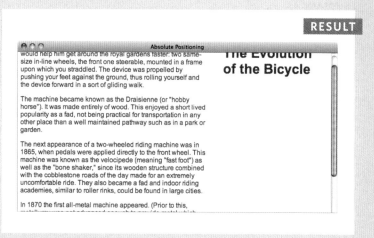

FIXED POSITIONING
position:fixed

HTML

```
<body>
  <h1>The Evolution of the Bicycle</h1>
  <p class="example">In 1817 Baron von Drais
    invented a walking machine that would help him
    get around the royal gardens faster...</p>
</body>
```

CSS

```
h1 {
  position: fixed;
  top: 0px;
  left: 0px;
  padding: 10px;
  margin: 0px;
  width: 100%;
  background-color: #efefef;}
p.example {
  margin-top: 100px;}
```

RESULT

Fixed positioning is a type of absolute positioning that requires the position property to have a value of fixed.

It positions the element in relation to the browser window. Therefore, when a user scrolls down the page, it stays in the exact same place. It is a good idea to try this example in your browser to see the effect.

To control where the fixed position box appears in relation to the browser window, the box offset properties are used.

In this example, the heading has been positioned to the top left hand corner of the browser window. When the user scrolls down the page, the paragraphs disappear behind the heading.

The <p> elements are in normal flow and ignore the space that the <h1> element would have taken up. Therefore, the margin-top property has been used to push the first <p> element below where the fixed position <h1> element is sitting.

OVERLAPPING ELEMENTS
z-index

When you use relative, fixed, or absolute positioning, boxes can overlap. If boxes do overlap, the elements that appear later in the HTML code sit on top of those that are earlier in the page.

If you want to control which element sits on top, you can use the z-index property. Its value is a number, and the higher the number the closer that element is to the front. For example, an element with a z-index of 10 will appear over the top of one with a z-index of 5.

This example looks similar to the one on page 368, but it uses relative positioning for the <p> elements. Because the paragraphs are relatively positioned, by default they would appear over the top of the heading as the user scrolls down the page. To ensure that the <h1> element stays on top, we use the z-index property on the rule for the <h1> element.

The z-index is sometimes referred to as the **stacking context** (as if the blocks have been stacked on top of each other on a z axis). If you are familiar with desktop publishing packages, it is the equivalent of using the 'bring to front' and 'send to back' features.

chapter-15/z-index.html `CSS`

```css
h1 {
  position: fixed;
  top: 0px;
  left: 0px;
  margin: 0px;
  padding: 10px;
  width: 100%;
  background-color: #efefef;
  z-index: 10;}
p {
  position: relative;
  top: 70px;
  left: 70px;}
```

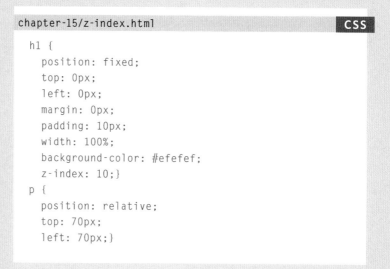

RESULT WITHOUT Z-INDEX

RESULT WITH Z-INDEX

FLOATING ELEMENTS
float

```
<h1>The Evolution of the Bicycle</h1>
<blockquote>"Life is like riding a bicycle.
    To keep your balance you must keep moving." -
    Albert Einstein</blockquote>
<p>In 1817 Baron von Drais invented a walking
    machine that would help him get around the royal
    gardens faster: two same-size in-line wheels, the
    front one steerable, mounted in a frame ... </p>
```

CSS

```
blockquote {
        float: right;
        width: 275px;
        font-size: 130%;
        font-style: italic;
        font-family: Georgia, Times, serif;
        margin: 0px 0px 10px 10px;
        padding: 10px;
        border-top: 1px solid #665544;
        border-bottom: 1px solid #665544;}
```

RESULT

The Evolution of the Bicycle

In 1817 Baron von Drais invented a walking machine that
would help him get around the royal gardens faster: two same-
size in-line wheels, the front one steerable, mounted in a
frame upon which you straddled. The device was propelled by
pushing your feet against the ground, thus rolling yourself and
the device forward in a sort of gliding walk.

*"Life is like riding a bicycle.
To keep your balance you
must keep moving." - Albert
Einstein*

The machine became known as the Draisienne (or "hobby
horse"). It was made entirely of wood. This enjoyed a short lived popularity as a fad, not being practical
for transportation in any other place than a well maintained pathway such as in a park or garden.

The next appearance of a two-wheeled riding machine was in 1865, when pedals were applied directly to
the front wheel. This machine was known as the velocipede (meaning "fast foot") as well as the "bone
shaker," since its wooden structure combined with the cobblestone roads of the day made for an
extremely uncomfortable ride. They also became a fad and indoor riding academies, similar to roller rinks,
could be found in large cities.

The float property allows you to take an element in normal flow and place it as far to the left or right of the containing element as possible.

Anything else that sits inside the containing element will flow around the element that is floated.

When you use the float property, you should also use the width property to indicate how wide the floated element should be. If you do not, results can be inconsistent but the box is likely to take up the full width of the containing element (just like it would in normal flow).

In this example, a <blockquote> element is used to hold a quotation. It's containing element is the <body> element.

The <blockquote> element is floated to the right, and the paragraphs that follow the quote flow around the floated element.

USING FLOAT TO PLACE ELEMENTS SIDE-BY-SIDE

A lot of layouts place boxes next to each other. The `float` property is commonly used to achieve this.

When elements are floated, the height of the boxes can affect where the following elements sit.

In this example, you can see six paragraphs, each of which has a `width` and a `float` property set.

The fourth paragraph (which begins "In 1865, the velocipede...") does not go across to the left hand edge of the page as one might expect. Rather it sits right under the third paragraph.

The reason for this is that the fourth paragraph has space to start under the third paragraph, but it cannot go any further to the left because the second paragraph is in the way.

Setting the height of the paragraphs to be the same height as the tallest paragraph would solve this issue, but it is rarely suited to real world designs where the amount of text in a paragraph or column may vary. It is more common to use the `clear` property (discussed on the next page) to solve this issue.

chapter-15/using-float.html

```html
<body>
  <h1>The Evolution of the Bicycle</h1>
  <p>In 1817 Baron von Drais invented a walking
     machine that would help him get around...</p>
</body>
```

```css
body {
  width: 750px;
  font-family: Arial, Verdana, sans-serif;
  color: #665544;}
p {
  width: 230px;
  float: left;
  margin: 5px;
  padding: 5px;
  background-color: #efefef;}
```

The Evolution of the Bicycle

In 1817 Baron von Drais invented a walking machine that would help him get around the royal gardens faster.

The device know as the Draisienne (or "hobby horse") was made of wood, and propelled by pushing your feet on the ground in a gliding movement.

It was not seen as suitable for any place other than a well maintained pathway.

In 1865, the velocipede (meaning "fast foot") attached pedals to the front wheel, but its wooden structure made it extremely uncomfortable.

In 1870 the first all-metal machine appeared. The pedals were attached directly to the front wheel.

Solid rubber tires and the long spokes of the large front wheel provided a much smoother ride than its predecessor.

CLEARING FLOATS
clear

```
<p class="clear">In 1865, the velocipede (meaning
   "fast foot") attached pedals to the front wheel,
   but its wooden structure made it extremely
   uncomfortable.</p>
```

CSS

```
body {
   width: 750px;
   font-family: Arial, Verdana, sans-serif;
   color: #665544;}
p {
   width: 230px;
   float: left;
   margin: 5px;
   padding: 5px;
   background-color: #efefef;}
.clear {
   clear: left;}
```

RESULT

The Evolution of the Bicycle

In 1817 Baron von Drais invented a walking machine that would help him get around the royal gardens faster.

The device know as the Draisienne (or "hobby horse") was made of wood, and propelled by pushing your feet on the ground in a gliding movement.

It was not seen as suitable for any place other than a well maintained pathway.

In 1865, the velocipede (meaning "fast foot") attached pedals to the front wheel, but its wooden structure made it extremely uncomfortable.

In 1870 the first all-metal machine appeared. The pedals were atttached directly to the front wheel.

Solid rubber tires and the long spokes of the large front wheel provided a much smoother ride than its predecessor.

The clear property allows you to say that no element (within the same containing element) should touch the left or right-hand sides of a box. It can take the following values:

left
The left-hand side of the box should not touch any other elements appearing in the same containing element.

right
The right-hand side of the box will not touch elements appearing in the same containing element.

both
Neither the left nor right-hand sides of the box will touch elements appearing in the same containing element.

none
Elements can touch either side.

In this example, the fourth paragraph has a class called clear. The CSS rule for this class uses the clear property to indicate that nothing should touch the left-hand side of it. The fourth paragraph is therefore moved further down the page so no other element touches its left-hand side.

PARENTS OF FLOATED ELEMENTS: PROBLEM

If a containing element *only* contains floated elements, some browsers will treat it as if it is zero pixels tall.

As you can see in this example, the one pixel border assigned to the containing element has collapsed, so the box looks like a two pixel line.

chapter-15/float-problem.html

```
<body>
  <h1>The Evolution of the Bicycle</h1>
  <div>
    <p>In 1817 Baron von Drais invented a walking
       machine that would help him get around the
       royal gardens faster...</p>
  </div>
</body>
```

CSS

```
div {
  border: 1px solid #665544;}
```

RESULT

The Evolution of the Bicycle

In 1817 Baron von Drais invented a walking machine that would help him get around the royal gardens faster.

The device know as the Draisienne (or "hobby horse") was made of wood, and propelled by pushing your feet on the ground in a gliding movement.

It was not seen as suitable for any place other than a well maintained pathway.

In 1865, the velocipede (meaning "fast foot") attached pedals to the front wheel, but its wooden structure made it extremely uncomfortable.

In 1870 the first all-metal machine appeared. The pedals were atttached directly to the front wheel.

Solid rubber tires and the long spokes of the large front wheel provided a much smoother ride than its predecessor.

PARENTS OF FLOATED ELEMENTS: SOLUTION

chapter-15/float-solution.html

```
<body>
  <h1>The Evolution of the Bicycle</h1>
  <div>
    <p>In 1817 Baron von Drais invented a walking
       machine that would help him get around the
       royal gardens faster...</p>
  </div>
</body>
```

CSS

```
div {
  border: 1px solid #665544;
  overflow: auto;
  width: 100%;}
```

RESULT

The Evolution of the Bicycle

In 1817 Baron von Drais invented a walking machine that would help him get around the royal gardens faster.

The device know as the Draisienne (or "hobby horse") was made of wood, and propelled by pushing your feet on the ground in a gliding movement.

It was not seen as suitable for any place other than a well maintained pathway.

In 1865, the velocipede (meaning "fast foot") attached pedals to the front wheel, but its wooden structure made it extremely uncomfortable.

In 1870 the first all-metal machine appeared. The pedals were atttached directly to the front wheel.

Solid rubber tires and the long spokes of the large front wheel provided a much smoother ride than its predecessor.

Traditionally, developers got around this problem by adding an extra element after the last floated box (inside the containing element). A CSS rule would be applied to this additional element setting the clear property to have a value of both. But this meant that an extra element was added to the HTML just to fix the height of the containing element.

More recently, developers have opted for a purely CSS-based solution because it means that there is no need to add an extra element to the HTML page after the floated elements. The pure CSS solution adds two CSS rules to the containing element (in this example the <div> element):

- The overflow property is given a value auto.

- The width property is set to 100%.

CREATING MULTI-COLUMN LAYOUTS WITH FLOATS

Many web pages use multiple columns in their design. This is achieved by using a `<div>` element to represent each column. The following three CSS properties are used to position the columns next to each other:

width
This sets the width of the columns.

float
This positions the columns next to each other.

margin
This creates a gap between the columns.

A two-column layout like the one shown on this page would need two `<div>` elements, one for the main content of the page and one for the sidebar.

Inside each of the `<div>` elements there can be headings, paragraphs, images, and even other `<div>` elements.

chapter-15/columns-two.html HTML

```html
<h1>The Evolution of the Bicycle</h1>
<div class="column1of2">
  <h3>The First Bicycle</h3>
  <p>In 1817 Baron von Drais invented a walking
    machine that would help him get around the
    royal gardens faster: two same-size ...</p>
</div>
<div class="column2of2">
  <h3>Bicycle Timeline</h3> ...
</div>
```

CSS

```css
.column1of2 {
  float: left;
  width: 620px;
  margin: 10px;}
.column2of2 {
  float: left;
  width: 300px;
  margin: 10px;}
```

RESULT

The Evolution of the Bicycle

The First Bicycle

In 1817 Baron von Drais invented a walking machine that would help him get around the royal gardens faster: two same-size in-line wheels, the front one steerable, mounted in a frame upon which you straddled. The device was propelled by pushing your feet against the ground, thus rolling yourself and the device forward in a sort of gliding walk.

The machine became known as the Draisienne (or "hobby horse"). It was made entirely of wood. This enjoyed a short lived popularity as a fad, not being practical for transportation in any other place than a well maintained pathway such as in a park or garden.

Further Innovations

The next appearance of a two-wheeled riding machine was in 1865, when pedals were applied directly to the front wheel. This machine was known as the velocipede (meaning "fast foot") as well as the "bone shaker," since its wooden structure combined with the cobblestone roads of the day made for an extremely uncomfortable ride. They also became a fad and indoor riding academies, similar to roller rinks, could be found in large cities.

In 1870 the first all-metal machine appeared. (Prior to this, metallurgy was not advanced enough to provide metal which was strong enough to make small, light parts out of.) The pedals were attached directly to the front wheel with no freewheeling mechanism. Solid rubber tires and the long spokes of the large front wheel provided a much smoother ride than its predecessor.

Bicycle Timeline

- 1817: Draisienne
- 1865: Velocipede
- 1870: High-wheel bicycle
- 1876: High-wheel safety
- 1885: Hard-tired safety
- 1888: Pneumatic safety

```
<h1>The Evolution of the Bicycle</h1>
<div class="column1of3">
  <h3>The First Bicycle</h3> ...
</div>
<div class="column2of3">
  <h3>Further Innovations</h3> ...
</div>
<div class="column3of3">
  <h3>Bicycle Timeline</h3> ...
</div>
```

CSS

```
.column1of3, .column2of3, .column3of3 {
  width: 300px;
  float: left;
  margin: 10px;}
```

Similarly, a three column layout could be created by floating three <div> elements next to each other, as shown on this page.

RESULT

The Evolution of the Bicycle

The First Bicycle

In 1817 Baron von Drais invented a walking machine that would help him get around the royal gardens faster: two same-size in-line wheels, the front one steerable, mounted in a frame upon which you straddled. The device was propelled by pushing your feet against the ground, thus rolling yourself and the device forward in a sort of gliding walk.

The machine became known as the Draisienne (or "hobby horse"). It was made entirely of wood. This enjoyed a short lived popularity as a fad, not being practical for transportation in any other place than a well maintained pathway such as in a park or garden.

Further Innovations

The next appearance of a two-wheeled riding machine was in 1865, when pedals were applied directly to the front wheel. This machine was known as the velocipede (meaning "fast foot") as well as the "bone shaker," since its wooden structure combined with the cobblestone roads of the day made for an extremely uncomfortable ride. They also became a fad and indoor riding academies, similar to roller rinks, could be found in large cities.

In 1870 the first all-metal machine appeared. (Prior to this, metallurgy was not advanced enough to provide metal which was strong enough to make small, light parts out of.) The pedals were attached directly to the front wheel with no freewheeling mechanism. Solid rubber tires and the long spokes of the large front wheel provided a much smoother ride than its predecessor.

Bicycle Timeline

- 1817: Draisienne
- 1865: Velocipede
- 1870: High-wheel bicycle
- 1876: High-wheel safety
- 1885: Hard-tired safety
- 1888: Pneumatic safety

SCREEN SIZES

Different visitors to your site will have different sized screens that show different amounts of information, so your design needs to be able to work on a range of different sized screens.

iPhone 4
Size: 3.5 inches
Resolution: 960 x 640 pixels

iPad 2
Size: 9.7 inches
Resolution: 1024 x 768 pixels

When designing for print, you always know the size of the piece of paper that your design will be printed on. However, when it comes to designing for the web, you are faced with the unique challenge that different users will have different sized screens.

Since computers have been sold to the public, the size of screens has been steadily increasing. This means that some people viewing your site might have 13 inch monitors while others may have 27+ inch monitors.

The size of a user's screen affects how big they can open their windows and how much of the page they will see. There is also an increasing number of handheld devices (mobile phones and tablets) that have smaller screens.

Resolution refers to the number of dots a screen shows per inch. Some devices have a higher resolution than desktop computers and most operating systems allow users to adjust the resolution of their screens.

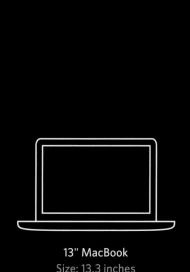

13" MacBook
Size: 13.3 inches
Resolution: 1280 x 800 pixels

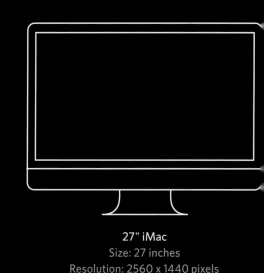

27" iMac
Size: 27 inches
Resolution: 2560 x 1440 pixels

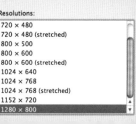

Most computers will allow owners to adjust the resolution of the display or the number of pixels that are shown on the screen. For example, here you can see the options to change the screen size from 720 x 480 pixels up to 1280 x 800 pixels.

It is interesting to note that the higher the resolution, the smaller the text appears. Many mobile devices have screens that are higher resolution than their desktop counterparts.

PAGE SIZES

Because screen sizes and display resolutions vary so much, web designers often try to create pages of around 960-1000 pixels wide (since most users will be able to see designs this wide on their screens).

Judging the height that people are likely to see on the screen without scrolling down the page is much harder. For several years, designers assumed that users would see the top 570-600 pixels of a page without having to scroll and some tried to fit all of the key messages in this area (fearing that people would not scroll down the page).

As screen sizes have increased and handheld devices have become more popular, the area users will see is far more variable.

The area of the page that users would see without scrolling was often referred to as being "above the fold" (a term newspapers had originally coined to describe the area of the front page you would see if the paper were folded in half).

It is now recognized that if someone is interested in the content of the page, they are likely to scroll down to see more. Having said which, usability studies have shown that visitors can judge a page in under a second so it is still important to let new visitors know that the site is relevant to them and their interests.

As a result, many designers still try to let the user know what the site is about within the top 570-600 pixels, as well as hint at more content below this point. But do not try to cram too much into that top area.

At the time of writing, there was a growing trend for people to create adaptive or responsive designs that could change depending on the size of the screen.

The shaded area is hidden by the constraints of the browser window, so the user must scroll in order to view the lower region.

However, the user gets a taste for what is lower on the page and can tell that there will be more to see if they scroll down.

1000 px

570 px

flickr® from YAHOO!

The Tour   Explore   Sign In   Sign Up   Search

Share your life
in photos

Sign up now
or login with your ID:

© by peterbaker

Upload
More ways to get your photos online.

Multiple ways to upload your photos to Flickr—through the web, your mobile device, email or your favorite photo applications.

Discover
See what's going on in your world.

Keep up with your friends and share your stories with comments & notes. Add rich information like tags, locations & people.

Share
Your photos are everywhere you are.

Upload your photos once to Flickr, then easily and safely share them through Facebook, Twitter, email, blogs and more.

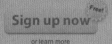 Free!
or learn more

It takes less than a minute to create your free account & start sharing!

Have a Google or Facebook account? You can use them to sign in!

Community
Flickr is made of people.

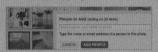

Join one of over 10 million active groups to take part in the conversation, learn from our

Privacy
Your photos are safe with us.

Share photos only with the people you want to with our easy privacy settings. Flickr's multiple-

Flickr on the go
Mobile options to keep you going.

Flickr is always in your back pocket with apps for iPhone, Windows 7, and more. Or use

FIXED WIDTH LAYOUTS

Fixed width layout designs do not change size as the user increases or decreases the size of their browser window. Measurements tend to be given in pixels.

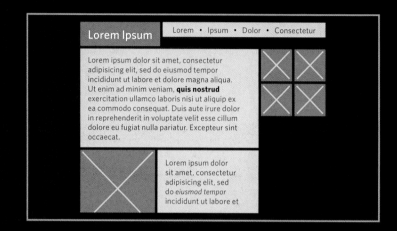

ADVANTAGES

- Pixel values are accurate at controlling size and positioning of elements.

- The designer has far greater control over the appearance and position of items on the page than with liquid layouts.

- You can control the lengths of lines of text regardless of the size of the user's window.

- The size of an image will always remain the same relative to the rest of the page.

DISADVANTAGES

- You can end up with big gaps around the edge of a page.

- If the user's screen is a much higher resolution than the designer's screen, the page can look smaller and text can be harder to read.

- If a user increases font sizes, text might not fit into the allotted spaces.

- The design works best on devices that have a site or resolution similar to that of desktop or laptop computers.

- The page will often take up more vertical space than a liquid layout with the same content.

LIQUID LAYOUTS

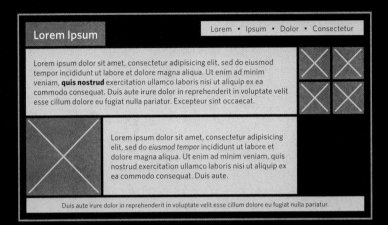

Liquid layout designs stretch and contract as the user increases or decreases the size of their browser window. They tend to use percentages.

ADVANTAGES

- Pages expand to fill the entire browser window so there are no spaces around the page on a large screen.

- If the user has a small window, the page can contract to fit it without the user having to scroll to the side.

- The design is tolerant of users setting font sizes larger than the designer intended (because the page can stretch).

DISADVANTAGES

- If you do not control the width of sections of the page then the design can look very different than you intended, with unexpected gaps around certain elements or items squashed together.

- If the user has a wide window, lines of text can become very long, which makes them harder to read.

- If the user has a very narrow window, words may be squashed and you can end up with few words on each line.

- If a fixed width item (such as an image) is in a box that is too small to hold it (because the user has made the window smaller) the image can overflow over the text.

Because liquid layouts can stretch the entire width of the browser, resulting in long lines of text that are hard to read, some liquid layouts only let part of the page expand and contract. Other parts of the page have minimum and maximum widths.

A FIXED WIDTH LAYOUT

To create a fixed width layout, the width of the main boxes on a page will usually be specified in pixels (and sometimes their height, too).

Here you can see several `<div>` elements, each of which uses an `id` or `class` attribute to indicate its purpose on the page.

In a book like this, the result of both the fixed and liquid layouts look similar. To get a real feel for them, you need to view them in your browser and see how they react when you adjust the size of the browser window.

The fixed width layout will stay the same width no matter what size the browser window is, whereas the liquid layout will stretch (or shrink) to fill the screen.

The HTML is the same for both the fixed width layout example on this page and the liquid layout example you see next.

chapter-15/fixed-width-layout.html

`HTML`

```html
<body>
  <div id="header">
    <h1>Logo</h1>
    <div id="nav">
      <ul>
        <li><a href="">Home</a></li>
        <li><a href="">Products</a></li>
        <li><a href="">Services</a></li>
        <li><a href="">About</a></li>
        <li><a href="">Contact</a></li>
      </ul>
    </div>
  </div>
  <div id="content">
    <div id="feature">
      <p>Feature</p>
    </div>
    <div class="article column1">
      <p>Column One</p>
    </div>
    <div class="article column2">
      <p>Column Two</p>
    </div>
    <div class="article column3">
      <p>Column Three</p>
    </div>
  </div>
  <div id="footer">
    <p>&copy; Copyright 2011</p>
  </div>
</body>
```

```
body {
  width: 960px;
  margin: 0 auto;}
#content {
  overflow: auto;
  height: 100%;}
#nav, #feature, #footer {
  background-color: #efefef;
  padding: 10px;
  margin: 10px;}
.column1, .column2, .column3 {
  background-color: #efefef;
  width: 300px;
  float: left;
  margin: 10px;}
li {
  display: inline;
  padding: 5px;}
```

The rule for the <body> element is used to fix the width of the page at 960 pixels, and it is centered by setting the left and right margins to auto.

The main boxes on the page have a margin of 10 pixels to create a gap between them.

The navigation, feature, and footer panels stretch to the width of the containing element (which in this instance is the <body> element), so we do not need to specify a width for them.

The three columns are each 300 pixels wide and use the float property, which allows them to sit next to each other.

Sometimes an extra HTML element is used to contain the page, rather than fixing the width of the <body>. This allows the background of the browser window to have a different color than the background of the content.

RESULT

Logo

Home Products Services About Contact

Feature

Column One   Column Two   Column Three

© Copyright 2011

A LIQUID LAYOUT

The liquid layout uses percentages to specify the width of each box so that the design will stretch to fit the size of the screen.

When trying this in your browser, remember to make the window smaller and larger.

```
<body>
  <div id="header">
    <h1>Logo</h1>
    <div id="nav">
      <ul>
        <li><a href="">Home</a></li>
        <li><a href="">Products</a></li>
        <li><a href="">Services</a></li>
        <li><a href="">About</a></li>
        <li><a href="">Contact</a></li>
      </ul>
    </div>
  </div>
  <div id="content">
    <div id="feature">
      <p>Feature</p>
    </div>
    <div class="article column1">
      <p>Column One</p>
    </div>
    <div class="article column2">
      <p>Column Two</p>
    </div>
    <div class="article column3">
      <p>Column Three</p>
    </div>
  </div>
  <div id="footer">
    <p>&copy; Copyright 2011</p>
  </div>
</body>
```

```css
body {
  width: 90%;
  margin: 0 auto;}
#content {overflow: auto;}
#nav, #feature, #footer {
  margin: 1%;}
.column1, .column2, .column3 {
  width: 31.3%;
  float: left;
  margin: 1%;}
.column3 {margin-right: 0%;}
li {
  display: inline;
  padding: 0.5em;}
#nav, #footer {
  background-color: #efefef;
  padding: 0.5em 0;}
#feature, .article {
  height: 10em;
  margin-bottom: 1em;
  background-color: #efefef;}
```

Logo

Home   Products   Services   About   Contact

Feature

Column One   Column Two   Column Three

© Copyright 2011

There is a rule on the `<body>` element to set the width of the page to 90% so that there is a small gap between the left and right-hand sides of the browser window and the main content.

The three columns are all given a margin of 1% and a width of 31.3%. This adds up to 99.9% of the width of the `<body>` element, so some browsers might not perfectly align the right-hand side of the third column with other elements on the page.

The `<div>` elements that hold the navigation, feature, and footer will stretch to fill the width of the containing `<body>` element. They are given a 1% margin to help them align with the columns.

If you imagine the browser window to be very wide or very narrow, you can see how lines of text could become very long or very short.

This is where the `min-width` and `max-width` properties help create boundaries within which the layout can stretch (although Internet Explorer 7 was the first version of IE to support these properties).

LAYOUT GRIDS

Composition in any visual art (such as design, painting, or photography) is the placement or arrangement of visual elements — how they are organized on a page. Many designers use a grid structure to help them position items on a page, and the same is true for web designers.

On the right, you can see a set of thick vertical lines superimposed over the top of a newspaper website to show you how the page was designed according to a grid. This grid is called the **960 pixel grid** and is widely used by web designers.

Grids set consistent proportions and spaces between items which helps to create a professional looking design.

If you flick back through the pages of this book you will see that it, too, has been constructed according to a grid (comprising three columns).

As you will see on pages 389-390, it is possible to create many different layouts using this one versatile grid.

While a grid might seem like a restriction, in actual fact it:

- Creates a continuity between different pages which may use different designs

- Helps users predict where to find information on various pages

- Makes it easier to add new content to the site in a consistent way

- Helps people collaborate on the design of a site in a consistent way

EXAMPLE GRID

POSSIBLE LAYOUTS:
960 PIXEL WIDE
12 COLUMN GRID

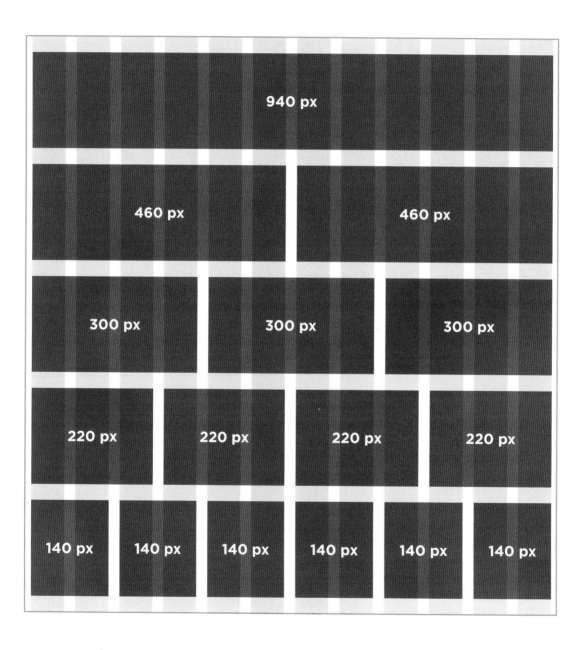

These two pages illustrate a 960 pixel wide, 12 column grid. They demonstrate how it is possible to create a wide range of column layouts using this one grid.

The page is 960 pixels wide and there are 12 equal sized columns (shown in gray), each of which is is 60 pixels wide.

Each column has a margin set to 10 pixels, which creates a gap of 20 pixels between each column and 10 pixels to the left and right-hand sides of the page.

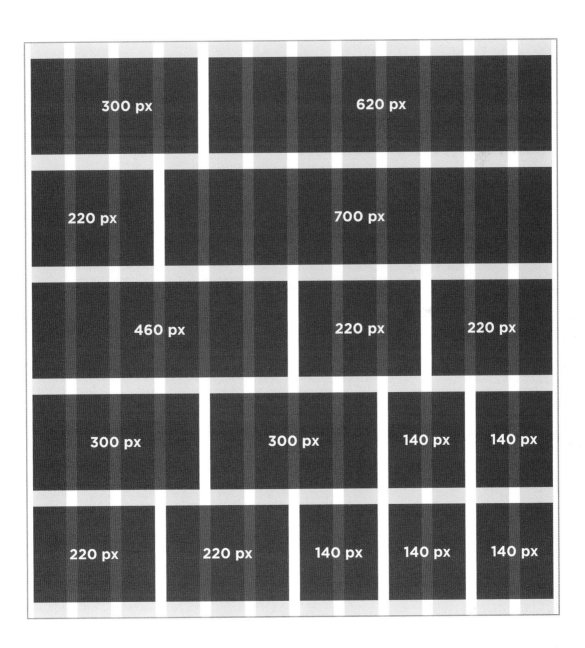

CSS FRAMEWORKS

CSS frameworks aim to make your life easier by providing the code for common tasks, such as creating layout grids, styling forms, creating printer-friendly versions of pages and so on. You can include the CSS framework code in your projects rather than writing the CSS from scratch.

ADVANTAGES

- They save you from repeatedly writing code for the same tasks.

- They will have been tested across different browser versions (which helps avoid browser bugs).

DISADVANTAGES

- They often require that you use class names in your HTML code that only control the presentation of the page (rather than describe its content).

- In order to satisfy a wide variety of needs, they often contain more code than you need for your particular web page (commonly referred to as code "bloat").

INTRODUCING THE 960.GS CSS FRAMEWORK

One of the most popular uses of CSS frameworks is in creating grids to layout pages. There are several grid frameworks out there, but the one we will be looking at over the next few pages is the 960 Grid System (available at www.960.gs).

960.gs provides a style sheet that you can include in your HTML pages. Once our page links to this style sheet, you can provide the appropriate classes to your HTML code and it will create multiple column layouts for you. The 960.gs website also provides templates you can

download to help design your pages using a 12 column grid. (In addition, there is a variation on the grid that uses 16 columns.)

To create a 12 column grid, an element that contains the entire page is given a class attibute whose value is container_12. This sets the content of the page to be 960 pixels wide and indicates that we are using a 12 column grid.

There are different classes for blocks that take up 1, 2, 3, 4, and up to 12 columns of the grid. Each block uses class names

such as grid_3 (for a block that stretches over three columns), grid_4 (for a block that stretches over 4 columns) and and so on through to grid_12 (for a box that is the full width of the page). These columns all float to the left, and there is a 10 pixel margin to the left and the right of each one.

There are several other grid-based CSS frameworks available online, such as those at:
blueprintcss.org
lessframework.com
developer.yahoo.com/yui/grids/

USING THE 960.GS GRID

Below you can see a sample layout of a page just like the fixed width page example. On the next page, we will recreate this using the 960.gs stylesheet. Instead of writing our own CSS to control layout, we will need to add classes to the HTML indicating how wide each section should be.

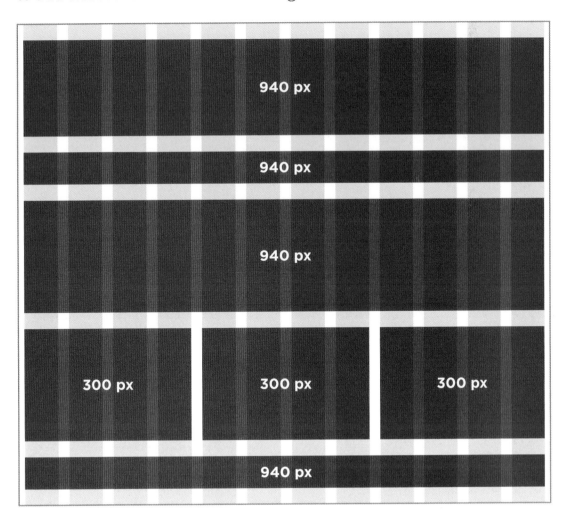

A GRID-BASED LAYOUT USING 960.GS

Let's take a look at an HTML page and how it has been marked up to use the 960.gs grid system.

You can see that we include the CSS for the grid using the `<link>` element inside the `<head>` of the page.

The styles we are writing ourselves are shown on the right hand page.

The `960_12_col.css` stylesheet contains all of the rules we need to control the grid layout. The HTML uses the class names:

`container_12` to act as a container for the whole page and indicate that we are using a 12 column grid

`clearfix` to ensure that browsers know the height of the containing box, because it only contains floated elements (this addresses the issue you met on pages 371-372)

`grid_12` to create a block that is twelve columns wide

`grid_4` to create a block that is four columns wide

chapter-15/grid-layout.html `HTML`

```
<head>
  <title>Grid Layout</title>
  <link rel="stylesheet" type="text/css"
      href="css/960_12_col.css" />
  <style>See the right hand page</style>
</head>
<body>
  <div class="container_12 clearfix">
    <div id="header" class="grid_12">
      <h1>Logo</h1>
        <div id="nav">
          <ul>
            <li><a href="">Home</a></li>
            <li><a href="">Products</a></li>
            <li><a href="">Services</a></li>
            <li><a href="">About</a></li>
            <li><a href="">Contact</a></li>
          </ul>
        </div>
    </div>
    <div id="feature" class="grid_12">
      <p>Feature</p>
    </div>
    <div class="article grid_4">
      <p>Column One</p>
    </div>
    <div class="article grid_4">
      <p>Column Two</p>
    </div>
    <div class="article grid_4">
      <p>Column Three</p>
    </div>
    <div id="footer" class="grid_12">
      <p>&copy; Copyright 2011</p>
    </div>
  </div><!-- .container_12 -->
</body>
```

```
* {
  font-family: Arial, Verdana, sans-serif;
  color: #665544;
  text-align: center;}
#nav, #feature, .article, #footer {
  background-color: #efefef;
  margin-top: 20px;
  padding: 10px 0px 5px 0px;}
#feature, .article {
  height: 100px;}
li {
  display: inline;
  padding: 5px;}
```

Logo

Home Products Services About Contact

Feature

Column One   Column Two   Column Three

© Copyright 2011

The 960.gs style sheet has taken care of the layout, creating the correct width for the columns and setting the spaces between them. Therefore, the only rules we needed to add are shown on this page. These rules:

- Control the font and the position of the text in the boxes

- Set the background colors for the boxes

- Set the height of the feature and article boxes

- Add a margin to the top and bottom of each box

MULTIPLE STYLE SHEETS
@import

Some web page authors split up their CSS style rules into separate style sheets. For example, they might use one style sheet to control the layout and another to control fonts, colors and so on.

Some authors take an even more **modular** approach to stylesheets, creating separate stylesheets to control typography, layout, forms, tables, even different styles for each sub-section of a site.

There are two ways to add multiple style sheets to a page:

1: Your HTML page can link to one style sheet and that stylesheet can use the @import rule to import other style sheets.

2: In the HTML you can use a separate <link> element for each style sheet.

The example on this page uses one <link> element in the HTML to link to a style sheet called styles.css. This stylesheet then uses the @import rule to import the typography.css and tables.css files.

If a styesheet uses the @import rule, it should appear before the other rules.

chapter-15/multiple-style-sheets-import.html `HTML`

```
<!DOCTYPE html>
<html>
  <head>
    <title>Multiple Style Sheets - Import</title>
    <link rel="stylesheet" type="text/css"
      href="css/styles.css" />
  </head>
  <body>
    <!-- HTML page content here -->
  </body>
</html>
```

chapter-15/styles.css `CSS`

```
@import url("tables.css");
@import url("typography.css");
body {
  color: #666666;
  background-color: #f8f8f8;
  text-align: center;}
#page {
  width: 600px;
  text-align: left;
  margin-left: auto;
  margin-right: auto;
  border: 1px solid #d6d6d6;
  padding: 20px;}
h3 {
  color: #547ca0;}
```

MULTIPLE STYLE SHEETS
link

```html
<!DOCTYPE html>
<html>
  <head>
    <title>Multiple Style Sheets - Link</title>
    <link rel="stylesheet" type="text/css"
      href="css/site.css" />
    <link rel="stylesheet" type="text/css"
      href="css/tables.css" />
    <link rel="stylesheet" type="text/css"
        href="css/typography.css" />
  </head>
  <body>
    <!-- HTML page content here -->
  </body>
</html>
```

RESULT

Central Park Bike Hire

Rent a bicycle to ride around Central Park:

	Per hour	Per day
Cruiser	$9	$45
21 Speed	$15	$50

WHERE AND WHEN
Loeb Boathouse

From April to November bicycles are available on first come first serve basis for riding in Central Park.

DEPOSITS
Cash or credit card

A $200 deposit is required for the hire of any of our bicycles.

On this page you can see the other technique for including multiple style sheets. Inside the `<head>` element is a separate `<link>` element for each style sheet.

The contents of site.css are identical to styles.css on the left hand page, except the code does not contain @import rules.

As with all style sheets, if two rules apply to the same element then rules that appear later in a document will take precedence over previous rules.

In the example on this page, any rules in typography.css would take precedence over rules in site.css (because the typography rules are included after the other rules).

In the example on the previous page, the rules in styles.css would take precedence over the rules in typography.css. This is because when the @import rule is used, that is the point at which the browser considers the rules live.

EXAMPLE
LAYOUT

This example demonstrates a modern magazine-style layout using the 960.gs grid. Using this style sheet saves us from having to create all of the CSS code ourselves.

Several classes from the 960.gs style sheet have been added to the code to indicate how many columns of the grid each element should stretch across. As you saw in this chapter, the 960.gs stylesheet uses the float property to position the blocks next to each other.

At the start of the page, the header uses fixed positioning (meaning that it does not move when the user scrolls down the page). The z-index property is added to the header to keep it on top of the remaining content as the user scrolls down the page.

Both the header and footer are contained within <div> elements which stretch the entire width of the page. Inside those container elements sit other elements that use classes from the 960.gs style sheet to ensure that the items in the header and footer align with the rest of the content.

The feature article takes up the entire width of the page. The push_7 and push_9 classes are part of the 960.gs style sheet and are used in the feature article to move the header and the content for this article over to the right.

Under the main article you can see four blocks, each of which is 3 columns wide. These contain images followed by links to more articles.

This example also uses background images to create a textured background for the page and header, and also to contain the images for the feature article. You will learn more about these in the next chapter.

Please note: If you view this example in Internet Explorer 6, the transparent PNGs used in this design may have a gray background. To learn more about this issue, visit the website accompanying this book where you can find a simple JavaScript that fixes this problem.

EXAMPLE
LAYOUT

```
<!DOCTYPE html>
<html>
  <head>
    <title>Layout</title>
    <link rel="stylesheet" type="text/css" href="css/960_12_col.css" />
    <style type="text/css">
      @font-face {
        font-family: 'QuicksandBook';
        src: url('fonts/Quicksand_Book-webfont.eot');
        src: url('fonts/Quicksand_Book-webfont.eot?#iefix') format('embedded-opentype'),
          url('fonts/Quicksand_Book-webfont.woff') format('woff'),
          url('fonts/Quicksand_Book-webfont.ttf') format('truetype'),
          url('fonts/Quicksand_Book-webfont.svg#QuicksandBook') format('svg');
        font-weight: normal;
        font-style: normal;}
      body {
        color: #ffffff;
        background: #413f3b url("images/bg.jpg");
        font-family: Georgia, "Times New Roman", Times, serif;
        font-size: 90%;
        margin: 0px;
        text-align: center;}
      a {
        color: #b5c1ad;
        text-decoration: none;}
      a:hover {
        color: #ffffff;}
      .header {
        background-image: url("images/bg-header.jpg");
        padding: 0px 0px 0px 0px;
        height: 100px;
        position: fixed;
        top: 0px;
        width: 100%;
        z-index: 50;}
      .nav {
        float: right;
        font-family: QuicksandBook, Helvetica, Arial, sans-serif;
```

```
  padding: 45px 0px 0px 0px;
  text-align: right;}
.wrapper {
  width: 960px;
  margin: 0px auto;
  background-image: url("images/bg-triangle.png");
  background-repeat: no-repeat;
  background-position: 0px 0px;
  text-align: left;}
.logo {
  margin-bottom: 20px;}
h1, h2 {
  font-family: QuicksandBook, Helvetica, Arial, sans-serif;
  font-weight: normal;
  text-transform: uppercase;}
h1 {
  font-size: 240%;
  margin-top: 140px;}
.date {
  font-family: Arial, Helvetica, sans-serif;
  font-size: 75%;
  color: #b5c1ad;}
.intro {
  clear: left;
  font-size: 90%;
  line-height: 1.4em;}
.main-story {
  background-image: url("images/triangles.png");
  background-repeat: no-repeat;
  background-position: 122px 142px;
  height: 570px;}
.more-articles {
  border-top: 1px solid #ffffff;
  padding: 10px;}
.more-articles p {
  border-bottom: 1px solid #807c72;
  padding: 5px 0px 15px 0px;
  font-size: 80%;}
```

EXAMPLE
LAYOUT

```css
    .more-articles p:last-child {
      border-bottom: none;}
    .footer {
      clear: both;
      background: rgba(0, 0, 0, 0.2);
      padding: 5px 10px;}
    .footer p {
      font-family: Helvetica, Arial, sans-serif;
      font-size: 75%;
      text-align: right;}
    .footer a {
      color: #807c72;}
  </style>
</head>
<body>
  <div class="header">
    <div class="container_12">
      <div class="grid_5">
        <img src="images/logo.png" alt="Pedal Faster - The modern bicycle magazine"
          width="216" height="37" class="logo" />
        <img src="images/header-triangle.png" alt="" width="116" height="100" />
      </div>
      <div class="nav grid_7">
        <a href="">home</a> / <a href="">news</a> / <a href="">archives</a> /
          <a href="">about</a> / <a href="">contact</a>
      </div>
    </div>
  </div>
  <div class="wrapper">
    <div class="main-story container_12">
      <div class="grid_6 push_6">
        <h1><a href="">Fixed Gear Forever</a></h1>
      </div>
      <div class="intro grid_3 push_9">
        <p class="date">16 APRIL 2011</p>
        <p>The veloheld combines minimalist design with superb quality. Devoid of
          excessive graphics and gear shift components, the veloheld product range
          delights us with its beauty and simplicity ... </p>
```

```
          </div>
        </div><!-- .main-story -->
        <div class="more-articles container_12">
          <h2 class="grid_12"><a href="">More Articles</a></h2>
          <div class="grid_3">
            <img src="images/more1.jpg" alt="The road ahead" width="220" height="125" />
            <p><a href="">On the Road: From the fixed gear fanatic's point of view</a></p>
            <p><a href="">Brand History: Pashley Cycles - hand-built in England</a></p>
            <p><a href="">Frame Wars: Innovations in cycle manufacture and repair</a></p>
          </div>
          <div class="grid_3">
            <img src="images/more2.jpg" alt="Sketchbook" width="220" height="125" />
            <p><a href="">Touring Diary: A sketchbook in your basket</a></p>
            <p><a href="">Top Ten Newcomers for 2012: A peek at what's to come</a></p>
            <p><a href="">InnerTube: The best cycling videos on the web</a></p>
          </div>
          <div class="grid_3">
            <img src="images/more3.jpg" alt="Repair shop sign" width="220" height="125" />
            <p><a href="">Product Review: All baskets were not created equal</a></p>
            <p><a href="">Going Public: Out &amp; about with the founder of Public</a></p>
            <p><a href="">Cycle Lane Defence: Know your rights</a></p>
          </div>
          <div class="grid_3">
            <img src="images/more4.jpg" alt="Schwinn Spitfire" width="220" height="125" />
            <p><a href="">Bicycle Hall of Fame: The 1958 Schwinn Spitfire</a></p>
            <p><a href="">Reader Survey: Share your thoughts with us!</a></p>
            <p><a href="">Chain Gang: The evolution of the humble bike chain</a></p>
          </div>
        </div><!-- .more-articles -->
      </div><!-- .wrapper -->
      <div class="footer clearfix">
        <div class="container_12">
          <p class="grid_12"><a href="">Legal Information</a> | <a href="">Privacy
            Policy</a> | <a href="">Copyright &copy; Pedal Faster 2011</a></p>
        </div>
      </div>
    </div>
  </body>
</html>
```

- `<div>` elements are often used as containing elements to group together sections of a page.

- Browsers display pages in normal flow unless you specify relative, absolute, or fixed positioning.

- The `float` property moves content to the left or right of the page and can be used to create multi-column layouts. (Floated items require a defined width.)

- Pages can be fixed width or liquid (stretchy) layouts.

- Designers keep pages within 960-1000 pixels wide, and indicate what the site is about within the top 600 pixels (to demonstrate its relevance without scrolling).

- Grids help create professional and flexible designs.

- CSS Frameworks provide rules for common tasks.

- You can include multiple CSS files in one page.

16

IMAGES

- ▸ Controlling size of images in CSS
- ▸ Aligning images in CSS
- ▸ Adding background images

Controlling the size and alignment of your images using CSS keeps rules that affect the presentation of your page in the CSS and out of the HTML markup.

You can also achieve several interesting effects using background images. In this chapter you will learn how to:

- Specify the size and alignment of an image using CSS
- Add background images to boxes
- Create image rollovers in CSS

CONTROLLING SIZES OF IMAGES IN CSS

You can control the size of an image using the `width` and `height` properties in CSS, just like you can for any other box.

Specifying image sizes helps pages to load more smoothly because the HTML and CSS code will often load before the images, and telling the browser how much space to leave for an image allows it to render the rest of the page without waiting for the image to download.

You might think that your site is likely to have images of all different sizes, but a lot of sites use the same sized image across many of their pages.

For example, an e-commerce site tends to show product photos at the same size. Or, if your site is designed on a grid, then you might have a selection of image sizes that are commonly used on all pages, such as:

Small portrait: 220 x 360
Small landscape: 330 x 210
Feature photo: 620 x 400

Whenever you use consistently sized images across a site, you can use CSS to control the dimensions of the images, instead of putting the dimensions in the HTML.

chapter-16/image-sizes.html `HTML`

```html
<img src="images/magnolia-large.jpg"
    class="large" alt="Magnolia" />
<img src="images/magnolia-medium.jpg"
    class="medium" alt="Magnolia" />
<img src="images/magnolia-small.jpg"
    class="small" alt="Magnolia" />
```

`CSS`

```css
img.large {
  width: 500px;
  height: 500px;}
img.medium {
  width: 250px;
  height: 250px;}
img.small {
  width: 100px;
  height: 100px;}
```

RESULT

First you need to determine the sizes of images that will be used commonly throughout the site, then give each size a name.

For example:
small
medium
large

Where the `<img>` elements appear in the HTML, rather than using `width` and `height` attributes you can use these names as values for the `class` attribute.

In the CSS, you add selectors for each of the class names, then use the CSS `width` and `height` properties to control the image dimensions.

ALIGNING IMAGES USING CSS

In the last chapter, you saw how the `float` property can be used to move an element to the left or the right of its containing block, allowing text to flow around it.

Rather than using the `<img>` element's `align` attribute, web page authors are increasingly using the `float` property to align images. There are two ways that this is commonly achieved:

1: The `float` property is added to the class that was created to represent the size of the image (such as the `small` class in our example).

2: New classes are created with names such as `align-left` or `align-right` to align the images to the left or right of the page. These class names are used in addition to classes that indicate the size of the image.

In this example you can see the `align-left` and `align-right` classes used to align the image.

It is also common to add a margin to the image to ensure that the text does not touch their edges.

chapter-16/aligning-images.html

HTML

```
<p><img src="images/magnolia-medium.jpg"
  alt="Magnolia" class="align-left medium" />
  <b><i>Magnolia</i></b> is a large genus that
  contains over 200 flowering plant species...</p>
<p><img src="images/magnolia-medium.jpg"
  alt="Magnolia" class="align-right medium" />
  Some magnolias, such as <i>Magnolia stellata</i>
  and <i>Magnolia soulangeana</i>, flower quite
  early in the spring before the leaves open...</p>
```

CSS

```
img.align-left {
  float: left;
  margin-right: 10px;}
img.align-right {
  float: right;
  margin-left: 10px;}
img.medium {
  width: 250px;
  height: 250px;}
```

RESULT

Magnolia is a large genus that contains over 200 flowering plant species. It is named after French botanist Pierre Magnol, and having evolved before bees appeared the flowers were developed to encourage pollination by beetles.

Some magnolias, such as *Magnolia stellata* and *Magnolia soulangeana*, flower quite early in the spring before the leaves open. Others flower in late spring or early summer, such as *Magnolia grandiflora*.

CENTERING IMAGES USING CSS

`chapter-16/centering-images.html`

```html
<p><img src="images/magnolia-medium.jpg"
    alt="Magnolia" class="align-center medium" />
<b><i>Magnolia</i></b> is a large genus that
contains over 200 flowering plant species. It
is named after French botanist Pierre Magnol and,
having evolved before bees appeared, the
flowers were developed to encourage pollination
by beetles.</p>
```

CSS

```css
img.align-center {
  display: block;
  margin: 0px auto;}
img.medium {
  width: 250px;
  height: 250px;}
```

RESULT

Magnolia is a large genus that contains over 200 flowering plant species. It is named after French botanist Pierre Magnol and, having evolved before bees appeared, the flowers were developed to encourage pollination by beetles.

By default, images are inline elements. This means that they flow within the surrounding text. In order to center an image, it should be turned into a block-level element using the `display` property with a value of `block`.

Once it has been made into a block-level element, there are two common ways in which you can horizontally center an image:

1: On the containing element, you can use the `text-align` property with a value of `center`.

2: On the image itself, you can use the `margin` property and set the values of the left and right margins to `auto`.

You can specify class names that allow any element to be centered, in the same way that you can for the dimensions or alignment of images.

The techniques for specifying image size and alignment of images can also be used with the HTML5 `<figure>` element, which you met on page 120.

BACKGROUND IMAGES
background-image

The background-image property allows you to place an image behind any HTML element. This could be the entire page or just part of the page. By default, a background image will repeat to fill the entire box.

The path to the image follows the letters url, and it is put inside parentheses and quotes.

 Here is the image tile used in this example.

In the first example, you can see a background image being applied to an entire page (because the CSS selector applies to the <body> element). In the second example, the background image just applies to a paragraph.

If you search online, you will find lots of resources that offer background textures that you can use on your pages.

Background images are often the last thing on the page to load (which can make a website seem slow to load). As with any images you use online, if the size of the file is large it will take longer to download.

chapter-16/background-image-body.html `CSS`

```
body {
  background-image: url("images/pattern.gif");}
```

`RESULT`

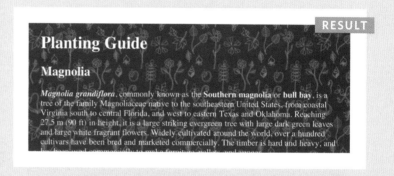

chapter-16/background-image-element.html `CSS`

```
p {
  background-image: url("images/pattern.gif");}
```

`RESULT`

Planting Guide

Magnolia

Magnolia grandiflora, commonly known as the **Southern magnolia** or bull bay, is a tree of the family Magnoliaceae native to the southeastern United States, from coastal Virginia south to central Florida, and west to eastern Texas and Oklahoma. Reaching 27.5 m (90 ft) in height, it is a large striking evergreen tree with large dark green leaves and large white fragrant flowers. Widely cultivated around the

REPEATING IMAGES
background-repeat
background-attachment

```
body {
  background-image: url("images/header.gif");
  background-repeat: repeat-x;}
```

RESULT

Planting Guide

Magnolia

Magnolia grandiflora, commonly known as the **Southern magnolia** or **bull bay**, is a tree of the family Magnoliaceae native to the southeastern United States, from coastal Virginia south to central Florida, and west to eastern Texas and Oklahoma. Reaching 27.5 m (90 ft) in height, it is a large striking evergreen tree with large dark green leaves and large white fragrant flowers. Widely cultivated around the world, over a hundred

```
body {
  background-image: url("images/tulip.gif");
  background-repeat: no-repeat;
  background-attachment: fixed;}
```

RESULT

Planting Guide

Magnolia

Magnolia grandiflora, commonly known as the **Southern magnolia** or **bull bay**, is a tree of the family Magnoliaceae native to the southeastern United States, from coastal Virginia south to central Florida, and west to eastern Texas and Oklahoma. Reaching 27.5 m (90 ft) in height, it is a large striking evergreen tree with large dark green leaves and large white fragrant flowers. Widely cultivated around the world, over a hundred

The background-repeat property can have four values:

repeat
The background image is repeated both horizontally and vertically (the default way it is shown if the background-repeat property isn't used).

repeat-x
The image is repeated horizontally only (as shown in the first example on the left).

repeat-y
The image is repeated vertically only.

no-repeat
The image is only shown once.

The background-attachment property specifies whether a background image should stay in one position or move as the user scrolls up and down the page. It can have one of two values:

fixed
The background image stays in the same position on the page.

scroll
The background image moves up and down as the user scrolls up and down the page.

BACKGROUND POSITION
background-position

When an image is not being repeated, you can use the `background-position` property to specify where in the browser window the background image should be placed.

This property usually has a pair of values. The first represents the horizontal position and the second represents the vertical.

left top

left center

left bottom

center top

center center

center bottom

right top

right center

right bottom

If you only specify one value, the second value will default to `center`.

You can also use a pair of pixels or percentages. These represent the distance from the top left corner of the browser window (or containing box). The top left corner is equal to `0% 0%`. The example shown, with values of `50% 50%`, centers the image horizontally and vertically.

`chapter-16/background-position.html` **CSS**

```
body {
  background-image: url("images/tulip.gif");
  background-repeat: no-repeat;
  background-position: center top;}
```

RESULT

Planting Guide

Magnolia

Magnolia grandiflora, commonly known as the **Southern magnolia** or **bull bay**, is a tree of the family Magnoliaceae native to the southeastern United States, from coastal Virginia south to central Florida, and west to eastern Texas and Oklahoma. Reaching 27.5 m (90 ft) in height, it is a large striking evergreen tree with large dark green leaves and large white fragrant flowers. Widely cultivated around the world, over a hundred

`chapter-16/background-position-percentage.html` **CSS**

```
body {
  background-image: url("images/tulip.gif");
  background-repeat: no-repeat;
  background-position: 50% 50%;}
```

RESULT

Planting Guide

Magnolia

Magnolia grandiflora, commonly known as the **Southern magnolia** or **bull bay**, is a tree of the family Magnoliaceae native to the southeastern United States, from coastal Virginia south to central Florida, and west to eastern Texas and Oklahoma. Reaching 27.5 m (90 ft) in height, it is a large striking evergreen tree with large dark green leaves and large white fragrant flowers. Widely cultivated around the world, over a hundred cultivars have been bred and marketed commercially. The timber is hard and heavy, and has been used commercially to make furniture, pallets, and veneer.

SHORTHAND
background

```css
body {
  background: #ffffff url("images/tulip.gif")
    no-repeat top right;}
```

The background property acts like a shorthand for all of the other background properties you have just seen, and also the background-color property.

The properties must be specified in the following order, but you can miss any value if you do not want to specify it.

```
1: background-color
2: background-image
3: background-repeat
4: background-attachment
5: background-position
```

CSS3 will also support the use of multiple background images by repeating the background shorthand. Because few browsers supported this property at the time of writing, it was not commonly used.

```css
div {
  background:
    url(example-1.jpg)
    no-repeat top left,
    url(example-2.jpg)
    no-repeat bottom left,
    url(example-3.jpg)
    repeat-x center top;}
```

The first image is shown on top, with the last one on the bottom.

RESULT

Planting Guide

Magnolia

Magnolia grandiflora, commonly known as the **Southern magnolia** or **bull bay**, is a tree of the family Magnoliaceae native to the southeastern United States, from coastal Virginia south to central Florida, and west to eastern Texas and Oklahoma. Reaching 27.5 m (90 ft) in height, it is a large striking evergreen tree with large dark green leaves and large white fragrant flowers. Widely cultivated around the world, over a hundred cultivars have been bred and marketed commercially. The timber is hard and heavy, and has been used commercially to make furniture, pallets, and veneer.

Ranunculus

Ranunculus asiaticus (Persian Buttercup) is a species of buttercup (Ranunculus) native to the eastern Mediterranean region in southwestern Asia, southeastern Europe (Crete, Karpathos and Rhodes), and northeastern Africa. It is a herbaceous perennial plant growing to 45 cm tall, with simple or branched stems. The basal leaves are three-lobed, with leaves higher on the stems more deeply divided; like the stems, they are downy or hairy. The flowers are 3-5 cm diameter, variably red to pink, yellow, or white, with one to several flowers on each stem.

Tulip

Tulipa gesneriana L. or "Didier's tulip" is a plant belonging to the family of Liliaceae. This species has uncertain origins, possibly from Asia, and has become naturalised in south-west Europe. Most of the cultivated species, subspecies and cultivars of tulip are derived from Tulipa gesneriana. The flower and bulb can cause dermatitis through the allergen, tuliposide A, even though the bulbs may be consumed with little ill-effect. The sweet-scented bisexual flowers appear during April and May. Bulbs are extremely resistant to frost, and can tolerate temperatures well below freezing - a period of low temperature is necessary to induce proper growth and flowering, triggered by an increase in sensitivity to the phytohormone auxin. The bulbs may be dried and pulverised and added to cereals or flour.

IMAGE ROLLOVERS
& SPRITES

Using CSS, it is possible to create a link or button that changes to a second style when a user moves their mouse over it (known as a **rollover**) and a third style when they click on it.

This is achieved by setting a background image for the link or button that has three different styles of the same button (but only allows enough space to show one of them at a time). You can see the image we are using in this example on the right. It actually features two buttons on the one image.

When the user moves their mouse over the element, or clicks on it, the position of the background image is moved to show the relevant image.

When a single image is used for several different parts of an interface, it is known as a **sprite**. You can add the logo and other interface elements, as well as buttons to the image.

The advantage of using sprites is that the web browser only needs to request one image rather than many images, which can make the web page load faster.

chapter-16/image-rollovers-and-sprites.html `HTML`

```html
<a class="button" id="add-to-basket">
   Add to basket</a>
<a class="button" id="framing-options">
   Framing options</a>
```

`CSS`

```css
a.button {
  height: 36px;
  background-image: url("images/button-sprite.jpg");
  text-indent: -9999px;
  display: inline-block;}
a#add-to-basket {
  width: 174px;
  background-position: 0px 0px;}
a#framing-options {
  width: 210px;
  background-position: -175px 0px;}
a#add-to-basket:hover {
  background-position: 0px -40px;}
a#framing-options:hover {
  background-position: -175px -40px;}
a#add-to-basket:active {
  background-position: 0px -80px;}
a#framing-options:active {
  background-position: -175px -80px;}
```

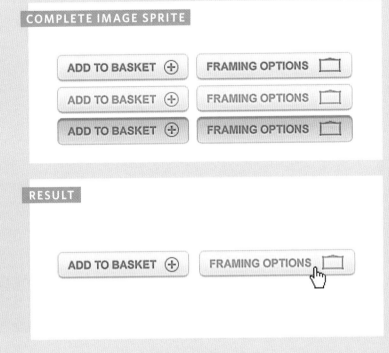

COMPLETE IMAGE SPRITE

RESULT

In this example, you can see two links that look like buttons. Each of the buttons has three different states. These are all represented in a single image.

Because the <a> element is an inline element, we set the display property of these links to indicate that they should be inline-block elements. This allows us to specify the width and height of each <a> element so that it matches the size of its corresponding button.

The background-position property is used to move the image in order to show the button in the right state.

When the user hovers over a link, the :hover pseudo-class has a rule that moves the background-position of the image to show a different state for that button.

Similarly, when the user clicks on the link, the :active pseudo-class has a rule to show the third state for that button.

Touch screen devices will not change a link's state when the user hovers over it, as the screens do not yet have a way to tell when the user is hovering. However, they will change their appearance when the user activates them.

CSS3: GRADIENTS
background-image

CSS3 is going to introduce the ability to specify a gradient for the background of a box. The gradient is created using the `background-image` property and, at the time of writing, different browsers required a different syntax.

Since it is not supported by all browsers, it is possible to specify a background image for the box first (which would represent the gradient) and then provide the CSS alternatives for browsers that support gradients.

On this page, we are focusing on linear gradients. You can see that in order to create a linear gradient, we need to specify two colors (that the gradient is between).

Some browsers allow you to specify the angle of the gradient, or even different types of gradients (such as radial gradients), but support is not as widespread as that for linear gradients.

chapter-16/gradient.html | CSS

```css
#gradient {
  /* fallback color */
  background-color: #66cccc;
  /* fallback image */
  background-image:url("images/fallback-image.png");
  /* Firefox 3.6+ */
  background-image: -moz-linear-gradient(#336666,
    #66cccc);
  /* Safari 4+, Chrome 1+ */
  background-image: -webkit-gradient(linear, 0% 0%,
    0% 100%, from(#66cccc), to(#336666));
  /* Safari 5.1+, Chrome 10+ */
  background-image: -webkit-linear-gradient(#336666,
    #66cccc);
  /* Opera 11.10+ */
  background-image: -o-linear-gradient(#336666,
    #66cccc);
  height: 150px;
  width: 300px;}
```

RESULT

CONTRAST OF BACKGROUND IMAGES

If you want to overlay text on a background image, the image must be low contrast in order for the text to be legible.

HIGH CONTRAST

A high contrast background image makes the text difficult to read.

LOW CONTRAST

A low contrast background image makes the text easier to read.

SCREEN

A screen added to a high contrast image makes the text easier to read.

The majority of photographs have quite a high contrast, which means that they are not ideal for use as a background image.

Image editing applications such as Photoshop and GIMP have tools that allow you to manually adjust your images to have lower contrast.

To overlay text on an image with high contrast, you can place a semi-transparent background color (or "screen") behind the text to improve legibility.

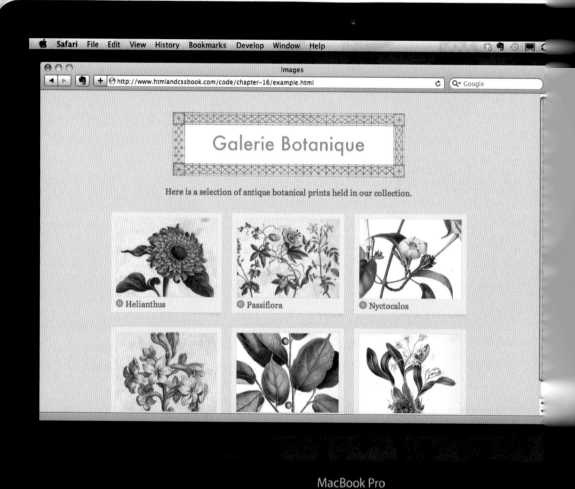

EXAMPLE
IMAGES

This example demonstrates how to use CSS to create a simple image gallery layout.

A background texture is applied to the whole page by repeating an image with the texture behind the <body> element. A repeating background image is sometimes referred to as **wallpaper**.

The content of the page is put inside a <div> element whose class is wrapper. This is used to fix the width of the page to 720 pixels. Its left and right margins are set to auto to center it in the middle of the screen.

The images sit inside an HTML5 <figure> element, and their captions are provided in the <figcaption> element. CSS is used to set the dimensions and background color for each <figure> element. The dimensions of the images themselves are also set using CSS, and they are given a single pixel gray border.

For the captions, a background image is used to the left of the text. We do not want this image to fill the background so we specify that it should not repeat. Padding is used to the left of the text so that the words do not go over the background image.

Each of the <figure> elements is contained within a <div>, which has two purposes. Firstly, it is used to create the three-column layout by specifying a width and margins for the element and then floating it to the left. Secondly, it adds a subtle shadow underneath each image. This creates a three-dimensional appearance making it look like a piece of card. To ensure that this sits underneath the image, the background-position property is used.

EXAMPLE
IMAGES

```html
<!DOCTYPE html>
<html>
  <head>
    <title>Images</title>
    <style type="text/css">
      body {
        color: #665544;
        background-color: #d4d0c6;
        background-image: url("images/backdrop.gif");
        font-family: Georgia, "Times New Roman", serif;
        text-align: center;}
      .wrapper {
        width: 720px;
        margin: 0px auto;}
      .header {
        margin: 40px 0px 20px 0px;}
      .entry {
        width: 220px;
        float: left;
        margin: 10px;
        height: 198px;
        background-image: url("images/shadow.png");
        background-repeat: no-repeat;
        background-position: bottom;}
      figure {
        display: block;
        width: 202px;
        height: 170px;
        background-color: #e7e3d8;
        margin: 0px;
        padding: 9px;
        text-align: left;}
      figure img {
        width: 200px;
        height: 150px;
        border: 1px solid #d6d6d6;}
      figcaption {
        background-image: url("images/icon.png") no-repeat;
        padding-left: 20px;}
    </style>
```

```
    </head>
    <body>
      <div class="wrapper">
        <div class="header">
          <img src="images/title.gif" alt="Galerie Botanique" width="456" height="122" />
          <p>Here is a selection of antique botanical prints held in our collection.</p>
        </div>
        <div class="entry">
          <figure><img src="images/print-01.jpg" alt="Helianthus" />
            <figcaption>Helianthus</figcaption>
          </figure>
        </div>
        <div class="entry">
          <figure><img src="images/print-02.jpg" alt="Passiflora" />
            <figcaption>Passiflora</figcaption>
          </figure>
        </div>
        <div class="entry">
          <figure><img src="images/print-03.jpg" alt="Nyctocalos" />
            <figcaption>Nyctocalos</figcaption>
          </figure>
        </div>
        <div class="entry">
          <figure><img src="images/print-04.jpg" alt="Polianthes" />
            <figcaption>Polianthes</figcaption>
          </figure>
        </div>
        <div class="entry">
          <figure><img src="images/print-05.jpg" alt="Ficus" />
            <figcaption>Ficus</figcaption>
          </figure>
        </div>
        <div class="entry">
          <figure><img src="images/print-06.jpg" alt="Dendrobium" />
            <figcaption>Dendrobium</figcaption>
          </figure>
        </div>
      </div>
    </body>
</html>
```

▸ You can specify the dimensions of images using CSS. This is very helpful when you use the same sized images on several pages of your site.

▸ Images can be aligned both horizontally and vertically using CSS.

▸ You can use a background image behind the box created by any element on a page.

▸ Background images can appear just once or be repeated across the background of the box.

▸ You can create image rollover effects by moving the background position of an image.

▸ To reduce the number of images your browser has to load, you can create image sprites.

17

HTML5 LAYOUT

- ▸ HTML5 layout elements
- ▸ How old browsers understand new elements
- ▸ Styling HTML5 layout elements with CSS

HTML5 is introducing a new set of elements that help define the structure of a page.

They are covered here (rather than with the other HTML elements you met earlier in the book) because you'll find it easier to understand how they can be used now that you have seen how CSS can control the layout of a page. These new elements are going to play an important part in creating layouts going forward. In this chapter you will see:

- The new HTML5 layout elements and their uses

- How they offer helpful alternatives to the `<div>` element

- How to ensure older browsers recognize these elements

As with all HTML5 and CSS3 content, its usage is still subject to change but it is already widely being used by web developers and it is likely that you will want to use them.

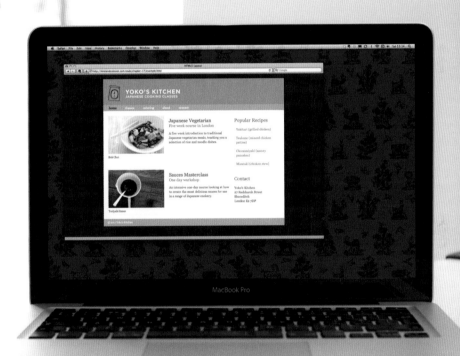

TRADITIONAL HTML LAYOUTS

For a long time, web page authors used `<div>` elements to group together related elements on the page (such as the elements that form a header, an article, footer or sidebar). Authors used `class` or `id` attributes to indicate the role of the `<div>` element in the structure of the page.

On the right you can see a layout that is quite common (particularly on blog sites).

At the top of the page is the header, containing a logo and the primary navigation.

Under this are one or more articles or posts. Sometimes these are summaries that link to individual posts.

There is a side bar on the right-hand side (perhaps featuring a search option, links to other recent articles, other sections of the site, or even ads).

When coding a site like this, developers would usually put these main sections of the page inside `<div>` elements and use the `class` or `id` attributes to indicate the purpose of that part of the page.

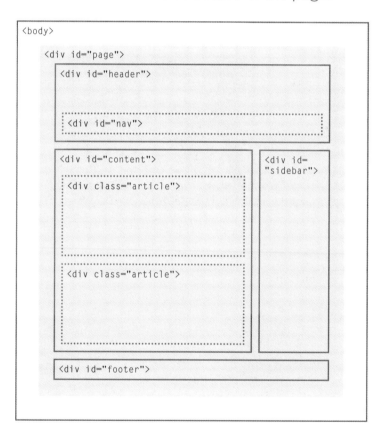

NEW HTML5 LAYOUT ELEMENTS

HTML5 introduces a new set of elements that allow you to divide up the parts of a page. The names of these elements indicate the kind of content you will find in them. They are still subject to change, but that has not stopped many web page authors from using them already.

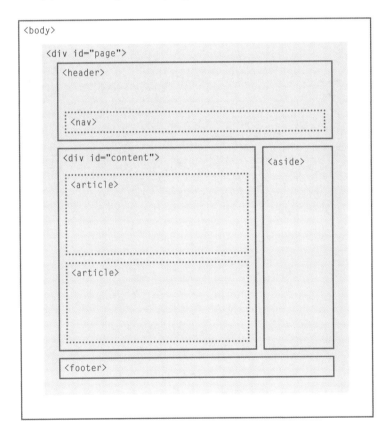

This example has exactly the same structure as seen on the previous page. However, many of the `<div>` elements have been replaced by new HTML5 layout elements.

For example, the header sits inside a new `<header>` element, the navigation in a `<nav>` element, and the articles are in individual `<article>` elements.

The point of creating these new elements is so that web page authors can use them to help describe the structure of the page. For example, screen reader software might allow users to ignore headers and footers and get straight to the content. Similarly, search engines might place more weight on the content in an `<article>` element than that in the `<header>` or `<footer>` elements. I think you will agree that it also makes the code easier to follow.

HEADERS & FOOTERS
<header> <footer>

The <header> and <footer> elements can be used for:

- The main header or footer that appears at the top or bottom of every page on the site
- A header or footer for an individual <article> or <section> within the page

In this example, the <header> element is used to contain the site name and the main navigation. The <footer> element contains copyright information.

Each individual <article> and <section> element can also have its own <header> and <footer> elements to hold the header or footer information for that section within the page.

For example, on a page with several blog posts, each individual post can be thought of as a separate section. The <header> element can therefore be used to contain the title and date of each individual post, and the <footer> might contain links to share the article on social networking sites.

Please note that all of the code shown in this chapter is referenced in one HTML document which is called: example.html

chapter-17/example.html `HTML`

```html
<header>
  <h1>Yoko's Kitchen</h1>
  <nav>
    <ul>
      <li><a href="" class="current">home</a></li>
      <li><a href="">classes</a></li>
      <li><a href="">catering</a></li>
      <li><a href="">about</a></li>
      <li><a href="">contact</a></li>
    </ul>
  </nav>
</header>
```

chapter-17/example.html `HTML`

```html
<footer>
  &copy; 2011 Yoko's Kitchen
</footer>
```

NAVIGATION
<nav>

```
HTML                                    chapter-17/example.html

<nav>
  <ul>
    <li><a href="" class="current">home</a></li>
    <li><a href="">classes</a></li>
    <li><a href="">catering</a></li>
    <li><a href="">about</a></li>
    <li><a href="">contact</a></li>
  </ul>
</nav>
```

The <nav> element is used to contain the major navigational blocks on the site such as the primary site navigation.

Going back to our blog example, if you wanted to finish an article with links to related blog posts, these would not be counted as major navigational blocks and therefore should not sit inside a <nav> element.

At the time of writing, some of the developers that were already using HTML5 decided to use the <nav> element for the links that appear at the bottom of every page (links to things like privacy policy, terms and conditions and accessibility information). Whether this will be widely adopted is still yet to be seen.

ARTICLES
\<article\>

The \<article\> element acts as
a container for any section of a
page that could stand alone and
potentially be syndicated.

This could be an individual
article or blog entry, a comment
or forum post, or any other
independent piece of content.

If a page contains several articles
(or even summaries of several
articles), then each individual
article would live inside its own
\<article\> element.

The \<article\> elements can
even be nested inside each
other. For example, a blog post
might live inside one \<article\>
element and each comment on
the article could live inside its
own child \<article\> element.

```
chapter-17/example.html                              HTML
<article>
  <figure>
    <img src="images/bok-choi.jpg" alt="Bok Choi" />
    <figcaption>Bok Choi</figcaption>
  </figure>
  <hgroup>
    <h2>Japanese Vegetarian</h2>
    <h3>Five week course in London</h3>
  </hgroup>
  <p>A five week introduction to traditional
    Japanese vegetarian meals, teaching you a
    selection of rice and noodle dishes.</p>
</article>
<article>
  <figure>
    <img src="images/teriyaki.jpg"
         alt="Teriyaki sauce" />
    <figcaption>Teriyaki Sauce</figcaption>
  </figure>
  <hgroup>
    <h2>Sauces Masterclass</h2>
    <h3>One day workshop</h3>
  </hgroup>
  <p>An intensive one-day course looking at how to
    create the most delicious sauces for use in a
    range of Japanese cookery.</p>
</article>
```

ASIDES
`<aside>`

```
<aside>
  <section class="popular-recipes">
    <h2>Popular Recipes</h2>
    <a href="">Yakitori (grilled chicken)</a>
    <a href="">Tsukune (minced chicken patties)</a>
    <a href="">Okonomiyaki (savory pancakes)</a>
    <a href="">Mizutaki (chicken stew)</a>
  </section>
  <section class="contact-details">
    <h2>Contact</h2>
    <p>Yoko's Kitchen<br />
       27 Redchurch Street<br />
       Shoreditch<br />
       London E2 7DP</p>
  </section>
</aside>
```

The `<aside>` element has two purposes, depending on whether it is inside an `<article>` element or not.

When the `<aside>` element is used inside an `<article>` element, it should contain information that is related to the article but not essential to its overall meaning. For example, a pullquote or glossary might be considered as an aside to the article it relates to.

When the `<aside>` element is used outside of an `<article>` element, it acts as a container for content that is related to the entire page. For example, it might contain links to other sections of the site, a list of recent posts, a search box, or recent tweets by the author.

SECTIONS
\<section\>

The \<section\> element groups related content together, and typically each section would have its own heading.

For example, on a homepage there may be several \<section\> elements to contain different sections of the page, such as latest news, top products, and newsletter signup.

Because the \<section\> element groups related items together, it may contain several distinct \<article\> elements that have a common theme or purpose.

Alternatively, if you have a page with a long article, the \<section\> element can be used to split the article up into separate sections.

The \<section\> element should not be used as a wrapper for the entire page (unless the page only contains one distinct piece of content). If you want a containing element for the entire page, that job is still best left to the \<div\> element.

```
chapter-17/example.html                              HTML

<section class="popular-recipes">
  <h2>Popular Recipes</h2>
  <a href="">Yakitori (grilled chicken)</a>
  <a href="">Tsukune (minced chicken patties)</a>
  <a href="">Okonomiyaki (savory pancakes)</a>
  <a href="">Mizutaki (chicken stew)</a>
</section>
<section class="contact-details">
  <h2>Contact</h2>
  <p>Yoko's Kitchen<br />
     27 Redchurch Street<br />
     Shoreditch<br />
     London E2 7DP</p>
</section>
```

HEADING GROUPS
<hgroup>

```
HTML                          chapter-17/example.html

<hgroup>
  <h2>Japanese Vegetarian</h2>
  <h3>Five week course in London</h3>
</hgroup>
```

The purpose of the <hgroup> element is to group together a set of one or more <h1> through <h6> elements so that they are treated as one single heading.

For example, the <hgroup> element could be used to contain both a title inside an <h2> element and a subtitle within an <h3> element.

This element has had a mixed reception. When it was first proposed by the people developing HTML5, there were some complaints and it was withdrawn from the HTML5 proposals. However, some people changed their minds and it has been added back into the language. Some developers do not like the use of the <hgroup> element and prefer to place a subtitle inside a <p> element (using an attribute to indicate that it is a subheading).

Some suggest that it is of little use other than as a styling hook. It has, however, been popular with those developers who believe that it is useful to group together the primary heading and the subheading (as both can be integral parts of a heading).

FIGURES
`<figure>` `<figcaption>`

You already met the `<figure>` element in Chapter 5 when we looked at images. It can be used to contain any content that is referenced from the main flow of an article (not just images).

It is important to note that the article should still make sense if the content of the `<figure>` element were moved (to another part of the page, or even to a different page altogether).

For this reason, it should only be used when the content simply references the element (and not for something that is absolutely integral to the flow of a page).

Examples of usage include:

- Images
- Videos
- Graphs
- Diagrams
- Code samples
- Text that supports the main body of an article

The `<figure>` element should also contain a `<figcaption>` element which provides a text decription for the content of the `<figure>` element. In this example, you can see a `<figure>` has been added inside the `<article>` element.

chapter-17/example.html   `HTML`

```html
<figure>
  <img src="images/bok-choi.jpg" alt="Bok Choi" />
  <figcaption>Bok Choi</figcaption>
</figure>
```

SECTIONING ELEMENTS
<div>

```
<div class="wrapper">
  <header>
    <h1>Yoko's Kitchen</h1>
    <nav>
      <!-- nav content here -->
    </nav>
  </header>
  <section class="courses">
    <!-- section content here -->
  </section>
  <aside>
    <!-- aside content here -->
  </aside>
  <footer>
    <!-- footer content here -->
  </footer>
</div><!-- .wrapper -->
```

It may seem strange to follow these new elements by revisiting the <div> element again. (After all, the new elements are often going to be used in its place.)

However, the <div> element will remain an important way to group together related elements, because you should not be using these new elements that you have just met for purposes other than those explicitly stated.

Where there is no suitable element to group a set of elements, the <div> element will still be used. In this example, it is used as a wrapper for the entire page.

Some people have asked why there is no <content> element to contain the main part of a page. The reason is that anything that lies outside of the <header>, <footer> or <aside> elements can be considered as the main content.

LINKING AROUND BLOCK-LEVEL ELEMENTS

HTML5 allows web page authors to place an <a> element around a block level element that contains child elements. This allows you to turn an entire block into a link.

This is not a new element in HTML5, but it was not seen as a correct usage of the <a> element in earlier versions of HTML.

Please note that this page uses slightly different code than the other examples in this chapter.

```
chapter-17/example-with-links.html                    HTML
<a href="introduction.html">
  <article>
    <figure>
      <img src="images/bok-choi.jpg"
           alt="Bok Choi" />
      <figcaption>Bok Choi</figcaption>
    </figure>
    <hgroup>
      <h2>Japanese Vegetarian</h2>
      <h3>Five week course in London</h3>
    </hgroup>
    <p>A five week introduction to traditional
     Japanese vegetarian meals, teaching you a
     selection of rice and noodle dishes.</p>
  </article>
</a>
```

HELPING OLDER BROWSERS UNDERSTAND

```css
header, section, footer, aside, nav, article,
figure, figcaption {
  display: block;}
```

```html
<!--[if lt IE 9]>
  <script src="http://html5shiv.googlecode.com/svn/
    trunk/html5.js"></script>
<![endif]-->
```

Older browsers that do not know the new HTML5 elements will automatically treat them as inline elements. Therefore, to help older browsers, you should include the line of CSS on the left which states which new elements should be rendered as block-level elements.

Also, IE9 was the first version of Internet Explorer to allow CSS rules to be associated with these new HTML5 layout elements. In order to style these elements using earlier versions of IE, you need to use a simple JavaScript known as the **HTML5 shiv** or **HTML5 shim**.

You do not need to understand JavaScript to use it. You can just link to a copy that Google hosts on its servers. It should be placed inside a **conditional comment** which checks if the browser version is less than (hence the 1t) IE9.

Unfortunately, this workaround does require that anyone using IE8 or earlier versions of IE has JavaScript enabled in their browser. If they do not have JavaScript enabled then they will not be able to see the content of these HTML5 elements.

EXAMPLE
HTML5 LAYOUT

This example shows a cooking site built using new HTML5 elements to describe the structure of the page (rather than just grouping items using <div> elements).

The header and footer of the page sit inside <header> and <footer> elements. The courses are grouped together inside a <section> element that has a class attribute whose value is courses (to distinguish it from other <section> elements on the page). The sidebar sits inside an <aside> element.

Each of the courses lives inside an <article> element, and use the <figure> and <figcaption> elements to contain an image. The headings for the courses have subheadings, so these are grouped inside an <hgroup> element. In the sidebar, the recipes and contact details are placed inside separate <section> elements.

The page is styled using CSS. The only difference is that our selectors are using the new HTML5 elements to allow us to create rules that target those elements. In order for the CSS to work in versions of IE before Internet Explorer 9, the HTML5 page contains a link to the HTML5 shiv JavaScript (hosted on Google's servers) inside a conditional comment.

EXAMPLE
HTML5 LAYOUT

```
<!DOCTYPE html>
<html>
  <head>
    <title>HTML5 Layout</title>
    <style type="text/css">
      header, section, footer, aside, nav, article, figure, figcaption {
        display: block;}
      body {
        color: #666666;
        background-color: #f9f8f6;
        background-image: url("images/dark-wood.jpg");
        background-position: center;
        font-family: Georgia, Times, serif;
        line-height: 1.4em;
        margin: 0px;}
      .wrapper {
        width: 940px;
        margin: 20px auto 20px auto;
        border: 2px solid #000000;
        background-color: #ffffff;}
      header {
        height: 160px;
        background-image: url("images/header.jpg");}
      h1 {
        text-indent: -9999px;
        width: 940px;
        height: 130px;
        margin: 0px;}
      nav, footer {
        clear: both;
        color: #ffffff;
        background-color: #aeaca8;
        height: 30px;}
      nav ul {
        margin: 0px;
        padding: 5px 0px 5px 30px;}
      nav li {
        display: inline;
        margin-right: 40px;}
      nav li a {
```

```
  color: #ffffff;}
nav li a:hover, nav li a.current {
  color: #000000;}
section.courses {
  float: left;
  width: 659px;
  border-right: 1px solid #eeeeee;}
article {
  clear: both;
  overflow: auto;
  width: 100%;}
hgroup {
  margin-top: 40px;}
figure {
  float: left;
  width: 290px;
  height: 220px;
  padding: 5px;
  margin: 20px;
  border: 1px solid #eeeeee;}
figcaption {
  font-size: 90%;
  text-align: left;}
aside {
  width: 230px;
  float: left;
  padding: 0px 0px 0px 20px;}
aside section a {
  display: block;
  padding: 10px;
  border-bottom: 1px solid #eeeeee;}
aside section a:hover {
  color: #985d6a;
  background-color: #efefef;}
a {
  color: #de6581;
  text-decoration: none;}
h1, h2, h3 {
  font-weight: normal;}
h2 {
```

```
      margin: 10px 0px 5px 0px;
      padding: 0px;}
    h3 {
      margin: 0px 0px 10px 0px;
      color: #de6581;}
    aside h2 {
      padding: 30px 0px 10px 0px;
      color: #de6581;}
    footer {
      font-size: 80%;
      padding: 7px 0px 0px 20px;}
  </style>
  <!--[if lt IE 9]>
  <script src="http://html5shiv.googlecode.com/svn/trunk/html5.js"></script>
  <![endif]-->
</head>
<body>
  <div class="wrapper">
    <header>
      <h1>Yoko's Kitchen</h1>
      <nav>
        <ul>
          <li><a href="" class="current">home</a></li>
          <li><a href="">classes</a></li>
          <li><a href="">catering</a></li>
          <li><a href="">about</a></li>
          <li><a href="">contact</a></li>
        </ul>
      </nav>
    </header>
    <section class="courses">
      <article>
        <figure>
          <img src="images/bok-choi.jpg" alt="Bok Choi" />
          <figcaption>Bok Choi</figcaption>
        </figure>
        <hgroup>
          <h2>Japanese Vegetarian</h2>
          <h3>Five week course in London</h3>
        </hgroup>
```

```
    <p>A five week introduction to traditional Japanese vegetarian meals,
        teaching you a selection of rice and noodle dishes.</p>
  </article>
  <article>
    <figure>
      <img src="images/teriyaki.jpg" alt="Teriyaki sauce" />
      <figcaption>Teriyaki Sauce</figcaption>
    </figure>
    <hgroup>
      <h2>Sauces Masterclass</h2>
      <h3>One day workshop</h3>
    </hgroup>
    <p>An intensive one-day course looking at how to create the most delicious
        sauces for use in a range of Japanese cookery.</p>
  </article>
</section>
<aside>
  <section class="popular-recipes">
    <h2>Popular Recipes</h2>
    <a href="">Yakitori (grilled chicken)</a>
    <a href="">Tsukune (minced chicken patties)</a>
    <a href="">Okonomiyaki (savory pancakes)</a>
    <a href="">Mizutaki (chicken stew)</a>
  </section>
  <section class="contact-details">
    <h2>Contact</h2>
    <p>Yoko's Kitchen<br />
        27 Redchurch Street<br />
        Shoreditch<br />
        London E2 7DP</p>
  </section>
</aside>
<footer>
  &copy; 2011 Yoko's Kitchen
</footer>
    </div><!-- .wrapper -->
  </body>
</html>
```

▸ The new HTML5 elements indicate the purpose of different parts of a web page and help to describe its structure.

▸ The new elements provide clearer code (compared with using multiple `<div>` elements).

▸ Older browsers that do not understand HTML5 elements need to be told which elements are block-level elements.

▸ To make HTML5 elements work in Internet Explorer 8 (and older versions of IE), extra JavaScript is needed, which is available free from Google.

18

PROCESS & DESIGN

- ▶ How to approach building a site
- ▶ Understanding your audience and their needs
- ▶ How to present information visitors want to see

This section discusses a process that you can use when you are creating a new website.

It looks at who might be visiting your site and how to ensure the pages feature the information those visitors need. It also covers some key aspects of design theory to help you create professional looking sites. In this chapter, we will look at:

- How to understand the audience your site may attract and what information they will expect to find on it

- How to organize information so that visitors can find what they are looking for

- Design theory for presenting information in a way that helps visitors achieve their goals

- Design tips to help you create more attractive and professional sites

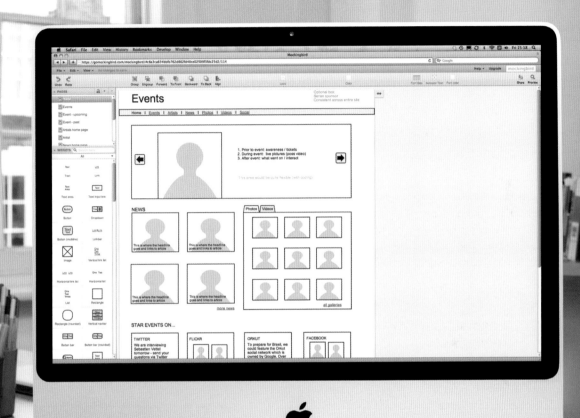

WHO IS THE SITE FOR?

Every website should be designed for the target audience—not just for yourself or the site owner. It is therefore very important to understand who your target audience is.

It can be helpful to ask some questions about the people you would expect to be interested in the subject of your site.

If you ask a client who a site is for, it is not uncommon for them to answer "the entire world."

Realistically, it is unlikely to be relevant to everyone. If your site sells light bulbs, even though most people using a computer probably use light bulbs, they are not likely to order them from someone in a different country.

Even if the site has a wide appeal, you can still think about the demographics of a sample of the target audience.

TARGET AUDIENCE: INDIVIDUALS

- What is the age range of your target audience?
- Will your site appeal to more women or men? What is the mix?
- Which country do your visitors live in?
- Do they live in urban or rural areas?
- What is the average income of visitors?
- What level of education do they have?
- What is their marital or family status?
- What is their occupation?
- How many hours do they work per week?
- How often do they use the web?
- What kind of device do they use to access the web?

TARGET AUDIENCE: COMPANIES

- What is the size of the company or relevant department?
- What is the position of people in the company who visit your site?
- Will visitors be using the site for themselves or for someone else?
- How large is the budget they control?

Invent some fictional visitors from your typical target audience. They will become your friends. They can influence design decisions from color palettes to level of detail in descriptions.

NAME	GORDON	MOLLY	JASPER	AYO	IVY
Gender	M	F	M	M	F
Age	28	47	19	32	35
Location	Chicago	San Francisco	New York	Miami	Boston
Occupation	Teacher	Attorney	Student	Retail	Journalist
Income	$62k	$180k	$24k	$160k	$75k
Web Use	2-3 days/wk	Daily	Daily	4-5 days/wk	Daily

If you have a question about how the site is going to be used, or what its priorities should be, you will be able to think back and ask yourself, "What would Gordon or Molly want in this situation?"

WHY PEOPLE VISIT YOUR WEBSITE

Now that you know who your visitors are, you need to consider **why** they are coming. While some people will simply chance across your website, most will visit for a specific reason.

Your content and design should be influenced by the goals of your users.

To help determine why people are coming to your website, there are two basic categories of questions you can ask:

1: The first attempts to discover the underlying **motivations** for why visitors come to the site.

2: The second examines the specific **goals** of the visitors. These are the triggers making them come to the site *now*.

KEY MOTIVATIONS

- Are they looking for general entertainment or do they need to achieve a specific goal?

- If there is a specific goal, is it a personal or professional one?

- Do they see spending time on this activity as essential or a luxury?

SPECIFIC GOALS

- Do they want general information / research (such as background on a topic / company), or are they after something specific (such as a particular fact or information on a product)?

- Are they already familiar with the service or product that you offer or do they need to be introduced to it?

- Are they looking for time sensitive information, such as the latest news or updates on a particular topic?

- Do they want to discover information about a specific product or service to help them decide whether to buy it or not?

- Do they need to contact you? If so, can they visit in person (which might require opening hours and a map)? Or might they need email or telephone contact details?

WHAT YOUR VISITORS ARE TRYING TO ACHIEVE

It is unlikely that you will be able to list every reason why someone visits your site but you are looking for key tasks and motivations. This information can help guide your site designs.

First you want to create a list of reasons why people would be coming to your site. You can then assign the list of tasks to the fictional visitors you created in the step described on the previous page.

GORDON bought a tennis racquet several years ago; now he wants to purchase one from your site for his girlfriend.

MOLLY has read about your new doggy daycare service in the press and wants to find out whether it would be suitable for her to use.

JASPER had a bad experience staying in a hotel when visiting Sydney, Australia, and wants to make a complaint.

AYO hopes to study architecture and wants to learn more about a new course that is being offered.

IVY is a picture editor and wants to look at a photographer's site to see examples of his work before deciding whether to commission him.

WHAT INFORMATION YOUR VISITORS NEED

You know who is coming to your site and why they are coming, so now you need to work out what information they need in order to achieve their goals quickly and effectively.

You may want to offer additional supporting information that you think they might find helpful.

Look at each of the reasons why people will be visiting your site and determine what they need to achieve their goals.

You can prioritize levels of information from key points down to non-essential or background information.

By ensuring that you provide the information that your visitors are looking for, they will consider your site more relevant to them.

Therefore, you will have more opportunity to tell them any extra information that you think would be helpful to them (or to expose them to other products and services you want to promote).

If you do not appear relevant to them by answering their needs, however, they are likely to go elsewhere.

Here are some questions to help you decide what information to provide for visitors to your site...

KEY INFORMATION

- Will visitors be familiar with your subject area / brand or do you need to introduce yourself?

- Will they be familiar with the product / service / information you are covering or do they need background information on it?

- What are the most important features of what you are offering?

- What is special about what you offer that differentiates you from other sites that offer something similar?

- Once people have achieved the goal that sent them to your site, are there common questions people ask about this subject area?

HOW OFTEN PEOPLE WILL VISIT YOUR SITE

Some sites benefit from being updated more frequently than others. Some information (such as news) may be constantly changing, while other content remains relatively static.

A website about fashion trends will need to change a lot more frequently than one that is promoting a service that people do not buy regularly (such as domestic plumbing or double glazing).

Once a site has been built, it can take a lot of time and resources to update it frequently.

Working out how often people are likely to revisit your site gives you an indication for how often you should update the site.

It can often be helpful to set a schedule for when a site will be updated (rather than doing it on an ad hoc basis).

You will often find that some parts of a site will benefit from being updated more frequently than others.

Here are some questions to help you decide how often to update your website content...

GOODS / SERVICES

- How often do the same people return to purchase from you?

- How often is your stock updated or your service changed?

INFORMATION

- How often is the subject updated?

- What percentage of your visitors would return for regular updates on the subject, compared with those who will just need the information once?

SITE MAPS

Now that you know what needs to appear on your site, you can start to organize the information into sections or pages.

The aim is to create a diagram of the pages that will be used to structure the site. This is known as a **site map** and it will show how those pages can be grouped.

To help you decide what information should go on each page, you can use a technique called **card sorting**.

This involves placing each piece of information that a visitor might need to know on a separate piece of paper and then organizing the related information into groups.

Each group relates to a page and, on larger sites, the pages can in turn be grouped together to create different sections of the website.

The groups of information are then turned into the diagram that is known as the site map.

Sometimes it can be helpful to ask people who are the target audience to help you group related information together.

A site map will usually begin with the homepage. Additionally, if the site is large and is compartmentalized into sections, each section might require its own section homepage to link to all of the information within it.

For example, most online shops have section homepages for each type of product, which then in turn link to individual product pages.

You may need to duplicate some information if it needs to appear on more than one page.

The pages (or groups of pages) will inform how users navigate through the site.

Remember to focus on the goals that your visitors want to achieve.

It is worth noting that the site owner might organize information in a way that is different to what the public expects. It is important to reflect the public's understanding of the subject (rather than just the site owner's understanding of it).

EXAMPLE SITE MAP

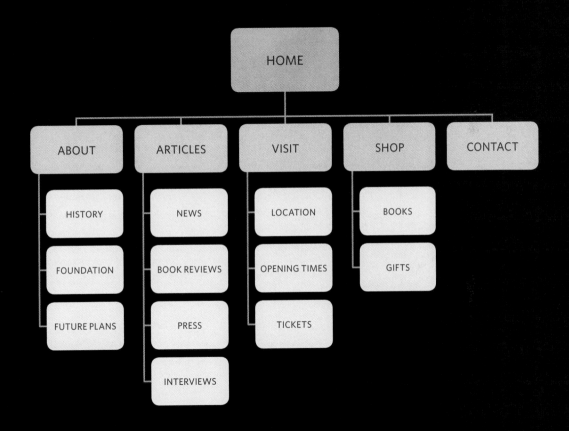

WIREFRAMES

A wireframe is a simple sketch of the key information that needs to go on each page of a site. It shows the hierarchy of the information and how much space it might require.

A lot of designers will take the elements that need to appear on each page and start by creating wireframes. This involves sketching or shading areas where each element of the page will go (such as the logo, primary navigation, headings and main bodies of text, user logins etc).

By creating a wireframe you can ensure that all of the information that needs to be on a page is included.

You should not include the color scheme, font choices, backgrounds or images for the website in the wireframe. It should focus on what information needs to be on each page and create a visual hierarchy to indicate the most important parts of each page.

The wireframes make design easier because you know what information needs to appear on which page before considering how the page should look.

It can be very helpful to show the wireframes of a site to a client before showing them a design. It enables the client to ensure the site has all the functions and information it needs to offer.

If you just present a site design to a client, it is common for them to focus on how the site looks, which means they may not raise issues about its function after the site has been built.

The example on the right was created in Photoshop using the templates that come with the 960.gs grid system.

You can sketch wireframes on paper or use a graphics application on your computer (such as Illustrator or InDesign).

There are also online wireframe tools such as those at:
http://gomockingbird.com
http://lovelycharts.com

EXAMPLE WIREFRAME

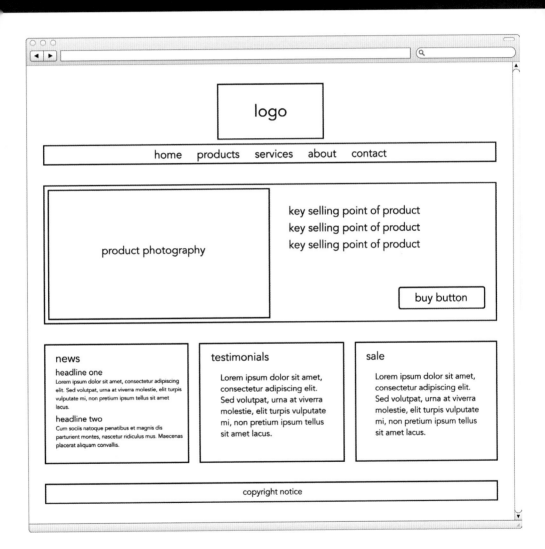

GETTING YOUR MESSAGE ACROSS USING DESIGN

The primary aim of any kind of visual design is to communicate. Organizing and prioritizing information on a page helps users understand its importance and what order to read it in.

CONTENT

Web pages often have a lot of information to communicate. For example, the pages of online newspapers will have information that does not appear on every page of the print equivalent:

- A masthead or logo
- Links to navigate the site
- Links to related content and other popular articles
- Login or membership options
- Ability for users to comment
- Copyright information
- Links to privacy policies, terms and conditions, advertising information, RSS feeds, subscription options

With so much on the page, the designer needs to **organize** and **prioritize** the information to communicate their message and help users find what they're looking for.

PRIORITIZING

If everything on a page appeared in the same style, it would be much harder to understand. (Key messages would not stand out.)

By making parts of the page look **distinct** from surrounding content, designers draw attention to (or away from) those items.

Designers create something known as a **visual hierarchy** to help users focus on the key messages that will draw people's attention, and then guide them to subsequent messages.

We look at visual hierarchy on pages 467-468.

ORGANIZING

Grouping together related content into **blocks** or **chunks** makes the page look simpler (and easier to understand).

Users should be able to identify the purpose of each block without processing each individual item.

By presenting certain types of information in a **similar** visual style (such as using the same style for all buttons or all links), users will learn to associate that style with a particular type of content.

We look at grouping and similarity on pages 469-470.

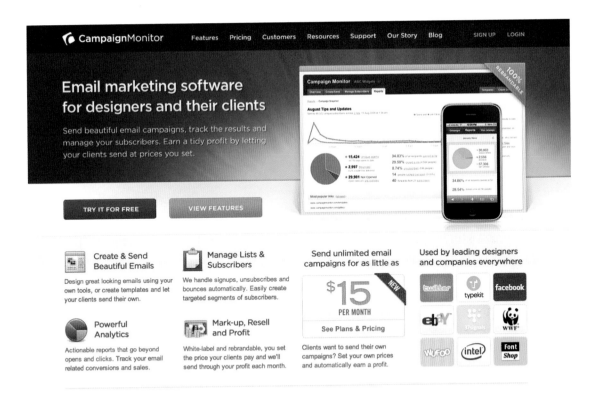

Let's look at an example of how design can be used to effectively communicate the services of a company.

VISUAL HIERARCHY

Attention is immediately drawn to a picture that shows the service this company offers and a headline to explain it. The size and colored background reinforce that this is the primary message on the page.

Should this service appeal to the user, below they can see more detail about what it does, how much it costs, and who uses it.

GROUPING

There are several chunks of information on this page.

At the top you can see the logo and navigation. Under this is the information that introduces the company's services.

Further down are three distinct groups showing you what the services do, the costs involved and some of the services' users.

SIMILARITY

There are several examples of similarity within this page.

The four points (at the bottom left of the screenshot) are all presented in a similar manner with consistent headings and icons.

All of the links in the body text are in blue so it is clear what text is clickable.

VISUAL HIERARCHY

Most web users do not read entire pages. Rather, they skim to find information. You can use contrast to create a visual hierarchy that gets across your key message and helps users find what they are looking for.

SIZE

Larger elements will grab users' attention first. For this reason it is a good idea to make headings and key points relatively large.

COLOR

Foreground and background color can draw attention to key messages. Brighter sections tend to draw users' attention first.

STYLE

An element may be the same size and color as surrounding content but have a different style applied to it to make it stand out.

Lorem ipsum
dolor sit amet, consectetur adipiscing elit. Lorem ipsum dolor sit amet, consectetur adipscing elit.

Lorem ipsum dolor sit amet, consectetur adipiscing elit. Lorem ipsum dolor sit amet, consectetur adipscing elit.

Lorem ipsum dolor sit amet, consectetur adipiscing elit. Lorem ipsum dolor sit amet, consectetur adipscing elit.

Visual hierarchy refers to the order in which your eyes perceive what they see. It is created by adding **visual contrast** between the items being displayed. Items with higher contrast are recognized and processed first.

IMAGES

Images create a high visual contrast and often attract the eye first. They can be used to draw attention to a specific message within the page. In some cases, the right image can succinctly reveal more than an entire page of text.

The effect of a well-designed visual hierarchy is largely subliminal. Achieving a good hierarchy requires balance; if nothing stands out a site can be rather uninteresting, and if too many aspects are competing for your attention, it can be hard to find the key messages. This example has a clear hierarchy which addresses the needs of visitors to the site.

GROUPING AND SIMILARITY

When making sense of a design, we tend to organize visual elements into groups. Grouping related pieces of information together can make a design easier to comprehend. Here are some ways this can be achieved.

PROXIMITY

When several items are placed close together, they are perceived as more related than items that are placed further apart. (You can also nest groups of information within larger groups of information.)

CLOSURE

When faced with a complicated arrangement of items, we will often look for a single or recognisable pattern or form. A real or imaginary box can be formed around elements due to their proximity and alignment.

CONTINUANCE

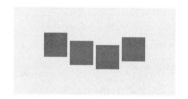

When elements are placed in a line or a curve then they are perceived to be more related than those that are not following the same direction. This can be used to direct a reader from one part of a page to the next.

WHITE SPACE

Placing related items closer together and leaving a bigger gap between unrelated items.

COLOR

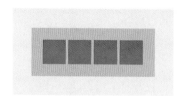

A background color placed behind related items to emphasize their connection.

BORDERS

A line can be drawn around the border of the group or between it and its neighbors.

We naturally observe similarities in design, and things that are similar are perceived to be more related than things that are dissimilar. Repetition of similar color, size, orientation, texture, font, or shape, suggests that matching elements have similar importance or meaning.

Book Reviews

Raw Creation
John Maizels

Raw Creation is the definitive book on outsider art and provides an indispensible guide to the self-taught art of this century and a fascinating account of human creativity. The chapter entitled *Wonders of the World* is mostly dedicated to Nek Chand's Rock Garden and includes a number of color photographs.
Buy on Amazon

Nek Chand Outsider Art
Lucienne Peiry, Philippe Lespinasse

This publication tells the story of Nek Chand and his life and takes the reader on a colorful journey through his Rock Garden, the world's most expansive work of environmental art.
Buy on Amazon

Fantasy Worlds
Deidi von Schaewen, John Maizels

Presenting the world's most unusual, colorful and poetic creations, some of which have never previously appeared in print. *Fantasy Worlds* includes the classics of fantasy architecture such as the Palais Ideal near Lyon and, of course, Nek Chand's Rock Garden in Chandigarh, India.
Buy on Amazon

The Rock Garden
M.S.Aulakh

This small black and white book is M.S. Aulakh's commentary on and tribute to the Rock Garden and is not widely available, but used copies can be found from time to time.
Buy on Amazon

CONSISTENCY

In this example each book review has a consistent style for the book titles, author names, and purchasing links. Having read just one of the blocks it is possible to infer the meaning of the other items in this box that follow the same style.

HEADINGS

Giving a chunk of information a heading clearly tells the user whether or not the content of the grouping is relevant to them. If not, they can ignore all of the elements within it. It also helps users of screen readers, as users often have the option to hear the headings on the page.

Each visual chunk can contain its own hierarchy as shown in this example, where the individual books have their own subsections of title, author, text and link.

DESIGNING NAVIGATION

Site navigation not only helps people find where they want to go, but also helps them understand what your site is about and how it is organized. Good navigation tends to follow these principles...

CONCISE

Ideally, the navigation should be quick and easy to read. It is a good idea to try to limit the number of options in a menu to no more than eight links. These can link to section homepages which in turn link to other pages.

CLEAR

Users should be able to predict the kind of information that they will find on the page before clicking on the link. Where possible, choose single descriptive words for each link rather than phrases.

SELECTIVE

The primary navigation should only reflect the sections or content of the site. Functions like logins and search, and legal information like terms and conditions and so on are best placed elsewhere on the page.

Home   Artist Profiles   Exhibitions and Events   Galleries   Books and Magazines
About this Website   Contact Us   Login   Register   Terms and Conditions   Privacy Policy

Home   Artist Profiles   Exhibitions   Galleries   Publications   About   Contact

A large site may have primary, secondary and even tertiary navigation. Primary navigation often appears across the top of the site from left to right, or down the left hand side of the page. Secondary navigation could be under the primary

navigation or down the side of the page. Tertiary navigation often sits in the footer of the page. The menu will not be the only way users navigate the site. They will also use links within each page. Some sites also offer a search function.

ONLINE EXTRA
Go to the website accompanying this book for information on how to implement search functionality for your site using Google Search.

CONTEXT

Good navigation provides context. It lets the user know where they are in the website at that moment. Using a different color or some kind of visual marker to indicate the current page is a good way to do this.

INTERACTIVE

Each link should be big enough to click on and the appearance of the link should change when the user hovers over each item or clicks on it. It should also be visually distinct from other content on the page.

CONSISTENT

The more pages a site contains, the larger the number of navigation items there will be. Although secondary navigation will change from page to page, it is best to keep the primary navigation exactly the same.

Home   Artist Profiles   Exhibitions   Galleries   Publications   About   Contact

Home   *Artist Profiles*   Exhibitions   Galleries   Publications   About   Contact

▸ It's important to understand who your target audience is, why they would come to your site, what information they want to find and when they are likely to return.

▸ Site maps allow you to plan the structure of a site.

▸ Wireframes allow you to organize the information that will need to go on each page.

▸ Design is about communication. Visual hierarchy helps visitors understand what you are trying to tell them.

▸ You can differentiate between pieces of information using size, color, and style.

▸ You can use grouping and similarity to help simplify the information you present.

19

PRACTICAL INFORMATION

- ▸ Search engine optimization
- ▸ Using analytics to understand visitors
- ▸ Putting your site on the web

To wrap up the book we are going to look at some practical information that will help you launch a successful site.

There are entire books written about each of the topics covered in this chapter but I will introduce you to the key themes that each subject deals with and give you pointers for what you need to be considering. You will see:

- The basics of search engine optimization

- Using analytics to understand how people are using your site after it has launched

- Putting your site on the web

SEARCH ENGINE OPTIMIZATION (SEO)

SEO is a huge topic and several books have been written on the subject. The following pages will help you understand the key concepts so you can improve your website's visibility on search engines.

THE BASICS

Search engine optimization (or SEO) is the practice of trying to help your site appear nearer the top of search engine results when people look for the topics that your website covers.

At the heart of SEO is the idea of working out which terms people are likely to enter into a search engine to find your site and then using these terms in the right places on your site to increase the chances that search engines will show a link to your site in their results.

In order to determine who comes first in the search results, search engines do not only look at what appears on your site. They also consider how many sites link to you (and how relevant those links are). For this reason, SEO is often split into two areas: on-page techniques and off-page techniques.

ON-PAGE TECHNIQUES

On-page techniques are the methods you can use on your web pages to improve their rating in search engines.

The main component of this is looking at keywords that people are likely to enter into a search engine if they wanted to find your site, and then including these in the text and HTML code for your site in order to help the search engines know that your site covers these topics.

Search engines rely very heavily on the text that is in your pages so it is important that the terms people are going to search for are in text. There are seven essential places where you want your keywords to appear.

Ensuring that any images have appropriate text in the value of their `alt` attribute also helps search engines understand the content of images.

OFF-PAGE TECHNIQUES

Getting other sites to link to you is just as important as on-page techniques. Search engines help determine how to rank your site by looking at the number of other sites that link to yours.

They are particularly interested in sites whose content is related to yours. For example, if you were running a website that sold fish bait, then a link from a hairdresser is not likely to be considered as relevant as one from an angling community.

Search engines also look at the words between the opening `<a>` tag and closing `</a>` tag in the link. If the text in the link contains keywords (rather than just *click here* or your website address) it may be considered more relevant.

The words that appear in links to your site should also appear in the text of the page that the site links to.

ON-PAGE SEO

In every page of your website there are seven key places where keywords (the words people might search on to find your site) can appear in order to improve its findability.

1: PAGE TITLE

The page title appears at the top of the browser window or on the tab of a browser. It is specified in the `<title>` element which lives inside the `<head>` element.

2: URL / WEB ADDRESS

The name of the file is part of the URL. Where possible, use keywords in the file name.

3: HEADINGS

If the keywords are in a heading `<hn>` element then a search engine will know that this page is all about that subject and give it greater weight than other text.

4: TEXT

Where possible, it helps to repeat the keywords in the main body of the text at least 2-3 times. Do not, however, over-use these terms, because the text must be easy for a human to read.

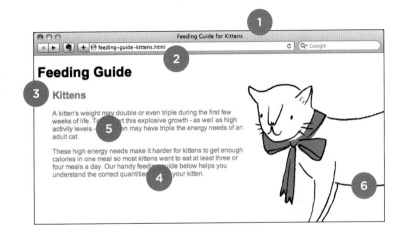

5: LINK TEXT

Use keywords in the text that create links between pages (rather than using generic expressions such as "click here").

6: IMAGE ALT TEXT

Search engines rely on you providing accurate descriptions of images in the alt text. This will also help your images show up in the results of image-based searches.

7: PAGE DESCRIPTIONS

The description also lives inside the `<head>` element and is specified using a `<meta>` tag. It should be a sentence that describes the content of the page. (These are not shown in the browser window but they may be displayed in the results pages of search engines.)

Never try to fool search engines! They will penalize you for it. For example, never add text in the same color as the background of the page as they can detect this.

HOW TO IDENTIFY KEYWORDS AND PHRASES

Determining which keywords to use on your site can be one of the hardest tasks when you start to think about SEO. Here are six steps that will help you identify the right keywords and phrases for your site.

1: BRAINSTORM

List down the words that someone might type into Google to find your site. Be sure to include the various topics, products or services your site is about.

It often helps to ask other people what words they would use to find your site because people less familiar with a topic might use different terms than you. (In particular, they are less likely to use industry-specific jargon.)

Your list may include some keyword phrases (not just individual words) if you have topics which are described by more than one word.

2: ORGANIZE

Group the keywords into separate lists for the different sections or categories of your website.

For example, if your website was a pet shop you might have different categories for different animals (such as dogs, cats and rabbits).

On a large site you may break this up further into sub-categories (for example, separate groups for different pet food brands).

3: RESEARCH

There are several tools that let you enter your keywords and then they will suggest additional keywords you might like to consider, such as:
adwords.google.co.uk/select/KeywordToolExternal (When using this tool, select the "exact match" option rather than "broad match.")
www.wordtracker.com
www.keyworddiscovery.com

Once these tools have suggested additional keywords, add the relevant options to your lists. (Keyword tools will most likely suggest some terms that are irrelevant so do omit any that do not seem appropriate).

4: COMPARE

It is very unlikely that your site will appear at the top of the search results for every keyword. This is especially true for topics where there is a lot of competition. The more sites out there that have already been optimized for a given keyword, the harder it will be for you to rise up the search results when people search on that term.

Some of the keyword research sites can tell you how many people have searched for a specific keyword to help you know how much competition those terms have.

You can also use Google's advanced search feature to just search the titles of web pages. This will help you to determine how many sites have that keyword in the title of their pages. (The more pages with the term in the title, the more competition there is.)

5: REFINE

Now you need to pick which keywords you will focus on. These should always be the ones that are most relevant to each section of your site.

If there is a phrase that is very relevant but you find there is a lot of competition, you should still use it. To improve the chances of your site being found you can look at whether there are other words that could be incorporated into a phrase. For example, if the information or service you offer on your website is location specific, then you will often find that incorporating your location into your keyword list will help people find you.

If your site is promoting a slate roofing company in Australia then it is better to get 100 people from Australia who are looking for a slate roof than 10,000 from the USA who are looking for other kinds of roofs.

6: MAP

Now that you have a refined list of keywords, you know which have the most competition, and which ones are most relevant, it is time to start picking which keywords you will use for each page.

Pick 3-5 keywords or phrases that map to each page of your website and use these as the keywords for each page.

You should not need to repeat the same keywords on all of the pages. It is also likely that, as you move further away from the homepage into the sections of the site, the keywords will become more specific to the individual topic dealt with on each page.

ANALYTICS: LEARNING ABOUT YOUR VISITORS

As soon as people start coming to your site, you can start analyzing how they found it, what they were looking at and at what point they are leaving. One of the best tools for doing this is a free service offered by Google called Google Analytics.

SIGNING UP

The Google Analytics service relies on you signing up for an account at:
www.google.com/analytics
The site will give you a piece of tracking code which you need to put on every page of your site.

HOW IT WORKS

Every time someone loads a page of your site, the tracking code sends data to the Google servers where it is stored. Google then provides a web-based interface that allows you to see how visitors use your site.

THE TRACKING CODE

A tracking code is provided by Google Analytics for each website you are tracking. It should appear just before the closing </head> tag. The code does not alter the appearance of your web pages.

At the time of writing, Google was updating their Analytics interface to Version 5. If you log into your account and see a different interface, look for a link in the top right-hand corner of the page that says 'New Version.'

HOW MANY PEOPLE ARE COMING TO YOUR SITE?

The overview page gives you a snapshot of the key information you are likely to want to know. In particular, it tells you how many people are coming to your site.

VISITS
This is the number of times people have come to your site. If someone is inactive on your site for 30 minutes and then looks at another page on your site, it will be counted as a new visit.

UNIQUE VISITS
This is the total number of people who have visited your site over the specified period. The number of unique visits will be lower than the number of visits if people have been returning to your site more than once in the defined period.

PAGE VIEWS
The total number of pages all visitors have viewed on your site.

PAGES PER VISIT
The average number of pages each visitor has looked at on your site per visit.

AVERAGE TIME ON SITE
The average amount of time each user has spent on the site per visit.

DATE SELECTOR
Using the date selector in the top right hand corner of the site, you can change the period of time the reports display. When you log in, this is usually set to the last month, but you can change it to report on a specific time period.

EXPORT
The export link just above the title that says "visitors overview" allows you to export the statistics on this page for other applications such as Excel.

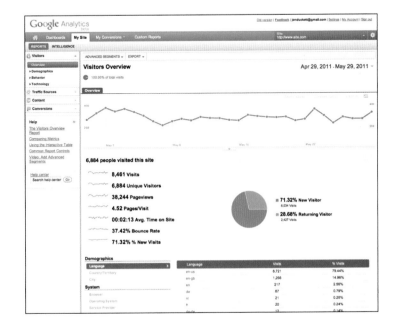

WHAT ARE YOUR VISITORS LOOKING AT?

The content link on the left-hand side allows you to learn more about what the visitors are looking at when they come to your site.

PAGES
This tells you which pages your visitors are looking at the most and also which pages they are spending the most time on.

LANDING PAGES
These are the pages that people arrive on when first visiting your site. This can be particularly helpful because you may find people are not always coming into your site via the homepage.

TOP EXIT PAGES
This shows which pages people most commonly leave from. If a lot of people are leaving from the same page then you might consider changing that page or improving it.

BOUNCE RATE
This shows the number of people who left on the same page that they arrived on. A high bounce rate suggests that the content is not what they were looking for or that the page did not sufficiently encourage them to look around the rest of the site. What counts as a bounce:

- Clicked a link to another site
- Clicked on an advertisement
- Entered a new URL
- Used the "back" button
- Closed the browser

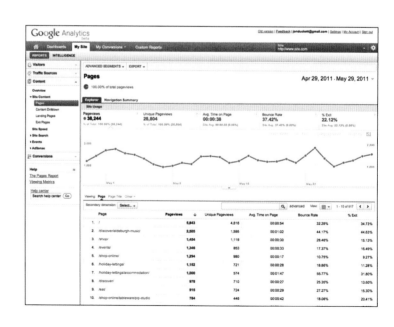

WHERE ARE YOUR VISITORS COMING FROM?

The traffic sources link on the left hand side allows you to learn where your visitors are coming from.

REFERRERS

This shows the sites that have linked to you and the number of people who have come via those sites. If a site sends a lot of traffic to you, get in touch and try to work together to ensure that traffic keeps flowing. You could also try to find similar sites and ask them to link to you. DIRECT

This shows which page a user arrived on if they did not come via a link on another site. They might have typed the URL into their browser, used a browser bookmark, or clicked a link in an email, PDF, or Word document.

SEARCH TERMS

This shows the terms users entered into a search engine to find your site. This can help you learn how visitors describe what they're looking for (which is often different to how someone might describe their own site). This can help you fine-tune your content and your SEO keywords.

ADVANCED FEATURES

We have only scratched the surface of what you can find out about your visitors from Google Analytics. Their help files tell you many more of the advanced features. If you run an online shop, it is well worth looking at their e-commerce tracking, which adds information about products sold, average basket size and much more. You can also set up goals where you specify the paths you want people to take, and then see how far they get through those paths, which is especially useful when gathering data from users.

DOMAIN NAMES & HOSTING

In order to put your site on the web you will need a domain name and web hosting.

DOMAIN NAMES

Your domain name is your web address (e.g. google.com or bbc. co.uk). There are many websites that allow you to register domain names. Usually you will have to pay an annual fee to keep that domain name.

These sites usually have a form that allows you to check whether your preferred domain name is available, and because millions of domain names have already been registered, it might take you a while to find the one that is right for your site.

A lot of sites that offer domain name registration also offer web hosting.

WEB HOSTING

So that other people can see your site, you will need to upload it to a web server. Web servers are special computers that are constantly connected to the Internet. They are specially set up to serve web pages when they are requested.

With the exception of some very large sites, most websites live on web servers run by web hosting companies. This is usually far cheaper and more reliable than trying to run your own web servers.

There are lots of different types of hosting on offer. We will now take a look at some of the key things that will help you choose which hosting company to use.

DISK SPACE
This refers to the total size of all of the files that make up your site (all of the HTML and CSS files, images and scripts).

BANDWIDTH
This is the amount of data the hosting company will send to your site's visitors. If you imagine 10 people looked at every page on your site, then it would be the equivalent to 10 times the amount of disk space you use.

BACKUPS
Check whether the hosting company performs backups on your site (and how often). Some only create backups so that they can restore your website in the event of a server breaking. Others allow access to backups (which can be helpful if you accidentally break the site when updating it).

EMAIL ACCOUNTS

Most hosting companies will provide email servers with their web hosting packages. You will want to check the size of mailbox you are allowed and the number of mailboxes you can use.

SERVER-SIDE LANGUAGES AND DATABASES

If you are using a content management system, it will likely use a server-side programming language and a database (such as PHP with a MySQL database, or ASP.Net with a SQL Server database). Be sure to check that your hosting company supports the technologies your software needs to run.

It is often worth searching for reviews of a hosting company to see what other people's experience has been with a hosting company. Unfortunately, you often can only tell how good a hosting company is when something goes wrong, at which point you find out how they are able to help you (so you can expect to see a few negative reviews for any company).

HOSTED SERVICES

There are a number of online services that allow you to point your domain name to their servers. Blogging platforms such as WordPress.com, Tumblr, and Posterous, or e-commerce platforms such as Big Cartel and Shopify provide the servers that your site is hosted on. If you are using a platform like this you will not need your own hosting for the website, although you often still need hosting for your email. If this is the case, some web hosting companies offer packages that will just offer email services.

FTP & THIRD PARTY TOOLS

To transfer your code and images from your computer to your hosting company, you use something known as File Transfer Protocol.

As the name suggests, File Transfer Protocol (or FTP) allows you to transfer files across the Internet from your computer to the web server hosting your site.

There are many FTP programs that offer a simple interface that shows you the files on your computer alongside the files that are on your web server. These allow you to drag and drop files from your computer to the server or vice versa.

There are a wide variety of sites that offer services commonly created by web developers (to save you having to build them yourself).

Some hosting companies offer tools to upload files to their servers using a web browser, but it is more common to use an FTP program as they are faster at transmitting files.

When you purchase your web hosting, you will be given FTP details that you enter into your FTP program in order to connect to the server. Usually this will be an address (such as `ftp://mydomain.com`), a username, and a password. It is important to keep this information secure in order to prevent strangers from gaining access to your server.

Here is a list of some popular FTP applications:

FileZilla
`filezilla-project.org`
Windows, Mac, Linux

FireFTP
`fireftp.mozdev.org`
Windows, Mac, Linux

CuteFTP
`cuteftp.com`
Windows, Mac

SmartFTP
`smartftp.com`
WIndows

Transmit
`panic.com/transmit`
Mac

Here is a list of some popular third party tools:

BLOGS
`wordpress.com`
`tumblr.com`
`posterous.com`

E-COMMERCE
`shopify.com`
`bigcartel.com`
`go.magento.com`

EMAIL NEWSLETTERS
`campaignmonitor.com`
`mailchimp.com`

SOCIAL NETWORKING
SHARING BUTTONS
`addthis.com`
`addtoany.com`

▸ Search engine optimization helps visitors find your sites when using search engines.

▸ Analytics tools such as Google Analytics allow you to see how many people visit your site, how they find it, and what they do when they get there.

▸ To put your site on the web, you will need to obtain a domain name and web hosting.

▸ FTP programs allow you to transfer files from your local computer to your web server.

▸ Many companies provide platforms for blogging, email newsletters, e-commerce and other popular website tools (to save you writing them from scratch).

INDEX

- A-Z
- HTML & CSS shortcuts
- Troubleshooting

TROUBLESHOOTING

Here are a few problems that beginners commonly face, along with the pages where you can find solutions to them.

STARTING OUT

The browser shows the markup typed in (not the result page).
Check the file extension is *.html* and not *.txt*. p 30, 32

Bold text, italics, headings, or link text are extending longer than expected.
Check you have closed the relevant tag e.g. </a>. p 21, 22

The page I linked to is not found.
Check the relative URL. p 83, 84

IMAGES

Images are not showing up.
Check the relative URL. p 83, 84

Images are looking blurry.
Check that you have saved your images in the right format and at the size you want to show them at. p 109-113

Border images are not showing.
This only works with latest browsers. (Also, check the relative URL). p 319

GIFs that were resized now look grainy or have jagged edges.
Check the color space in your image editing program. It should be RGB (not indexed color).

TEXT

Some text flashes up before showing the correct font.
You have a Flash Of Unstyled Content. p 278

When copying text from word processors, lots of extra tags are added to the markup.
Copy the text into a plain text editor (to remove formatting) then paste it into your HTML editor. p 49

The text looks bigger/smaller on some screens.
This is usually due to variances in screen resolutions. Also, check the type scale is set for the <body> element. p 377, 275, 276

The font size is wrong in IE when I use ems.
See above. p 276

The font I specified is not showing in some browsers.
The computer must have that font installed. p 269-272
If you use @font-face it must be in several formats. p 277, 278

My fonts look jagged on a PC.
Some fonts to do not anti-alias as well as others on a PC. Try a different typeface or try a thicker version. p 272

GENERAL CSS

A specified style is not showing.
Remember CSS selectors are case sensitive.

Check that your selectors are correct. p 238

The web developer toolbar can help you find the right selector. p 348

If the selectors are correct, do you have another selector that applies to the same element later in the CSS? p 239, 240

CSS varies in some browsers. There are a number of CSS bugs/browser quirks that mean they render the page slightly differently - try searching for the problem and see if it is a known CSS bug/quirk. p 242

HTML 5

The browser is not applying styles to HTML5 elements.
If it is IE, you might need to use the HTML5 shiv / shim. p442

Block-level elements are rendering as inline elements.
Use display:block to tell the browser which HTML5 elements are block-level elements. p 442

LAYOUT

The design looks bigger/smaller on some screens.
The resolution of a monitor affects how big the items appear on the page. p 377, 378

Margins above and below a box not showing.
Vertical margins collapse.
p 308, 314

My content does not fit in the containing box/browser window.
You can deal with this using the overflow property. p 306, 316

Boxes look a different size in IE.
Some versions of IE use a different box model than all other browsers. Use a DOCTYPE to make old versions of IE behave like other browsers. p 316

Boxes do not appear centered when using auto for left and right margins.
You may need to use the text-align property on the containing element. p 315

Elements are overlapping.
When you take elements out of normal flow, they can overlap. z-index helps you control which item goes on top. p 369

Why is the vertical-align property not vertically centering my block-level element?
This property is not designed for this purpose. It is used to center inline elements on the page. You will find several ways to vertically center block-level elements (depending on their context) if you search on Google.

A background image is not showing on my box.
Does the box you are applying the style to have a defined height and width? p 303

Does the containing box have an overflow property set to auto?
p 373, 374

My background images do not show when the page is printed.
Most browsers do not print background images by default to help save ink. You can adjust this in your print preferences.

There is a gap between the browser window and my content.
You may need to set margin and padding on the <body> element to 0. p 313, 314

FLOAT IN LAYOUT

A box is not sitting next to another floated element.
Ensure that there is enough space in the containing element for the two to sit side by side. p 303, 371, 372

Margins and padding are added to the width of the box (except for older versions of IE, which have a different box model). Therefore, the box might be wider than specified in the width property. p 316

Did you specify a width for the floated element? (See next point.)

My floated element takes up the full width of the browser window (or containing box).
Check that you have specified a width for the floated element. p 370, 371

The container around my floated elements are one pixel tall.
The containing element doesn't know the height of the floated elements inside it. You can either add an element that acts as a clearing box or use the overflow property with a value set to auto. p 373, 374

IE added an extra margin to my floated elements.
Set the display property to inline.

If you've come across a problem that you think belongs in this troubleshooting section, please feel welcome to email it to us at: hello@htmlandcssbook.com. We will endeavor to address the most common problems our readers have faced in future editions of this book. Thank you!

HTML ELEMENTS

HTML ATTRIBUTES

CSS PROPERTIES

PSEUDO-CLASSES, ELEMENTS & RULES